Become ITIL® 4 Foundation Certified in 7 Days

Understand and Prepare for the ITIL Foundation Exam with Real-life Examples

Second Edition

Abhinav Krishna Kaiser

apress®

Become ITIL® 4 Foundation Certified in 7 Days: Understand and Prepare for the ITIL Foundation Exam with Real-life Examples

Abhinav Krishna Kaiser
Staines, UK

ISBN-13 (pbk): 978-1-4842-6360-0
https://doi.org/10.1007/978-1-4842-6361-7

ISBN-13 (electronic): 978-1-4842-6361-7

Copyright © 2021 by Abhinav Krishna Kaiser

Managing Director, Apress Media LLC: Welmoed Spahr
Acquisitions Editor: Celestin Suresh John
Development Editor: Laura Berendson
Coordinating Editor: Aditee Mirashi

Cover designed by eStudioCalamar

Cover image designed by Freepik (www.freepik.com)

ITIL® is a (registered) trademark of AXELOS Limited. All rights reserved.

Distributed to the book trade worldwide by Springer Science+Business Media New York, 1 New York Plaza, Suite 4600, New York, NY 10004-1562, USA. Phone 1-800-SPRINGER, fax (201) 348-4505, e-mail orders-ny@springer-sbm.com, or visit www.springeronline.com. Apress Media, LLC is a California LLC and the sole member (owner) is Springer Science + Business Media Finance Inc (SSBM Finance Inc). SSBM Finance Inc is a **Delaware** corporation.

For information on translations, please e-mail booktranslations@springernature.com; for reprint, paperback, or audio rights, please e-mail bookpermissions@springernature.com.

Apress titles may be purchased in bulk for academic, corporate, or promotional use. eBook versions and licenses are also available for most titles. For more information, reference our Print and eBook Bulk Sales web page at www.apress.com/bulk-sales.

Any source code or other supplementary material referenced by the author in this book is available to readers on GitHub via the book's product page, located at www.apress.com/978-1-4842-6360-0. For more detailed information, please visit www.apress.com/source-code.

Printed on acid-free paper

*Dedicated to my wife Radhika and
my kids Anagha and Aadwik who endured
several hours away from me during "family time."*

Table of Contents

About the Author

Abhinav Krishna Kaiser is a well-known authority in DevOps, Agile, and ITIL frameworks. He has developed DevOps architectures and transformed client organizations into Agile ways of working by playing the roles of an Agile architect and an Agile coach. He continues to innovate with novel ways of working and automation opportunities. His name is widely associated with the ITIL framework.

His most notable ITIL designs have been in the configuration management practice, where he has designed architectures in complex environments involving multiple interfaces and tools such as ServiceNow and BMC Atrium.

Abhinav has delivered numerous trainings in ITIL, DevOps, and Agile across the globe. His trainings are particularly powerful with the use of day to day examples to explain tough concepts.

He works as a senior manager in a leading consulting firm. He consults with client organizations in his areas of expertise. Being a consultant, he is always on the move. He is from Bangalore but currently lives in Staines-upon-Thames, United Kingdom. Abhinav is happily married to Radhika, and they have a daughter (Anagha) and a son (Aadwik).

Abhinav started as a blogger in 2004 when the world was getting to know blogs, and graduated to writing on famed websites such as Tech Republic and Plural Sight. His first book was on soft skills: *Workshop in a Box: Communication Skills for IT Professionals*. Then he wrote *Become*

ITIL Foundation Certified in 7 Days, which is one of the top guides for the ITIL V3 framework. His previous book was *Reinventing ITIL in the Age of DevOps*, wherein he tweaks and customizes the ITIL V3 framework to fit the contours of DevOps projects. This tweaked framework has been implemented across industries with great success.

Abhinav blogs and writes guides and articles on DevOps, Agile, and ITIL at `http://abhinavpmp.com`. While most of his works are associated with IT, he has a passion for fiction as well. He has written a few short stories on `http://indiancritic.com` and hopes to write a full length novel someday—hopefully not too far off in the future.

About the Technical Reviewer

Jaya Tiwari is an ISTQB®, PRINCE2®, ITIL®, PSM™ I, Lean Six Sigma Green Belt Certified test lead who has been working in the software telecom industry for the last ten years, with a focus on software quality assurance and best practices. She has managed departments encompassing all aspects of the software life cycle, including requirement design and analysis, software development, database design, software quality assurance, software testing, technical documentation, and reviews.

In addition to working as a "Test Professional", Jaya is a Quality and Agile coach and provides trainings for ISTQB test certifications and Agile frameworks. She strongly believes that continuous learning and adaptation leads to a phenomenal transformation in every individual.

Preface

In 2017, two years before ITIL 4 hit the scene, I wrote *Become ITIL Foundation Certified in 7 Days*. When ITIL 4 was announced in 2018, I felt that I was hit by a crater. I had dodged several requests from publishers over the years, and when I finally decided to write a book on ITIL, the version was coming to a premature end. Nevertheless, my ITIL foundation book became an instant success within the year of publication and my publisher was soon knocking on my door again to write the second edition. I am thankful to all the readers of the first edition for extending their support in making my book the premier guide for taking up the ITIL Foundation examination. ITIL V3 may have been officially upgraded to ITIL 4, but the framework lives on. The logical sequence of developing a service from nothingness to a full-blooded beast is a journey that lives on in most organizations, and its greatest strength is that its application is still relevant to non-IT organizations. ITIL V3 is a beautiful framework that is evergreen and provides a strong foundation for ITIL 4 and DevOps to flourish.

When my publisher approached me for the second edition, I told them that the first and second editions are worlds apart. An edition change would generally have updates that are overshadowed by the remaining content of the book. In contrast, the book that I was asked to write as the second edition was going to be the polar opposite. I was going to rewrite at least 80 percent of the book; such was the change between the two ITIL versions.

Between my first and second editions, I wrote a book in 2018 on an ITIL framework that would work in DevOps projects. *Reinventing ITIL in the Age of DevOps* was built on ITIL V3 and considered tweaks and customizations to the organization structures, and most ITIL processes went under the scanner for DevOps refitting. Plus, special emphasis and opportunities were identified where technology and automation could be employed for increasing efficiency and reducing defects. The framework tweak that I proposed in the book is relevant with ITIL 4, as some of the tweaks that I had preempted in my framework have been considered in ITIL 4 and blend seamlessly.

One of the core principles of ITIL is to give liberty for service architects to come up with a framework design that fits the organization. *Reinventing ITIL in the Age of DevOps* adapts the ITIL framework to work for DevOps, in the process prescribing ITIL for projects that work in a DevOps mode. If you are looking to get into ITIL or transition into ITIL 4 from ITIL V3, *Become ITIL 4 Foundation Certified in 7 Days* is your go-to book. If you are looking to implement ITIL in a DevOps setting, *Reinventing ITIL in the Age of DevOps* should be your best bet.

I started my ITIL journey way back in 2005-2006 with the second version of ITIL. I grew rapidly from being an ITIL practitioner to an ITIL consultant and undertook several ITIL implementations over the years. My perspective of the world of services changed as I started donning the role of a service architect and then eventually the ITIL Expert track that I embarked on. As I started to explore ITIL and manipulate services to get the intended results, the ITIL framework workings seemed like second nature to me. I headed the training and consulting practice in an organization and conducted hundreds of Foundational and Expert-level trainings. I gained fame and positions of authority, and then something happened.

An organization change resulted in me getting grouped with DevOps consultants and the DevOps practice. At around the same time, my manager who was familiar with my expertise (which was ITIL at the time and not DevOps) quit the organization. A new manager took over and one day while I was packing up, walked up to me and said: "Abhinav, I am looking at you to be one of the DevOps trainers." I could have told him that I am not DevOps, but ITIL. I remained silent and accepted the assignment.

For the next month and a half, I ate, slept, and dreamed DevOps and DevOps alone. I studied everything on DevOps that I could get my hands on. In those days, DevOps resources were few and far between, unlike today.

The assignment started and I began with a bang. Combined with my training prowess, DevOps knowledge that I had acquired made me an instant success. I started training IT developers and testers across multiple continents for the next 12 months on various DevOps concepts and processes. My life had changed the moment I remained silent, and I never looked back at my decision to jump ship from one segment of IT to another. As I delved deeper into DevOps, it was apparent that DevOps and ITIL were not worlds apart, and there was a bridge that was believed to be too far. Through this and my *Reinventing* book, I hope that I have brought the two parcels of IT together.

As the world is getting flatter, so are the different branches in IT. They all seem to be converging under the DevOps umbrella. Prior to my DevOps career, I would have sworn that you are either in service management or in project management (development) and your career will go into either of these areas. These days, I see the convergence. I have designed DevOps architectures where both development and service management happen in the same hut, and the same set of people are responsible for both. When you read *Become ITIL 4 Foundation Certified in 7 Days*, have an open mind. Do not be of the view that this is something that you do not do, so it is not important. You may not be doing it today, but tomorrow's responsibilities are anybody's guess.

This book does not only prepare you for the exam, but a world that is dauntingly getting unified with DevOps. The book will help you become a fully rounded IT professional who is set for what the future has to offer.

Introduction

Predictability is a critical quality of planning in IT. Preparing for an IT certification is no different. I have tried to imbue this quality in *Become ITIL 4 Foundation Certified in 7 Days*. Working professionals need to know the kind of time commitments that need to be set aside for taking up new trainings for certification exams. The entire book is sliced into 7 unequal parts, and I have suggested how you could read the book and complete it in 7 days. I have gone one step ahead and also estimated the time that you may require to read and understand every chapter. This will give you a decent handle on planning your learning activities.

I must also remind you that ITIL is nonprescriptive; in the same spirit, the 7 days that I have put forth is a suggestion and not a prescription. I have considered a common working IT professional who has about an hour a day after office hours. If you have more time on your hands, then you can finish it faster. If you have only weekends, then two weekends may be what you need. Plan your study to suit your needs. At the end of the day, there is no point in getting stressed over setting targets that are not achievable. As they say, we must plan toward achieving success and not make the target so steep that failure seems imminent.

If you are new to ITIL, you might find the going a little rough getting used to the service management concepts. To help you wade through these waters, Chapters 1, 2, and 3 are especially for you. I have explained the basics of ITIL and DevOps with day to day examples to help you grasp the concepts.

ITIL 4 gets going from Chapter 4. If you are coming from ITIL V3, you will find that the concepts such as service value system, service value chain, and four dimensions are completely new. Yes, they have been introduced in ITIL 4. They are, however, not completely novel; they are derived from the service lifecycle that you are familiar with. When you read through Chapters 4 and 5, you will realize that ITIL V3 and ITIL 4 are not much different after all.

What we used to call processes in ITIL V3 is referred to as practices in ITIL 4. It is not the same though. There are no functions. ITIL 4 takes a different view of clubbing process and functions together to come up with practices.

Every chapter (3-14) ends with exercises. They are aimed toward helping you recollect the chapter contents and to prepare you for the upcoming examination. Remember that definitions are especially important in ITIL Foundation exams; this one is no different. Understanding concepts is necessary and, alongside memorizing the definitions, helps you in easy recall. Axelos provides a sample paper as well, which you must plan to attempt before the certification exam. I have provided these details in Chapter 14. For those who have questions on ITIL-based careers, I have answered a select few frequently asked questions in Chapter 14.

There are 34 practices in ITIL, and you will not be studying all of them for the examination. Fifteen practices are considered in the syllabus for ITIL 4 Foundation examination. If you are interested in the practices that are outside the scope of the exam, head over to my blog (`http://abhinavpmp.com`) where the remaining practices are laid out.

DAY 1

Approximate Study Time: 1 hour and 12 minutes

Chapter 1 - 25 minutes
Chapter 2 - 47 minutes

On the first day of your ITIL 4 Foundation journey you will get into the overview, history, and differences between ITIL 4 and ITIL V3, and you will learn DevOps concepts and processes. The details of the ITIL Foundation certification examination are covered, and the other ITIL certifications on offer are discussed.

CHAPTER 1

Introduction to the New ITIL

ITIL is in its fourth incarnation, and the new one has something exciting to offer. It not only offers a new variant of a framework to manage services but provides a fresh perspective into the world of services. This is especially interesting because the boundary between the development stage and operations stage is not razor thin but rather has vanished into thin air. With the absence of a barrier to distinguish the activities surrounding development stages and operational activities, the relevance of ITIL as a framework to manage operations has been scrutinized. The answer is a new version of ITIL that is tailored for the digital age.

ITIL is widely employed across IT organizations in various levels of maturity and implementation. It is the standard today to run IT operations. With the advent of the digital age and DevOps, the principles and the core understanding of management of services were somewhat shaken. A new version of ITIL was conceived to adapt to the fast-changing IT world and to keep the principal service management framework relevant.

In fact, several eulogies were written to extol the service management framework that stood guard for at least two and a half decades. It was felt that in this age of *digital everything*, the service-focused ITIL V3 was obsolete.

© Abhinav Krishna Kaiser 2021
A. K. Kaiser, *Become ITIL® 4 Foundation Certified in 7 Days*,
https://doi.org/10.1007/978-1-4842-6361-7_1

Why ITIL 4?

ITIL has come a long way. It started out being Information Technology Infrastructure Library (ITIL) and then moved into the realm of all things service management. Now in its fourth avatar as the digital ITIL, the framework is making a strong comeback.

When ITIL 4 was announced in 2017, more people feared than rejoiced. The primary concern was the certifications that people held. Traditionally, ITIL certifications become redundant with the advent of newer versions, and the bridge course is generally a bridge too far. "You might as well study the whole thing instead" was the talk of the town.

Apart from the certification pangs, others who knew the industry and where it was headed felt a tad happy to see a refresh. They felt that the refresh was late by at least 4 to 5 years; nevertheless, better late than never.

There was a question that everybody had. ITIL V3 was so much more successful than anything that was out there. Every organization practicing service management opted for it without a blink of an eye. The framework was rugged; nonprescriptive; technology neutral; and free to be adopted, adapted, and implemented. Why was a new framework needed? The answer is simple: it was out of touch with the times.

ITIL V3 Was Not for the Digital Age

ITIL V3 reminded me of Nokia. When the cell phone age started, the word cell phone was synonymous with Nokia and vice versa. And when the touchscreen phones became a reality, Nokia just faded into the background. The reason can be as straightforward as that the company did not keep up with the changing times, and they continued to invest in traditional phones with keys rather than with screens that are touch sensitive. The result was disastrous. They realized it a bit too late for them to return with a thumping roar, and they remain on the sidelines.

With ITIL too, the story would have been similar had it remained with ITIL V3. Like Nokia, ITIL V3 and service management mean the same. There is no alternative, absolutely no opposition or a competitor to it. Yet its mere existence was doubted as we embarked into the digital age. Many critics and digital champions wrote eulogies for ITIL and basically said that in the age when change happens at the speed of light, a traditional and process-driven framework has absolutely no room to play. The digital age needed plenty of agility, dynamism, and rapid decision making. ITIL V3 with its phases, processes, and functions was never going to cut it, they said.

It was then that the company behind ITIL, AXELOS, initiated a refresh by reaching out to about 2,000 professionals from various organizations to come together with the single objective of creating a framework that was agile and innovative. The outcome is ITIL 4.

Emergence of DevOps

There was an explosion that made tradition get locked up in a box, and two distinct parts of IT had to come together under the same umbrella. Development and operations had always been at loggerheads and had been the IT industry's favorite blame game. If too many incidents were reported, the development side of things was blamed. If resolution took too long, the developers pegged it on the operational inefficiencies. While the industry had accepted living with this arrangement, Patrick Debois had other plans. He proposed that all the inefficiencies could be put to rest and synergy amplified by asking development and operations to work as a single unit. No more blame games and no more passing the buck; only collaboration, he surmised.

Not that the industry fell all over the DevOps methodology when it was first socialized. But when it got into the biggies such as Accenture and IBM, every other company wanted to get into this model. In fact, running projects in a DevOps model became a sales pitch. The customers too wanted the new shiny thing and headed towards the DevOps methodology.

Underneath the game of development and operations, there was a major shift that the IT industry witnessed. It was no longer project management and service management that drove the combined parts that came together. It was rather replaced by product management. So, everything that we knew about project and service management became obsolete and there was hunger for the digital ways of thinking. It came in Agile flavors in the place of project management; then there was Lean that promised cutbacks and minimalism; and finally, on the operations front, there were hubbubs that operations was no longer needed if the product management was done brilliantly. They said that if you provide a perfect product without defects, then what incidents would operations resolve, and what was the need to go through the whole nine yards of service management? The industry did not really buy into the concept of no ops but instead started to look for options to take over from the mighty ITIL that had dominated the service management space. This is when the new ITIL was announced and this was the time when my work toward reinventing ITIL began.

In a DevOps project, essentially the development of a product happens alongside the operations. More often than not, there will be a single product backlog to feed off from, and the same set of people are tasked with working on both sets of activities. This changes the equation for ITIL V3 to work in a way that is most commonly implemented—take, for example, the change management process. It is meant to be a governance process that builds into a certain level of bureaucracy. And bureaucracy takes time to process due to various approvals and checks and balances. DevOps is like a startup company. It does not like bureaucracy. It does not believe in waiting unless there is a real dependency. In this situation, how do you implement change management for a DevOps project? How can you keep both sides happy? Maybe standardize all forms of changes? Think again! Does it defeat the purpose of the change management process if all changes are to be standardized? Perhaps. Most likely. Likewise, there are several conflicts and contradictions that came out while designing ITIL for a DevOps project. The major one was the ITIL's service lifecycle.

Incompatible Service Lifecycle

ITIL V3's biggest USP (Unique Selling Proposition) from its previous version was the logical beginning to identify services and its lifecycle. The definition of the entire lifecycle of a service brought a new meaning to how services were valued and defined. This literally was the game changer.

There are five phases in the ITIL V3 service lifecycle:

1. Service strategy

2. Service design

3. Service transition

4. Service operations

5. Continual service improvement

The five phases are represented in Figure 1-1.

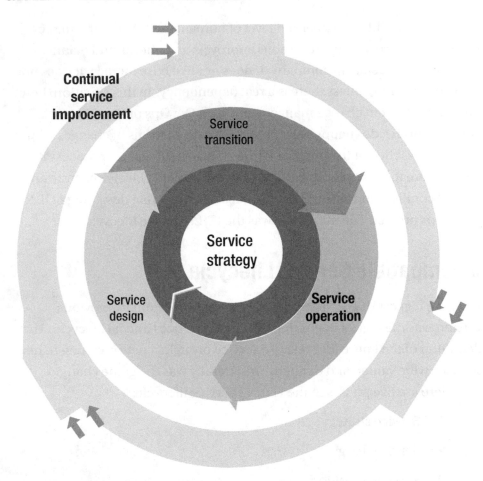

Figure 1-1. *ITIL V3 service lifecycle*

It shows service strategy at the core to indicate the importance
and involvement of a sound strategy in the inception of IT services.
Service strategy provides guidance around existing and new IT services.
Surrounding service strategy are service design, service transition, and
service operations. Service design provides the direction pertaining to
realization of a service. The IT services that are identified in the service
strategy are defined and designed, and blueprints are created for their
development. These designs are built, tested, and implemented in the

service transition phase. After implementation, the services move into a maintenance mode. Maintenance of services is handled by the service operations phase. Continual service operations envelop the other four phases. The depiction shows that all four phases present opportunities for improvement, and the continuous service improvement will provide the means to identify and implement improvements across the service lifecycle.

The life of a service, starting with its interception and watching it grow and improve, is a wonderful story. It is timeless. But today, service by itself does not have an identity. It is clubbed with the development story. So, when development and services are viewed as Siamese twins, the service and its lifecycle become irrelevant. This is one of the primary reasons why ITIL V3 did not come as a natural fit to the DevOps scheme of things.

The ITIL V3 service lifecycle is sequential in nature. It starts nicely with ideation in service strategy and moves logically and with purpose from one phase to another. DevOps on the other hand is not sequential. It is not parallel as well. It works in small iterations. The value is realized through bits and pieces of delivery rather than the whole giant fish. We cannot see a service shaping up in iterations. It is just not possible.

ITIL Reinvented

I started my career as a service management architect who embraced ITIL with both hands. After a decade of ITIL designs and implementations, I moved into the DevOps area. As a DevOps architect, I often had a chance to design the operations, and the ITIL in verbatim could not fit the scheme of things. So, I designed my own framework that was built on the pillars of core ITIL V3 while adapting to the nature of DevOps methodology.

The framework turned into a book called *Reinventing ITIL in the Age of DevOps* (Apress, 2018). Several ITIL V3 implementations have opted for my *reinvented* framework to fit their DevOps and Digital needs.

The demand coming in from DevOps projects was to construct an operations framework that was nimble and gelled well alongside development work. As we no longer had the luxury of staffing operations professionals, the new demand from service operations was to build a weighted system that measures development work against operations in an Agile manner. The framework would have to consider incidents and problems alongside the development user stories.

In *Reinventing ITIL in the Age of DevOps*, I offered suggestions on how the teams can be structured to suit DevOps and ITIL in conjunction, decoded each of the 26 processes, and provided implementable process tips and tricks for the processes that are most employed during operations (incident, problem, configuration, change, and release management processes).

If your interest is in operationalizing ITIL in DevOps projects, I would still recommend that you use the process that I put forth in my book.

Brief ITIL History

The history of ITIL is nebulous and inconsistent. It started sometime during the late 1980s as a collection of best practices in IT management. A department in the UK government, known as the OGC (Office of Government Commerce), sanctioned the coalition. Basically, the best practices of various IT departments and companies in the UK were studied and documented. It is believed that most of the initial practices that constituted ITIL came from IBM.

The first version of ITIL was bulky and lacked direction, with a compilation of over 30 books. The second version of ITIL was cut down to nine books in 2000, but mainly revolved around two books: service delivery and service support. The ITIL certifications were based on these two books as well. ITIL v2 introduced ten processes, five each from service delivery and service support. I started my ITIL journey with ITIL v2.

ITIL v2 was process centric. IT organizations were expected to operate around the ITIL processes. The processes were interconnected but lacked a broader vision and a flow to move things along.

The shortcomings and inadequacies in v2 gave rise to ITIL V3 in 2007. It had an excess of 20 processes, spanning across the entire lifecycle of a service, from conception up to a point where the service runs on regular improvement cycles.

ITIL V3 came out with five books, each book spanning a lifecycle phase of an IT service. ITIL V3 has penetrated most IT organizations. Even the conservative IT organizations have embraced the ITIL V3 service management framework with open arms. The framework is still rampant in the industry today and enjoys a monopolistic nature, except for Microsoft, which adheres to a derivative version of ITIL, the Microsoft Operations Framework.

In 2011, ITIL V3 received a minor update where a couple of new processes were added along with some minute changes in definitions and concepts. The 2011 framework has 26 processes and four functions. It is referred to as ITIL 2011 and some people refer to it as ITIL V3 2011, indicating the version and the revision year.

In 2017, a new version (V4) was announced. The date was set 2 years later, and in February 2019, a phase-wise release of ITIL 4 started. It started with the ITIL Foundation publication and announcement of the ITIL Foundation examination, and through the next few months, individual modules were announced. The entire set is expected to be released by the end of 2020.

ITIL V3 and ITIL 4: The Differences

ITIL 4 is not a new wine in an old bottle. Although the principles of the ITIL remain strong, the nuances of the framework are contrasting. While the former tries to build a story like Jeffrey Archer, the new is dynamic and explosive like Tim Ferriss' brilliance. In other words, the resemblance is limited to individual processes rather than the story and context built around them.

There are several changes, but I am not going to discuss all of them here. Maybe I need an entire book to start expounding on it. Here are the big-ticket items.

The Service Lifecycle Is Dead

On expected lines, the service lifecycle has been done away with. It was the lack of a traditional lifecycle that led the call for a new ITIL and the eventual coming to be of ITIL 4.

The void left by the service lifecycle has been taken up by not one concept but two. Service value system and service value chain are the new concepts that drive the delivery of services. The service value chain roughly tries to cover for service lifecycle but takes a PDCA (Plan-Do-Check-Act) flavor with planning, acting, vetting, and corrective actions.

More details on it are in Chapter 5.

Introducing Practices

In ITIL, processes rule the roost. All activities happen through processes. In fact, the service lifecycle too is comprised of various processes to deliver service phase objectives. However, in ITIL 4 it is practices that take center stage, but not as prominently as the processes did.

Practices are more than processes. One does not replace the other, nor is one a mere reflection of the other. A process was meant to take in certain inputs and when the trigger kicks in, a set of activities was designed to take place. And finally, there would be an output. A practice is an extension of a process. It not only defines the activities but also brings together various entities, capabilities, and tools to accomplish the set objectives.

We had a concept called functions in ITIL V3, which was the teams executing various processes. In the previous version, I had a section dedicated to fuse processes and functions. I imagined the functions running as horizontals, while the processes were verticals and they intersected as a mesh—because people and teams were needed to run the processes. I do not have that section in this book. Guess why? There are no functions in ITIL 4. The functions are fused within the process, and the outcome can roughly be termed as a practice.

Imagine having a problem management team in your organization. It is a function. What do they do? They work on the problem management process to meet its objectives. Besides the problem management team, you needed other technical teams to deliver the objectives. They were part of the different distinct functions.

To collaborate better and to deliver value efficiently, ITIL 4 has introduced the concept of practices. Problem management practice in this instance is a system on its whole whose objectives is to deliver all the problem management outputs.

Service Has a New Definition

ITIL V3 service definition read: *a means of delivering value to customers by facilitating outcomes customers want to achieve without the ownership of specific costs and risks.* The onus was on the service provider to create value for the customer, and the customer does not have to own up to the risks or individual costs for unit items. The customer pays a certain agreed amount for the service and gets the service without worrying about the service's inherent risks or underlying cost of individual elements that make up a service.

ITIL 4 has changed the definition of a service. *It is a means of enabling value co-creation by facilitating outcomes that customers want to achieve, without the customer having to manage specific costs and risks.* The difference might look trivial, but the meaning and implication is huge.

Today a service provider cannot tuck away services and deliver it to the customer in isolation. Any service can become valuable only if there is ample direction and feedback from the customer, the primary person who uses the service. Hence the definition has rightly included *co-creation*.

Governance Is a New Kid on the Block

Governance in ITIL V3 was not embraced with open arms in my opinion. Yes, we had the governance processes to ensure that the service management work was governed to the hilt and things did not go in unwanted directions. But my problem was that there was no explicit mention or a process or a function to define it. It was always the outsider who was looking in.

Things have changed for the better in ITIL 4. Governance has a proper seat at the table. The only way a service management framework or any other management framework can get governance defined and implemented right is by giving it focus and defining its objectives. You will find more on it in Chapter 5.

Automation Is In

Activities that do not require cognizance, intelligence, or decision-making brain cells can theoretically be run by machines. This makes even more sense if these activities are repeatable exercises. Automation is the key to launching and running any service because they are not simplistic anymore. There are multiple integrations, and handling every single driver can only be achieved if it is entrusted to the machines. So, automation is to be embraced and not be looked at as an opponent to job creation.

ITIL V3 toyed with the idea of event management tools. It was not full blown but the intentions were clear. ITIL 4 has taken it to the next level by defining a guiding principle coupling optimization and automation to allow ITIL to step through DevOps' doors.

ITIL 4 Certification Hierarchy

ITIL has matured with every release of its hierarchy of exams, and this is aimed to help service management professionals choose the right certification based on their job profile. In ITIL V3 too, it started with the basic foundation exam and moved into each of the specific areas/phases, and an expert level was defined for the person who was able to pass all the levels. Above the expert level was the pinnacle of ITIL certifications—the master level. It was like a PhD in ITIL, where the certification seeker was expected to write a thesis rather than answer a bunch of questions.

ITIL 4 is similar and has significantly changed, adapting to the times we live in. The certification levels are illustrated in Figure 1-2.

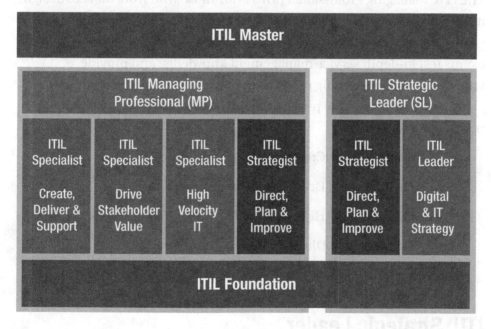

Figure 1-2. *ITIL 4 certification path*

Similar to ITIL V3, the new ITIL 4 too starts recognizing ITIL professionals through the ITIL Foundation certification. More on the certification is included in the next subsection.

After completing the foundation certification, ITIL practitioners can choose their certification based on the choice of career. There are two options:

1. ITIL Managing Professional (MP)

2. ITIL Strategic Leader (SL)

ITIL Managing Professional

The ITIL Managing Professional (MP) is for those who work on ITIL design, implementation, and operations. It is meant for pure service-management professionals who work in technology and digital streams. The certification exams test in-depth service management knowledge and provide knowledge around running projects, practices, teams, and workflows.

To become an MP, the practitioner must complete four individual modules:

1. ITIL Specialist: Create, Deliver, and Support

2. ITIL Specialist: Drive Stakeholder Value

3. ITIL Specialist: High Velocity IT

4. ITIL Strategist: Direct, Plan, and Improve

ITIL MP is equivalent to ITIL Expert in the V3 certification scheme.

ITIL Strategic Leader

While ITIL MP looks primarily inward toward the cogs of the ITIL engine, the ITIL SL certification is meant to look outward toward business—business needs, expectations, and everything related to them.

The certification tests the knowledge of ITIL from the perspective of the understanding of the influence ITIL has on the business strategy.

To become an SL, the practitioner must complete two modules:

1. ITIL Strategist: Direct, Plan, and Improve (common with MP)

2. ITIL Leader: Digital and IT Strategy

ITIL Master

Not much is known about the ITIL 4 Master certification. Currently, the master certification available is only for the ITIL V3 certification.

We believe that the ITIL 4 Master certification will be eligible for ITIL practitioners who have completed MP and SL certifications and must appear for an interview or prove a design/theory based on empirical facts and assumed data.

The existing Master certification has an eligibility of ITIL Expert certification and minimum 5 years' experience in service management.

ITIL Foundation Certification

The ITIL Foundation certification is a test of understanding of the various ITIL concepts, philosophy, framework, and underlying ideas. The certification skims the surface across the entire framework. The candidate gets an entire overview of the framework, the principle of IT services, the delivery mechanisms, and the continuous improvements it endures.

The ITIL 4 Foundation certification was opened on the 28th of February, 2019.

Eligibility Criteria

Anybody can take up the ITIL 4 certification. There are no criteria for minimum experience, education, or other prerequisite certifications. Although there are accredited training organizations that deliver ITIL Foundation trainings, you can self-study using a study guide such as this one and appear for the exam.

Your existing ITIL V3 Foundation certification does not count toward the ITIL 4 certification exam, as there is no bridge program that is available. So, everybody needs to take up the ITIL 4 Foundation certification examination, whether or not they have an equivalent certification in ITIL V3.

This is an entry level certification program into the world of ITIL. I encourage everybody in IT to take up the certification, as DevOps and ITIL are not mutually exclusive. What better way to get a firmer grip on DevOps than by getting a solid understanding of the operations side of it.

Most ITIL-based jobs are in service operations, and for a service operations role, the ITIL Foundation certification is considered adequate. Even in traditional organizations delivering IT services, most employers expect employees to hit the ground running when they start. For this to happen, there needs to be an alignment of processes, terminology, and the ways of working. This is primarily the reason for employers to insist on the ITIL Foundation certification.

People often change career paths within the same organization. To change into a service management role, organizations insist that employees undergo ITIL training and probably be certified before the transition.

I have also had students who are primarily from the projects side of the industry. They were keen to understand how the services operate, and to get a general awareness of IT service management, they took the ITIL Foundation certification course.

Certification Examination

The ITIL Foundation certification can be taken up through an online examination or a paper-based exam.

Here are some highlights of the ITIL Foundation Exam:

- Closed book: You cannot refer to any books, notes, or cheat sheets.

- There are 40 multiple choice questions; every question comes with a choice of four possible answers.

- Exam duration: 60 minutes

- Each question carries one mark; wrong answers do not bog you down with negative scoring.

- You are required to give 26 correct answers to pass the exam: 65 percent.

- The Foundation certificate only showcases that you have passed the exam and does not display the score you obtained on the exam.

- You get instant results when you opt for online exams.

You will find ITIL Foundation examination tips, tricks, and FAQs on ITIL and ITIL-based careers in Chapter 15.

CHAPTER 2

Brief Overview of DevOps

New ways of working, or new methodologies, begin to unearth because of a problem—yes, it all starts with a problem. DevOps too had its own reasons. Businesses craved fast turnarounds of their solutions. And often businesses found out in the midst of development that they did not have all the information they needed to make the right decisions. They wanted to recommend a few more changes to the requirements and still expected the delivery to happen on time. DevOps was born to solve this problem.

Well, DevOps did not just show up as the DevOps we have today. It has evolved over time. It was clear to those who started solving the problem around agility that DevOps has a lot of potential to not just solve the problem of agility but also increase productivity by leaps and bounds. Further, the quality of the software developed had the potential to be at a historic best. Thus, to this day, DevOps keeps changing and changing for the better.

DevOps is not just a methodology for developers. Operations too gets its share of the benefits pie. With increased automation, operations went from being a mundane job to an innovative one. Operations folks just got themselves a new lease on life through various tools that can make their working lives a whole lot better, and they could start looking forward to integrating and configuring tools to do advanced stuff, rather than the repetitive workload that is generally associated with operations. Here too, the productivity shot up, and human errors became a rarity.

© Abhinav Krishna Kaiser 2021
A. K. Kaiser, *Become ITIL® 4 Foundation Certified in 7 Days*,
https://doi.org/10.1007/978-1-4842-6361-7_2

The software development was carried out on the back of the software delivery life cycle (SDLC) and managed through waterfall project management. On the operations front, ITIL ruled the roost. Through DevOps, development and operations essentially came together to form a union. In the mix, the waterfall methodology gave way to Agile methodologies, and still people who design DevOps processes did not have a good understanding of how ITIL would come into DevOps. So, a lot of noise started to circulate that the dawn of DevOps is the end for ITIL. This is plainly noise without any substance.

What Exactly Is DevOps

There are multiple perceptions about DevOps. In fact, if you search the Web, you will be surprised to find multiple definitions for DevOps and that no two original definitions converge on common aspects and elements.

I have trained thousands in the area of DevOps, and the best answer I have is that it brings together the development and operations teams, and that's about it. Does bringing two teams together create such a strong buzz across the globe? In fact, if it was just the culmination of two teams, then probably DevOps would have been talked of in the human resources ecosphere, and it would have remained a semicomplex HR management process.

During the beginning of the DevOps era, to amuse my curiosity, I spoke to a number of people to understand what DevOps is. Most bent toward automation; some spoke of that thing they do in startups; and there were very few who spoke of it as a cultural change. Interesting! Who talks of culture these days, when the edge of our seats burns a hole if we don't act on our commitments? A particular example made me sit up and start joining the DevOps dots, and it all made sense eventually.

DevOps Explained with an Example

Let us say that you are a project manager for an Internet banking product. The past weekend you deployed a change to update a critical component of the system after weeks of development and testing. The change was deployed successfully; however, during the postimplementation review, it threw out an error that forced you to roll back the change.

The rollback was successful, and all the artifacts pertaining to the release were brought to the table to examine and identify the root cause the following Monday. Now what happens? The root cause is identified, a developer is pressed into action to fix the bug, and the code goes through the scrutiny of various tests, including the tests that were not originally done that could have caught the bug in the functional testing stage rather than in production. All tests run OK; a new change is planned; it gets approved by the change advisory board; and the change gets implemented, tested, and is given all green lights.

These are the typical process activities that are undertaken when a deployment fails and has to be replanned. However, the moment things go south, what is the first thing that comes to your mind as the project manager? Is it what objective action you should take next, or do you start thinking of the developer who worked in this area, the person responsible for the bug in the first place? Or do you think about the tester who identified the scenarios, wrote the scripts, and performed exploratory testing? Yes, it is true that you start to think about the people responsible for the mess. Why? It is because of our culture. We live in a culture that blames people and tries to pass the buck.

I mentioned earlier about some respondents telling me that DevOps is about culture. So, what culture am I talking about within the context of this example? The example depicts a blameful culture where the project manager is trying to pin the blame on the people within his team directly responsible for the failure. He could be factually right in pinning the blame on people directly responsible, but I am focusing on the practice of blaming individuals.

How is this practice different from a DevOps culture? In DevOps, the responsibility of completing a task is not considered as an individual responsibility but rather a shared responsibility. Although an individual works on a task, if the person fails or succeeds, the entire team gets the carrot or the stick. Individuals are not made responsible when we look at the overall DevOps scheme of things, and we do not blame individuals. We follow a blameless culture. This culture of blamelessness arises from the fact that we all make mistakes because we are humans after all and far from being perfect. We make mistakes. So, what is the point in blaming people? In fact, we expect that people do make mistakes—not based on negligence but from the experimentation mindset.

This acceptance (of developers making mistakes) has led us to develop a system where the mistakes that are made get identified and rectified in the developmental stages, well before they reach production.

How is this system (to catch mistakes) built? To make it happen, we brought the development and operations teams together (to avoid disconnect); we developed processes that are far more effective and efficient than what was out there; and finally we took umbrage under automation to efficiently provide us with feedback on how we are doing (as speed is one of the main objectives we intend to achieve).

DevOps is a common phrase, and with its spread reaching far and wide, there are multiple definitions coming from various quarters. No two definitions will be alike, but they will have a common theme: culture. So, for me, DevOps is a cultural transformation that brings together people from across disciplines to work under a single umbrella to collaborate and work as one unit with an open mind and to remove inefficiencies.

Note   Blameless culture does not mean that the individuals who make repeated mistakes go scot-free. Individuals will be appraised justly and appropriately but in a constructive manner.

Why DevOps

You might ask what gave rise to a new culture called DevOps. The answer is evolution. If you take a timeline view of software, from the 1960s up to the advent of the Internet in the 1990s, developing software was equivalent to a building project or launching a space shuttle. It required meticulous planning and activities that were planned to be executed sequentially. The waterfall project management methodology was thus born with five sequential steps, as indicated in Figure 2-1.

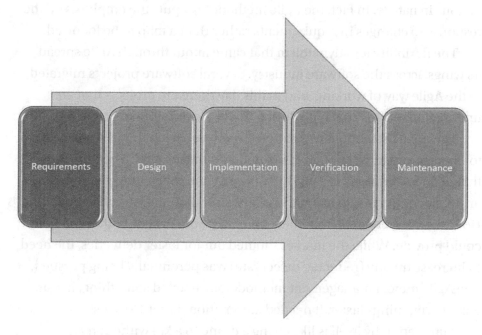

Figure 2-1. *Waterfall project management methodology*

When the Internet boomed, the software was far more accessible than the earlier era, and this generated demand not seen earlier. When the software industry started to expand, the waterfall model's limitations were exposed. The need to complete a detailed planning exercise and the sequential practice of flow did seem like an impediment to the advancement of the software industry.

Then in 2001 at a ski resort in Utah, the Agile Manifesto was born. Several prevalent Agile methodologies came together to form a common goal that would remove the cast-in-stone waterfall sequential activities.

Agile was more fluid because it did not conceive of all the requirements at the beginning and try to solve everything overnight. It was an approach that was based on iterations, where all the activities of project management just cycled repeatedly.

In between, if a requirement were to change, that's OK because there were provisions to make changes that were neither bureaucratic nor tedious in nature. In fact, the Agile methodology puts the emphasis on the response to changes in requirements rather than a map to be followed.

The flexibility and dynamism that came about through Agile spread its wings across the software industry. Several software projects migrated to the Agile way of working, and to this day there are projects that are undergoing serious coaching during this transformational phase.

The Agile methodology is simple, where you keep things small enough to manage and large enough to be rendered meaningful. The time frames that defined iterations in Agile did not carry too much wriggle room. From an efficiency perspective, Agile was far better than the waterfall model. However, the demands from the market were out of sync with what Agile could provide. While the market shouted out for faster deliveries, the need to increase quality (reducing defect rate) was perennially being pursued. The Agile project management methodology needed something, like an elixir to run things faster. It needed automation. Enter DevOps!

Automation by itself is like giving a drone to a kid without really teaching him the process to make it fly. Generally speaking, technology by itself has no meaning if there are no underlying functional architecture, process, and embedded principles. DevOps, therefore, is not just automation but a whole lot more. You will find out the nitty-gritty details in the coming sections.

A Note on DevOps Scope

The word DevOps gives away the scope through its conjunction of two parts of a software life cycle. While Agile existed mainly to put an end to the rigidity brought forth by the waterfall model, it was said that the methodology can be used for operations as well. But, without an overarching process or a framework, using Agile for operations with the same rigor was not going to work. DevOps bridged this gap by bringing in the operational phases along with the developmental activities under a single umbrella, and applying common processes and principles to be employed across the board.

DevOps comes into play when you get started with the software development process, which is the requirement gathering phase. It ends when the software retires from service. DevOps spans the entire wavelength of a software life cycle, and if you read between the lines, you cannot just implement and execute DevOps until deployment and be done with it. It will continue to function until the software is used by its designated users. In other words, DevOps is here to stay, and stay for as long as services are delivered. So, in practice, the operational phase runs perpetually, and DevOps will deliver the required optimization and automation. The processes to run operations will be borrowed from the ITIL service management framework.

Note   The word DevOps came into existence thanks to Twitter. The first Devopsdays conference was held in Ghent, Belgium, in 2009. While people tweeted about it, the #devopsdays tag ate way 11 characters out of a possible 140. In a way of shortening it, one of the tweeters used #devops, and others followed suit. This led to the advent of what we know today as DevOps.

Benefits of Transforming into DevOps

Several software companies have been delivering applications for a number of years now. Why do we need DevOps to tell us how we must develop now?

Our services are being delivered to several customers including top banks and mines around the globe. I am running simply fine with my service management framework. Why DevOps?

People have lived for thousands of years now. They did just fine, reproducing and surviving. What has changed in the past 100 years? We have changed the modes of transport for better efficiency; we communicate faster today; and overall, our quality of life has gone up several notches. The fact that something is working is not a barrier for improvements to be brought about and to transform. DevOps introduces several enhancements in the areas of working culture, process, technology, and organization structure. The transformation has been rooted in practices that were developed by some like-minded organizations that were willing to experiment, and the results have vastly gone in favor of DevOps over other ancient methodologies that still exist today.

Amazon, Netflix, Etsy, and Facebook are some of the organizations that have taken their software deliveries to a whole new level, and they don't compete anymore with the laggards. They have set new benchmarks that are impossible to meet with any of the other methodologies.

At the 2011 Velocity conference, Amazon's director of platform analysis, Jon Jenkins, provided a brief insight into Amazon's ways of working. He supported it with the following statistics.

During weekdays, Amazon can deploy every 11.6 seconds on average. Most organizations struggle to deploy weekly consistently, but Amazon does more than 1,000 deployments every hour (1,079 deployments to be precise). Further, 10,000 hosts receive deployments simultaneously on average, and the highest Amazon has been able to achieve is 30,000 hosts simultaneously receiving deployments. Wow! These numbers are really out of this world. And these are the statistics from May 2011. Imagine what they can do today!

It's not just the speed of deployments. There are several added advantages that Amazon went on to claim during the conference:

- Outages owing to software deployments have reduced by a whopping 75 percent since 2006. Most outages are caused by new changes (read software deployments), and the reduction in outages points to the success achieved in deploying software changes.

- The downtime owing to software deployments too has reduced drastically, by about 90 percent.

- On an average, there has been an outage for every 1,000 software deployments, which is about a 0.1 percent failure rate. This looks great for a moderate software delivery organization, but for Amazon, the number seems high because of the 1,000+ deployments every hour.

- Through automation, Amazon has introduced automatic failovers whenever hosts go down.

- Architecture complexity has reduced significantly.

DevOps Principles

DevOps principles or the guidance toward *true north* are in a state of constant evolution. In fact, there are multiple versions of the principles. The most widely believed set of principles is represented with the acronym CALMS. Figure 2-2 represents a mug from a marketing campaign for DevOps featuring CALMS.

Figure 2-2. *DevOps principles (image credit: devopsnet.com)*

CALMS stands for the following:

- Culture

- Automation

- Lean

- Measurement

- Sharing

Culture

There is a popular urban legend that the late Peter Drucker, known as the founder of modern management, famously said, "Culture eats strategy for breakfast." If you want to make a massive mind-boggling earth-shaking change, start by changing the culture that can make it happen and adapt to the proposed new way of working. Culture is something that cannot be changed by a swift switching process. It is embedded into human behavior and requires an overhaul of people's behavior.

These are some of the behavioral traits that we want to change with DevOps:

- Take responsibility for the entire product and not just the work that you perform.

- Step out of your comfort zone and innovate.

- Experiment as much as you want; there's a safety net to catch you if you fall

- Communicate, collaborate, and develop affinity with the involved teams.

- For developers especially: you build it, you run it.

Automation

Automation is a key component in the DevOps methodology. It is a massive enabler for faster delivery and also crucial for providing rapid feedback. Under the culture principle, I talked about a safety net with respect to experimentation. This safety net is made possible through automation.

The objective is to automate whatever possible in the software delivery life cycle. The kinds of activities that can be efficiently automated are those that are repetitive and those that don't ask for human intelligence. For example, building infrastructure was a major task that involved hardware architects and administrators; and most importantly, building servers took a significant amount of time. This was time that was added to the overall software delivery. Thanks to the advancement of technology, we have cloud infrastructure today, and servers can be spun up through code. Additionally, we don't need hardware administrators to do it. Developers can do it themselves. Wait, there's more! Once the environment provisioning script is written, it can be used to automate spinning up servers as many times as necessary. Automation has really changed the way we see infrastructure.

Activities involving executing tasks such as running a build or running a test script can be automated. But, the activities that involve human cognizance are hard to automate today. The art of writing the code or test scripts requires the use of human intelligence, and the machines of today are not in a position to do it. Tomorrow, artificial intelligence can be a threat to the activities that are dependent on humans today.

Lean

DevOps has borrowed heavily from Lean methodology and the Toyota Production System (TPS). The thinking behind the Lean methodology is to keep things simple and not to overcomplicate them. It is natural that the advent of automation can decrease the complexity of architecture and simplify complicated workflows. The Lean principle aids in keeping us on the ground so we can continue working with things that are easy to comprehend and simple to work with.

There are two parts to the Lean principle. The primary one is not to bloat the logic or the way we do things; keep it straightforward and minimal. An example is the use of microservices, which support the cause by not overcomplicating the architecture. We are no longer looking to build monolithic architectures that are cumbersome when it comes to enhancements, maintenance, and upgrades. A microservice architecture solves all the problems that we faced yesterday with monolithic architectures; it is easy to upgrade, troubleshoot (maintain), and enhance.

The second part of the principle is to reduce the wastage arising from the methodology. Defects are one of the key wastes. Defects are a nuisance. They delay the overall delivery, and the amount of effort that goes into fixing them is just a sheer waste of time and money. The next type of waste focuses on convoluted processes. If something can be done by passing the ball from A to B, why does it have to bounce off C? There are many such wastes that can be addressed to make the software delivery more efficient and effective.

Measurement

If you seek to automate everything, then you probably need a system to provide feedback whenever something goes wrong. Feedback is possible if you know what the optimum results are and what aren't. The only way you can find out whether the outcome is optimum or not is by measuring it. So, it is essential that you measure everything if you are going to automate everything!

Measurement principle provides direction on the measures to implement and keep tabs on the pulse of the overall software delivery. It is not a simple task to measure everything. Many times we do not even know what we should measure.

Even if we do it, the how part can be an obstacle. A good DevOps process architect can help solve this problem. For example, if you are running static analysis on your code, the extent of passable code must be predetermined. It is not a random number, but a scientific reasoning must be behind it. Several companies allow a unit test to pass even if it parses 90 percent of the code. We know that ideally it must be 100 percent, so why should anybody compromise for 90 percent? That is the kind of logic that must go behind measuring everything and enabling fast feedback, to be realistic about the kind of feedback that you want to receive.

In operations, monitoring applications, infrastructure, performance, and other parameters come under this principle. Measurements in monitoring will imply when an event will be categorized as a warning or an exception. With automation in place, it is extremely important that all the critical activities, and the infrastructure that supports them, be monitored and optimized for measurement.

There are other measurements as well that are attached to contracts and SLAs and are used for reporting on a regular basis. These measurements are important as well in the overall scheme of things.

Sharing

The final principle is sharing, which hinges on the need for collaboration and knowledge sharing between people. If we aim to significantly hasten the process of software delivery, it is only possible if people don't work in silos anymore. The knowledge, experience, thoughts, and ideas must be put out into the open for others to join in the process of making them better, enhanced, and profound.

One of the key takeaways of this principle is to put everyone who works on a product or a service onto a single team and promote knowledge sharing. This will lead to collaboration rather than competition and skepticism.

There are a number of collaboration tools on the market today that help support the cause. People do not even have to be colocated to share and collaborate. Tools such as Microsoft Teams and Slack help in getting the information across not only to a single person but to all those who matter (such as the entire team). With information being transparent, there will be no reason for others to worry or be skeptical about the dependencies or the outcome of the process.

Elements of DevOps

DevOps is not a framework; it is a set of good practices. It got started out of a perfect storm that pooled several practices together (which is discussed later in this chapter), and today we consider them under the DevOps umbrella. You might have seen a graphic with an elephant (Andrew Clay Shafer's "The Panel Experiment and Ignite DevOps," May 16, 2010, devopsdays.org). The IT industry around software development is so vast that several practices are followed across the board. This is depicted as the elephant. DevOps, which is a cultural change, can be applied to any part of the software industry and to any activity that is being carried out today. So, you can identify any part of the elephant (say testing) and design DevOps-related practices and implement them and you are doing DevOps!

No matter where you want to implement DevOps, there are three common elements that support and enable the culture change. The three sections are indicated by a Venn diagram in Figure 2-3.

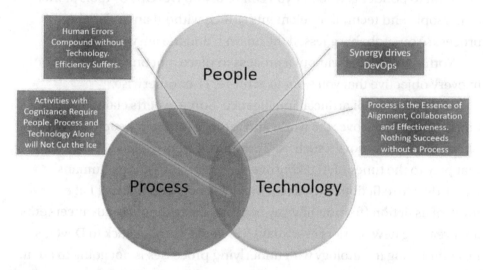

Figure 2-3. *Three elements of DevOps*

People, process, and technology are the three elements that are common to all DevOps practices. In fact, they are the enablers to effect change in the DevOps culture. Only when the three elements come together in unison are we able to realize the complete benefits of DevOps.

Let's examine the three elements and see how they fit together. To bring in a cultural change, we most definitely need people, and people cannot operate without the aid of processes. By bringing in people and processes, we have achieved the functional design to implement a DevOps solution. However, the question to ask is whether it is efficient.

Humans are known to make mistakes. We cannot avoid it. How can processes alone support humans in identifying the mistakes committed? There may be a way to do it, but it is most definitely not efficient. To make things move faster and in an efficient manner, we need the technology stack to help us achieve the process objectives.

Today, people talk of DevOps through the lens of technology. They throw around several tool names and claim that they do DevOps. So, the question to ponder is whether you can really do DevOps by tools alone. Can people and technology elements suffice without an underlying process? You probably guessed the answer, and the answer is no.

Nothing succeeds without a process in place, not only in DevOps but in every objective that you want to achieve, IT or otherwise.

This is the age of artificial intelligence. Some experts claim that the machines will take over the world and replace the work people used to do. There are several movies such as "Terminator Genisys" and "Ex Machina" that play to the tunes of AI taking over the reins and putting humans in jeopardy. I love fiction, and AI making decisions is something I like to think of as fiction (for now anyway because the technology advancements are breaking new barriers every day). However, coming back to DevOps, just employing technology with underlying processes is not going to cut it. Without people, creation does not happen. Yes, technology can automate a number of preprogrammed activities, but can it develop new solutions on its own? I don't think so; not today anyway. People are the driving force of creation and the agents of cultural change.

All the three elements of people, process, and technology are essential to build the DevOps methodology and to achieve the objectives that are set forth before us. By the union of all three elements, we can create an unmatched synergy that can fuel developments at an unparalleled pace

People

The word *DevOps* is derived from the conjunction of two words, development, and operations. I have already familiarized you with what DevOps is all about: a change of culture in the way we deliver and operate software. People are at the heart of this cultural transformation, and they are one of the three critical elements that enable the DevOps culture.

The development and operation teams are amalgamated to bring about a change in culture. The thinking behind it is quite straightforward. Let's say that an application is developed, and it comes to the change advisory board (CAB) for approval. One of the parties on the CAB is the operational teams. They specifically ask questions around the testing that has been performed for this software, and even though the answer from development is yes for the success rate of all the tests, the operational teams tend to be critical. They don't want to be blockers, yet they find themselves in a position where they have to support software that they haven't been familiarized with yet. The bugs and defects that come with the software will become their problem after the warranty period (usually between 1 and 3 months). Most importantly, they only have the confirmation of the developers to go with when the quality of the software is put on the line.

In the same scenario, imagine if the operational teams were already part of the same team as development. Being on the same team will give them an opportunity to become familiar with the development process and the quality controls put in place. Instead of asking questions in the CAB, they can work progressively with the development teams in ensuring that the software is maintainable, and all possible operational aspects are undertaken beforehand. This is one such case study that showcases the benefit of having a single team.

In Figure 2-4, you can visualize the development team on the edge of one cliff, while the operations team is on the opposite. In between the two cliffs lies an area of uncertainty where activities that fall between the two

37

teams have a knack for being unpredictable and they are usually sparred over, generally over ownership. In other words, you want things to be either with the development team or with the operations team. There is no bridge between the teams, meaning there can be a lot of confusion, miscommunication, and mistrust between the two opposing teams.

Figure 2-4. *Conflict between development and operations*

Let's play out the priorities for both teams. The development team still has a job because there is a need to develop new features. That is their core area, and that is what they must do to remain relevant. The operations team's big-ticket goal is to keep the environment stable, in the most basic sense. They need to ensure that even if something was to go wrong, they are tasked to bring it back to normal, in other words, maintain the status quo. So, here we have a development team intending to create new features and an operations team looking to keep the environment stable.

Does it have to be rocket science to have evolved into a methodology called DevOps that promises to shake the industry from its roots? Well, the environment is going to remain stable if there are no changes introduced to it. As long as it stays stagnant, nothing ever will bother its stability, and the operations team would have been awarded for a stellar job. But we have the development team waiting in the wings to develop new features. New features that are developed will be deployed in the production environment, and there is every chance that the deployment of new features could impact stability. So, stability is something that can never be achieved as long as new features are introduced, and no software will remain stagnant without enhancements and expansion.

A decent way to tackle this conundrum between the development and operation teams is to put them together and create channels of communication within the team members. Both the development and operations teams have a shared responsibility to ensure that development, testing, deployment, and other support activities happen smoothly and without glitches. Every team member takes responsibility for all the activities being carried out, which translates to the development and operation teams jointly working on the solution that begins with coding and ends with deployment. The operations teams will have no reason to mistrust the test results and can confidently deploy onto the production environment.

Process

Processes are a key component in ensuring the success of any project. However, we often find that most DevOps implementations focus more on automation and technology and give a backseat to processes that are supposed to be the basis for automation. They say that backseat driving is dangerous, so placing processes in this position and hoping that the destination would be reached in record time with no mishaps is a gamble that plays with unpredictability. Therefore, it is important that processes are defined first along with a functional DevOps architecture and then translated into tooling and automation. *The process must always drive tools and never the other way around.*

With DevOps combining different disciplines under a single banner, the processes too need to be rejigged to fit the new objectives. This section covers the processes pertaining to the development area.

Waterfall project management methodology (such as PMI-backed Project Management and PRINCE for projects in controlled environments) are not favored in the IT field anymore. There are various reasons going against this methodology, mainly stemming from the rigidity it brings into the project management structure.

Most IT projects are run on Agile project management methodologies because of the flexibility it offers in this ever-changing market. According to PMI's "Pulse of Profession" 2017 publication (`www.pmi.org/-/media/pmi/documents/public/pdf/learning/thought-leadership/pulse/pulse-of-the-profession-2017.pdf`), 71 percent of organizations have been leveraging Agile. Another study by PricewaterhouseCoopers, named "Agile Project Delivery Confidence (July 2017)" (`www.pwc.com/gx/en/actuarial-insurance-services/assets/agile-project-delivery-confidence.pdf`), reported that Agile projects are 28 percent more successful than their waterfall counterparts. This is huge considering that Agile is still new and emerging and the waterfall methodology has existed since the 1960s.

When we talk about Agile project management, there are a number of methodologies to pick from. Scrum, Kanban, Scrumban, Extreme Programming (XP), Dynamic Systems Development Method (DSDM), Crystal, and Feature Driven Development (FDD) are some examples. However, all the methodologies are aligned by a manifesto that was formulated in a ski resort in Utah in 2001. And there are a set of 12 Agile principles that provide guidance in setting up the project management processes.

Technology

Technology is the third element of DevOps and is often regarded as the most important. It is true in a sense that without automation, we cannot possibly achieve the fast results that I have shared earlier through some statistics. It is also true that technology on its own, without the proper synchrony of people (roles) and processes, is like a spaceship in the hands of kindergarteners. It is a must that the people and process sides of DevOps are sorted out first before heading this way.

The number of tools that claim to support DevOps activities is enormous—too many to count.

DevOps Practices

The word DevOps has become synonymous with certain practices such as continuous integration, continuous delivery, and continuous deployment. This section explains and declutters the practices and the differences between them.

Continuous Integration

Several developers work together on the same piece of code, which is referred to as the mainline in software development lingo. When multiple developers are at work, conflicts arising due to changes performed on pieces of code and the employed logic are quite common. Software developers generally integrate their pieces of code into the mainline once a day.

When conflicts arise, they discuss and sort it out. This process here of integrating the code manually at a defined time slows down the development. Conflicts at times can have drastic results, with hundreds of lines of code having to be rewritten. Imagine the time and effort lost due to manual integration. If I can integrate code in almost real time with the rest of the developers, the potential amount of rework can significantly be reduced. This is the concept of continuous integration.

To be more specific, continuous integration is a process whereby developers integrate their code into the source code repository (mainline) on a regular basis, say multiple times a day. When the code is integrated with the mainline, any conflicts will come out into the open as soon as it is integrated. The resolution of conflicts does not have to be an affair where all developers sit across the codebase and break their heads. Only those who have conflicts need to sort them out manually. By doing this conflict resolution multiple times a day, the extent of conflicts is drastically minimized.

Note   The best definition of continuous integration was coined by Martin Fowler from ThoughtWorks, who is also one of the founding members of the Agile Manifesto.

Continuous integration is a software development practice where members of a team integrate their work frequently, usually each person integrates at least daily, leading to multiple integrations per day. Each integration is verified by an automated build (including tests) to detect integration errors as quickly as possible. Many teams find that this approach leads to significantly reduced integration problems and allows a team to develop cohesive software more rapidly (source: `www.martinfowler.com/articles/continuousIntegration.html`).

Integrating the code with the mainline is just the beginning. Whenever the code is integrated, the entire mainline is built, and other quality checks such as unit testing and code-quality checks (static and dynamic analysis) also are carried out.

Note   Build is a process where the human-readable code is converted into machine-readable language (executable code), and the output of a build activity is a binary.

Unit testing is a quality check where the smallest testable parts of an application are tested individually and in a componentized manner.

Static analysis is an examination of the source code against the coding standards set forth by the industry/software company, such as naming conventions, blank spaces, and comments.

Dynamic analysis is an examination of the binary during runtime. Such an examination will help identify runtime errors such as memory leaks.

Let us say a particular project has three developers, and each developer integrates their code three times a day. Daily, this equates to nine integrations every day. As per Figure 2-5, code that is integrated gets unit tested first, followed by software build and code quality checks. All this happens automatically whenever code gets integrated.

With nine integrations on a daily basis, we are staring at a possibility of having nine unit tests, nine builds on the entire mainline, and nine code quality checks.

Suppose one of the builds or unit tests or code quality checks fail. The flow gets interrupted, and the developer gets down to work to fix the defect at the earliest. This ensures that the flow of code does not get hampered and other coders can continue coding and integrate their work onto the mainline.

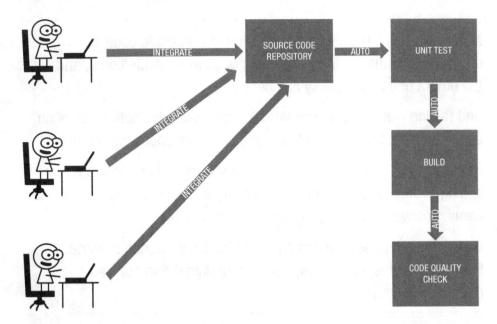

Figure 2-5. *Continuous integration*

Continuous integration allows for fast delivery of software, and any roadblocks are avoided or identified as early as possible, thanks to rapid feedback and automation. The objective of continuous integration is to hasten the coding process and to generate a binary without integration bugs.

Continuous Delivery

With continuous integration we have achieved these two things:

- A binary is generated successfully.

- Code-level and runtime checks and analysis are completed.

The next item in the SDLC is to test the generated binary from various angles, aspects, and perspectives. Yes, I am referring to the tests such as system tests, integration tests, regression tests, user acceptance tests, performance tests, and security tests; this list is quite endless. When we are done with the agreed number of tests, the binary is deemed to be of quality and deployable into production. The qualified binary can be deployed into production with a click of a button. The qualification of any of the binaries as releasable into production is termed as continuous delivery (see Figure 2-6). It is generally seen as a natural extension of the continuous integration process.

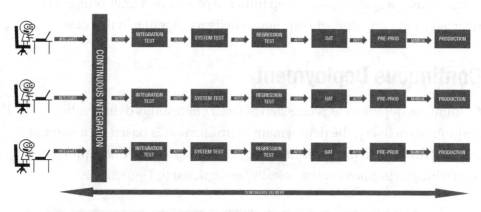

Figure 2-6. *Continuous delivery*

Figure 2-6 depicts a continuous delivery pipeline. After every successful cycle of continuous integration, the binary is automatically subjected to an integration test. When the integration test is successful, the same binary is automatically system tested. The cycle passes on up to the preproduction environment as long as the tests (regression and user acceptance testing [UAT] in this illustration) are successful. When the same binary is successfully deployed in the preproduction environment (in this illustration) or any other environment that comes before the production environment, the binary becomes qualified to be deployed on to production. The deployment into the production environment is not done automatically but requires a trigger to make it happen. The entire cycle starting from the code push into the source code repository up to the manual deployment into the production environment is continuous delivery.

In the illustration, I have shown three developers integrating their code and three deployable binaries. Continuous delivery does not dictate that all three binaries have to be deployed into production. The release management process can decide to deploy only the latest binary every week. Remember that the latest binary will consist of the code changes performed by all the developers up until that point in time.

The sequence of automation for the activities beginning in the continuous integration process up until the production environment is referred to as a pipeline, or continuous delivery pipeline in this case.

Continuous Deployment

Continuous deployment is one step beyond continuous delivery. In continuous delivery, the deployment to production is based on a manual trigger. However, in the continuous deployment process, the deployment to production happens automatically, as depicted in Figure 2-7.

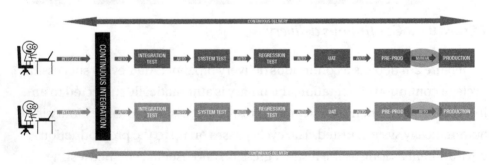

Figure 2-7. *Continuous deployment*

As soon as all the tests are successful, the binary is deployed to the preproduction environment. When the deployment to preproduction goes as planned, the same binary is deployed into production directly. In continuous delivery (Figure 2-7), the binaries were qualified as deployable, and the release manager was in a position to not deploy every single qualified binary into production. On the contrary, in continuous deployment, every single qualified binary gets deployed onto the production instance.

You might think that this is far too risky. How can you deploy something into production without any checks and balances and approvals from all stakeholders? Well, every single test that is performed and all the quality checks executed are the checks that are qualifying binaries as deployables. It is all happening in an automated fashion. You would do the same set of things otherwise but manually. Instead of deploying multiple times a day, you might deploy once a week. All the benefits that you derive from going early into the market are missing from the manual processes.

Let us say that one of the deployments were to fail. No problem! There is an automated rollback mechanism built into the system that rolls back the deployment within seconds. And it is important to note that the changes that are being discussed here are tiny changes. So, the chances of these binaries bringing down a system are remote.

Continuous Delivery vs. Continuous Deployment

The difference lies in the final sequence, where the deployment to production instance is automatic in continuous deployment and has a manual trigger for continuous delivery, as depicted in Figure 2-8.

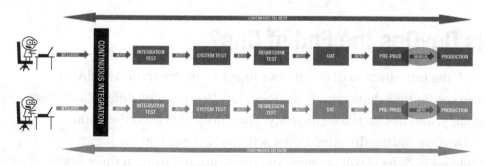

Figure 2-8. *Continuous delivery vs. continuous deployment*

Any organization on a journey of implementing DevOps will implement the continuous delivery process and upon gaining sufficient maturity will move toward the pinnacle of DevOps maturity: the continuous deployment process.

Organizations that feel a need to keep total control of their production environment through a formal structure of approvals and visibility tend to opt for continuous delivery. Banking and other financial segments fall into this category.

There are other organizations that have scaled the DevOps maturity ladder and are quite confident that the automatic deployment doesn't cause significant impact to their production environment. Even if something was to fail, the rollback will be rapid too, even before anybody can notice it. Companies like Amazon, Netflix, and Google have been in this space for a while now. I shared a statistic earlier about Amazon managing a deployment every 11.6 seconds. How is it even possible? Look no further than continuous deployment.

Note   Here is a cheat sheet for continuous delivery and continuous deployment:

Continuous delivery: You can deploy.

Continuous deployment: You will deploy

Is DevOps the End of Ops?

With the introduction of continuous integration, continuous delivery, and continuous deployment, the focus has been to plug defects, increase quality, and not sacrifice efficiency. The thinking behind the notion of DevOps ending the operational activities is based on the premise that lack of defects will not give rise to operational work. If there are no defects, there are potentially no incidents or problems, which translates to a massive reduction in operational work. Another example is if we implement continuous deployment, the change and release management processes as we know them will be automated to a great extent and will diminish the need for approvals and subsequent approvals, release planning, and release deployment.

Let's get one thing straight: no matter how much we try with the use of technology and automation, defects will always exist. The number of defects will come down due to the rapid feedback and automation, but to state that all the defects would be identified and rectified is absurd. With the reduction of defects, the amount of operational work will definitely go down. With the argument around change and release management processes, the execution of changes and releases can be automated through continuous delivery and continuous deployment, but the planning bit will always remain the cognizance of human experience. To an extent, the operational work involving change and release management processes are starting to go down as well.

Innovation is a double-edged sword. With the introduction of tools and automation, there is a new operational requirement to set up and configure the tool stack and to maintain it as long as the project is underway. This is an operational activity that is added to the traditional operations work. While some areas have seen a reduction, there are new ones that have sprouted to take their place. The manual, repetitive, and boring activities are going away. In their place, exciting DevOps tooling work has come to the fore and is making the operational roles all the more lucrative.

So, if you are an operational person, it is time to scale up and scale beyond managerial activities alone. The new wave of role mapping requires people to be techno-managerial in talent and be multiskilled. T-shaped resources, not only for operations but also in development, are being sought after. I-shaped resources must look toward getting acquainted with areas of expertise that complement their line of work.

With the advent of DevOps, there is a turbulence created in software projects. This is a good turbulence because it seeks to raise the level of delivery and to make teams, rather than individuals, accountable for the outcomes. From an operations front, it is clear that their role has gone up a couple of notches where the mundane, boring, repetitive activities have been replaced with imaginative and challenging jobs such as configuring pipelines, integrating toolsets, and automating configuration management. The nature of work for operations has changed but not the role they play as guardians of environments and troubleshooters of incidents and problems. DevOps has not spelled the end of operations but rather rejuvenated it to an exciting journey that will keep the wits of people working in operations alive.

DAY 2

Approximate Study Time: 1 hour and 37 minutes

Chapter 3 - 53 minutes
Chapter 4 - 44 minutes

On day 2 we jump into ITIL concepts: products, services, value, and service relationships. We also study the four dimensions of ITIL, which are the pillars that hold the ITIL fort steady.

CHAPTER 3

ITIL 101: Concepts and Core Foundation

The ITIL 4 Foundation Certification exam study guide starts with this chapter. While Chapter 1 went into the nuances and history of ITIL, Chapter 2 provided an insight into the world of DevOps and its practices.

From this point on, I will not be referring to ITIL 4 but just ITIL. I will try and avoid comparing ITIL concepts against the incumbent version. All the comparisons and commentary are in Chapter 1.

In this chapter, you will learn about the underlying concepts of service management, which includes services and roles that are pivotal. I will further delve into value, outcomes, costs, and risks. The evergreen concept of marrying services with value is done under the banner of utility and warranty. Finally, I will talk about service relationships.

Exam Tip   Beginning with this chapter, you can expect to see a few questions at the end of the chapter. These are the typical questions you can expect to see on your ITIL Foundation exam. Answer keys to the questions are provided at the end of the book.

© Abhinav Krishna Kaiser 2021
A. K. Kaiser, *Become ITIL® 4 Foundation Certified in 7 Days*,
https://doi.org/10.1007/978-1-4842-6361-7_3

Service Management

When you buy a product, say a smartphone, what are some of the things that you will consider? You would look at the features, brand, and price for sure. But what else comes up on the list? Perhaps service-related options such as cost of servicing, warranty, availability of service centers, parts covered under the service, and turnaround times are important. In fact, today, a brand gets its value not only from the products it has on the market but also on the service factor. Apple makes the most popular phone today in iPhone. What else makes the iPhone click? The international warranty, proximity to Apple stores across the globe, professional approach to fixing problems, and the no nonsense approach to keeping the customer happy are of foremost importance.

I repeat. A brand gets its value from the services it offers. Think of all the cars you have owned and the service comfort you have had within the service provider. Yes, the service provider plays a major role in keeping things in motion. It could be the tangibles such as your latest iPhone phone or your Tesla car. Or it could be intangibles such as electricity, mobile internet, and landscaping. The services offered collectively fall under service management, which branches out toward various specializations like IT, hospitality, and medicine.

ITIL Definition of Service Management

A set of specialized organizational capabilities for enabling value for customers in the form of services.

The specialized organizational capabilities point to the technical maturity, experience, customer service, and management frameworks that the service provider brings to the table in servicing the customers, meeting their needs, and creating value.

Exam Tip   In the ITIL Foundation examination, understanding the definition in verbatim is essential. Questions appear on the exam asking you to identify the correct definition of, *say*, service management. You will be in a position to do it only if you have memorized the definitions. Although I am not a big fan of memorizing anything, I would recommend that you do it from an examination standpoint.

The specialized organizational capabilities do not come easy. It is a long and arduous process to gain knowledge from past experiences, capabilities (skills), and a clear direction to move forward. Leadership in service management starts with identifying the nature of true value, reading the stakeholders accurately, and drawing boundaries of support and improvement.

Although service management is the core of the ITIL framework, it is very much a part of the complete framework of product management. We cannot look at service management without the context of a product. A product drives the service's success. A lousy product, for example, clubbed with exemplary service does not influence the customer's perception. Both need to walk hand in hand and tango like an Argentine.

Products and Services

The gulf between a product and a service has been closing since the dawn of the digital age. While we all know the basic difference between the two, such as a product being tangible and something that a customer can buy and potentially snap all ties with the manufacturer, a service is more about the relationship between a customer and a service provider. Services are generally intangible and time-bound.

The digital age has seen a trend where products are camouflaged and sold as services. In other words, products are no longer products—they are products in services' form and shape—like a wolf in sheep's clothing. Take for example the ever popular MS Office application. In my college days, I used to pay a certain sum and buy the application. I used it for a number of years until a new version came in and I discarded the old for the new. Today, this product from yesteryear is not sold as a product anymore. Well, you can buy it as a product but it is no longer a knight in shining armor. Office is sold in the garb of Office 365, where I pay a fraction of the money that I normally pay for the product, and I pay every month (or annually). The benefits (although over a period of time, I end up paying a whole lot more than the product itself) are the free upgrades and the number of licenses that I get with a single subscription— plus humongous amount of space on OneDrive. All that Microsoft had to do was repackage the product with some glitters and lollipops and they came out on the other side with a constant flow of revenue and substantial profits. Welcome to the digital age!

ITIL is primarily about services and how services make customers create outcomes. Creating services cannot be done in the absence of a strategy for product management. So this section touches upon both products and services, but delves deep into services while we skim the product's surface.

ITIL Definition of a Product

A configuration of an organization's resources designed to offer value for a consumer.

An organization's resources can come in multiple forms and shapes. It could be the people working in it, the processes, or the products that are manufactured or developed. These resources can be sold to a consumer in a number of ways:

- It could be sold at a one-time price.

- It can be leased or rented for a certain period of time.

- The customer could use the product on a subscription basis.

- People in an organization could work as contractors in a staff augmentation role.

No matter how the company offers its products, the end goal is to provide value through the resources that it has at its disposal.

Services are a different beast. They are easier to initiate but a lot tougher to hold onto for the organization providing services. Being a successful service provider is a task that's fueled with imagination and continuous learning and improvement. With products eating away into the services' pie, ITIL has done a rethink on the meaning of a service.

ITIL Definition of a Service

A means of enabling value co-creation by facilitating outcomes that customers want to achieve, without the customer having to manage specific costs and risks.

The definition of a service is a wonderful reflection of how a service is created—not in isolation. No organization can claim to create value through a service without active involvement of the customer who is leveraging the service. In the preceding definition, a service enables value that is co-created by the service provider, the customer, and perhaps other parties as well.

Going back to the example of Office 365, how did it outweigh the benefits that the Office product offered? Office 365, although expensive with continuous usage over a period, is successful. It offers free product updates, and in the world we live in where people jump into upgrading to the latest wiz, this is a fairly good magnet. To top it off, multiple licenses are offered depending on the type of subscription. And in the age of cloud, an additional feature of 1TB of space on OneDrive is salivating. I have stopped buying hard drives since I bumped into Office 365 and several hundreds of GB is there at my disposal wherever I go. Imagine how I had to carry it with me on hard drives whenever my life as a management consultant required travel.

While I enjoy the service by paying a certain fee, I, as a customer, do not have the weight on my shoulders of bearing the risks that come with the service. The service provider owns the risks completely and does not expose the customer to it. Let us say a document was corrupted while being stored on OneDrive. It is the responsibility of Microsoft to take frequent backups to ensure that a customer does not end up losing it. What good is a service if it is not reliable, right? Likewise, a service consumes various individual costs—like costs for servers, specific licenses, developers, support personnel, etc. The service provider does not ask the customer to pay a certain percentage for each of these elements but rather a service cost for enjoying the services. In other words, the service provider works with their expenses and capital investments and identifies a fair value that the customer needs to shell out that is competitive, as well as ensuring that costs do not break the service provider's bank. The second half of the service definition is about the service provider owning the risks and specific costs and not passing them directly to the customer.

Exam Tip   Understanding what a service means is extremely critical to further progressing in the ITIL Foundation Certification study. If you still have lingering doubts, read the service definition again. Without a proper understanding of it, you will not be well placed to grasp the remaining concepts.

Organization

I mentioned earlier that value cannot be created in isolation. I meant that an organization creating value on its own is not possible; rather, with the support and feedback of other entities that consume the service, it is possible to create value. In this section let's try to understand what an organization is.

An organization is an entity that is either made up of a single person or multiple people. It can be made up of a simple flat structure with numbers in tens and hundreds or be humongous multinationals in hundreds of thousands.

Yes, you read it right. Even individuals can act as organizations. For example, a freelance consultant who comes into an organization to conduct a preaudit assessment can run their own company and be the only person on the payroll.

ITIL Definition of an Organization

A person or a group of people that has its own functions with responsibilities, authorities, and relationships to achieve its objectives.

An organization has its own set of objectives and they work toward a common goal, no matter how big and complex they are. Larger organizations tend to have multiple hierarchies, and with that comes the authorities and chain of command. Nevertheless, the objective they are trying to achieve does not change.

An organization in the context of service management can play two distinct roles:

- Service provider

- Service consumer

A service provider is an organization that offers services to customers. Microsoft is the service provider and since I am paying for the services, I am the customer; and because I consume the services offered, I can also take on the role of a service consumer. On the other hand, when I take up a freelance job to conduct a DevOps feasibility assessment for Company Alpha, I put on the hat of a service provider while Company Alpha becomes the service consumer. To summarize, the organizational roles, service provider and service consumer, are contextual. The same organization plays the role of a service provider for a customer and can be the customer or a service consumer for another service provider. It is even possible that two organizations can play both service provider and service consumer roles for different sets of services. Say, for example, Microsoft provides Office 365 service for a telecom company like Verizon and could end up consuming Verizon's fiber connectivity between two Microsoft offices. In this example, Microsoft and Verizon put on different hats for different sets of services.

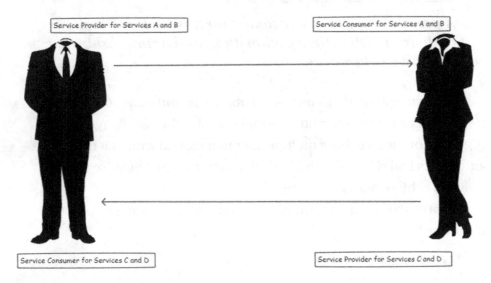

Figure 3-1. *Service provider and service consumer mutual relationship illustration*

Figure 3-1 illustrates a mutual relationship between a service provider and a service consumer. While the organization on the left is the service provider for services A and B, it is also the service consumer for services C and D. Likewise, the organization on the right plays the part of a service provider for services C and D and enjoys the services offered for services A and B.

People Roles

Within an organization there are multiple roles. Some generic ones from an ITIL standpoint that are of interest are:

- Customer

- Sponsor

- User

They say that the customer is always right because he/she knows exactly what they want. This is not exactly true, because they figure out what they really need during the course of development. So, in DevOps projects, the customer becomes a part of the development team and the role that is defined is called a product owner. From a service management perspective, it is exactly the same as he/she defines the requirements of a service and is pivotal to the service's final form and shape.

ITIL Definition of a Customer

A person who defines the requirements for a service and takes responsibility for the outcomes of service consumption.

The customer is able to define the requirements because he/she knows how the outcome of the service is going to be leveraged to meet the business' goals and objectives. Therefore, a lot of weight falls on the customer's shoulder to give the right direction to the service development teams.

A sponsor generally comes from the customer's organization and holds the keys to the budgetary approval. The sponsor is generally a senior person in the organization to whom finances are entrusted. They need to judge the budgetary release based on the requirements and a fair price for the services in scope.

ITIL Definition of a Sponsor

A person who authorizes budget for service consumption.

The person or persons who enjoy the service are defined by the role User.

ITIL Definition of a User

A person who uses services.

A user plays a part in two distinct ways.

1. A user leverages the service for the job that needs to be done.

2. Most importantly, the user provides feedback on the service, which will be used as an input for improving the service. Remember the definition of a service where value is co-created. Users play their part in providing valuable feedback on the service and thereby help the customer in shaping the service.

Consider an example where a multinational organization decides to buy laptops to replace its aging fleet. Requirements for the laptop for the sake of this example will be defined by the CTO, who in this case is a customer. The sponsor, or the person who holds the budgetary approval, is the CFO. Based on the requirements, the cost of laptops varies and the CFO tallies the budget set aside for capital investment and decides if he can sponsor the laptops. When the laptops are procured, they are distributed to several employees who are the users. They don't generally have a deciding say in the requirements, nor do they hold the keys to the money locker.

Tweaking this example to a mom and pop grocery shop, the convenience store owner has a desire to replace his laptop. He decides on a certain configuration. He knows exactly whether he can afford the laptop (although generally the authorization comes from the wife) that matches his needs. Finally, after buying it, he is the one who uses it. In this case the same person plays the role of a customer, sponsor, and user.

Exam Tip   From this section (Service Management), you can expect a minimum of one question and a maximum of two questions to appear in your ITIL Foundation Certification exam.

Defining Value

How do you know that you have created value for the customer through IT services? There is no easy answer for this. Perhaps, if you were running a courier company, you could have confidently claimed that you delivered the tendered papers to a government organization, there were no delays, you charged economically, and you have quantified value to your customer.

What if you are running a service whose value cannot be quantified, like an insurance company where customers have not yet filed claims? How will the customer know that you have created value? You could say that you have given your customers peace of mind by covering all eventualities. But the reality is that you don't know if the customer has perceived your definition of value.

So, in effect, whether value is created for the customer is judged and perceived by the customer. The service provider, at best, can research his customers and come up with possible solutions that can make the customer happy. And in the end, he still cannot be sure that value was created for the customer. This is because value is always measured through the eyes of the customer. There are two other components that define value apart from customer perception: the outcomes that business obtains and customer preferences. They are illustrated in Figure 3-2.

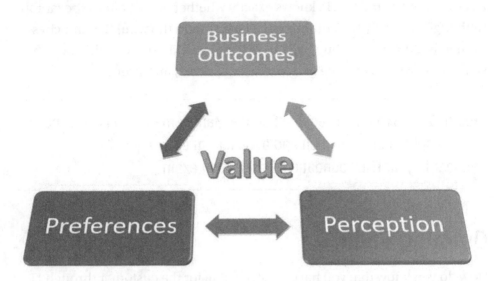

Figure 3-2. *Elements of value*

<u>ITIL Definition of Value</u>

The perceived benefits, usefulness, and importance of something.

At the end of the day, what stands out when it comes to weighing value is perception, because as a wise man once said: "always deliver more in perceived value than you take in cash value."

Although the actual business outcome that a customer gets and their preferences play a significant part in determining the value of a service, the *perception* of it trumps more often than not. Read the definition again. It says that rather than actual benefits, usefulness and importance of a service is secondary; how a customer sees it along with the inherent biases play a rather crucial role in determining the value of a service.

As I mentioned earlier in the chapter, value is not created in isolation. It is co-created between the service provider and the customer. There were days when the service provider developed services that perhaps could benefit the customer. It did in some cases and didn't in the rest. This became a game of hit or miss. Today, it's about surety. If a service provider is going to invest a certain amount of money, then it needs to know it is going to pull it off. So it becomes a *partner* with the customer rather than a service provider. This mere perception of seeing the service provider not as a service provider but as a partner (in crime!) does a world of difference in building trust that is the bedrock of value creation. The customer openly asks for what he wants and seeks advice where he needs. The service provider is no longer looking over his shoulder and opens up with ideas and sparks creating value. Thus value is born not from one entity but through the natural process of co-creation, like all of us are.

Here's a real-life example of co-creating value. Nokia made some of the best and greatest cell phones during the 90s and early 2000s. With other players jumping into the market with innovations and Nokia sticking to its successful guns, it lost the market dearly. Then we know the story of Microsoft buying it out and plugging the Windows operating system into the Nokia infrastructure. These phones were terrible— not because of the hardware but due to a failed operating system.

Then the unthinkable happened. In a quest to reconquer the market, Nokia had to create value to its consumers. The hardware was great, so changing it was out of the question. Although Microsoft is defined through the Windows operating system, they decided to switch the Windows operating system with Android, a giant that was ruling the market in its clique and was and is a serious competitor to iOS.

By bringing two disparate entities together, Microsoft hoped to create value for its consumers. The end result although not chest thumping was better than its former experience. Value is about co-creating and with the customer playing a centric role.

Outcomes

Value so far has been defined as something that gets co-created between the service provider and the customer. Alongside, we know that value is highly subjective. Two customers can have varying perceptions of the same service and it all depends on the customer, so co-creating such a service has its definite benefits in tailoring it to that customer's needs.

> ### *ITIL Definition of Output*
>
> *A tangible or intangible deliverable of an activity.*
>
> ### *ITIL Definition of Outcome*
>
> *A result for a stakeholder enabled by one or more outputs.*

The customer bases their judgement on the outcomes that they can derive from a service. The objective that the customer can achieve because of the service is more important and pertinent compared to the actual output.

What is the difference between outcome and output you might ask!

Netflix is an entertainment service that provides on-demand video in the form of movies, TV shows, and documentaries. The outputs are these videos per se. Each of these movies or episodes of a TV show can be considered as outputs.

While outputs are tangible or measurable, outcomes are intangible. An outcome is generally a result based on one or more outputs. In this Netflix example, the outcome is whether you were thoroughly entertained or not, or whether you were able to bond with your kids over a family movie. This outcome could be because of one episode of a TV show such as "Anne with an E" or the entire season consisting of multiple episodes. Your entertainment taste is yours alone. You might have a wonderful time with this show, while the family next door hates the concept of a show that is based in the mid-1900s and prefers something scientific like "Star Trek: Picard." You see that the same show that one customer loves might just not be a winner for another.

Exam Tip   Remember that the services facilitate outcome through one or more outputs. The difference between an outcome and an output is a probable question on the exam. If you have any lingering doubts, read the section again.

Another aspect to remember with respect to outcomes is that the value proposition changes when the underlying or surrounding factors come into play. On a Sunday morning with the Wimbledon final being aired on live TV, the same "Star Trek: Picard" family will prefer to tune into the live TV rather than the recorded show. At that moment, due to the factors involved (a sport that they like), their preference has changed. Their perception of a service that is of value has changed.

While I end this section, regarding setting up of metrics—define metrics for the outcomes and not for the outputs. Nobody cares if Netflix has more than 10,000 movies on their shelf but what matters is its popularity with its viewers. Remember that unless you measure an outcome, you will never feel the true pulse of a customer.

Costs

Costs in ITIL generally pertain to the finances transactions from the service consumer to the service provider.

ITIL Definition of Costs

The amount of money spent on a specific activity or resource.

As per the service definition, the customer purchases services for a certain price. This topic focuses on the elements that determine the cost of a service.

In any service organization, most expenses go toward employing people. People costs are calculated either on a monthly or a quarterly basis, and along with the other direct and indirect costs, the overall cost of a service is determined. A common terminology we employ in the IT industry for people is FTE, which stands for full time effort. A person's FTE for a certain period is the factor that determines the cost of a service. For example, if we are calculating the costs for a monthly period, we use the term man months. The number of man months needed to deliver a service to a consumer plus the added direct and indirect costs determines the cost of a service.

Delving a little deeper into the different types of costs:

1. Direct costs that are imposed on the customer. The cost of the service itself comes under the direct costs, plus the consumer might be provided other bells and whistles like add-ons such as priority support and training that will be charged extra.

2. Indirect costs are those costs that are generally behind the price of a service. This could include the cost of infrastructure, man hours, resources, or any of the other costs that are not directly imposed on the customer but rather charged under the guise of a service charge.

This is a competitive world. The service provider is wary of the service costs and more often than not, the costs are derived not only on the internal factors but also based on their competitors. While they try to keep the prices competitive, it is important for service providers and service consumers to be in a win-win service relationship. The service provider should not be in a position where he breaks his bank while he provides services. Think about Uber, which offered cheap rides to quickly gain market but in the process, they bled quite badly. The service consumer on the other hand should not feel that costs paid toward services are a burden but rather should view it as a necessary investment. This happens when the consumer perceives that the price paid is justified. So, to summarize on this, the costing of services must be commensurate with the market, the service expenses, and customers' expectations.

From a consumer's perspective, they need to analyze the service offered based on their needs. This will give them grounds to choose a service that is beneficial to them. I subscribe to the HP Instant Ink program wherein I do not pay directly for ink cartridges but pay on the number of pages that I print. When I started the program, I used to subscribe to 100 pages a month; after a couple of months, going through the reports available on their website, it was apparent to me that I was not even meeting half the target that I was paying for. So, I switched to a lower band where I paid a fraction of the costs for printing 50 pages a month. As a consumer, keeping tabs on the numbers helped me make a decision that saves me from unnecessary bills that I can avoid.

Risks

Risks are inherent in every business, including the business of providing IT services. The world's most popular entrepreneurs would not have reached peaking heights if they had not taken risks at various instances. An IT service provider must take risks to come out on top.

When a service is conceived, it comes with inherent risks. They cannot be avoided. The smart thing would be to identify and manage them. It is like harnessing the sun's rays for power generation rather than staying indoors during the day.

ITIL Definition of Risk

A possible event that could cause harm or loss or make it more difficult to achieve objectives.

Broadly speaking, risks are either borne by service providers or service consumers. Yet in both cases, the service consumer needs to be concerned/aware of the risks that affect a service:

1. There are risks that the service provider reduces or removes from a service. Let us consider the example of a cab-hailing service such as Uber. They reduce the risks and hazards of driving and parking in cities by providing point to point rides for a certain cost. Yet there are risks that a consumer might face: say, for example, the consumer's data connection is lost. The consumer will lose the ability to book taxis. To mitigate it, an Indian company called Ola has a risk mitigator in booking taxis using the short messaging system.

2. There are risks that are inherent with the service provider for which the impact on services would be felt by the service consumer. Considering the same example, say there are not any available cabs in the area. Although the cellphone and the Internet are working fine, the lack of cabs will render the service unusable.

Risk-Related Conversations

In reality, in business to business services, the risks are not imposed from one side to another and the other side does not take it lying down. Remember that value is co-created. So are the risks, by way of discussions followed by agreements. Although the management of risks is owned by the service provider, the consumer has plenty of skin in the game and normally engages in the following ways to be an active partner in curbing risks:

1. Defining the requirements is an art. Customer organizations employ professional requirement consultants to define the requirements, including spelling out the risk appetite. When the desired outcomes are drafted, the risks that can possibly be defined and managed are also identified, discussed, and agreed by the customer and the service provider.

2. While defining requirements and the desired outcomes, the customer needs to spell out what the critical success factors are and the constraints that are in place. For example, a customer employing an auditing agency might list timely delivery of audit reports as a critical success factor, and the government regulations that apply are identified as the constraints in place. The auditing agency (service provider) will have to work around the constraint rather than finding a solution to mitigate the constraint.

3. It comes back to the customer and the service provider working hand in hand. Unless a customer trusts the service provider to have the best interests behind their actions, the mitigation of risks will not be entirely possible. The customer must come clean by stating all factors and providing accesses to all possible resources to make the service delivery successful. If a service provider is expected to work with a part of a business, the customer has to provide all the pertinent information such as stakeholder list, the underlying architecture, et al.

Note   A critical success factor (CSF) is something that must happen if an IT service, process, plan, project, or other activity is to succeed.

Risk Mitigation Options

Although most matured organizations identify the risks that can plague a service, it is not practical to believe that the risks can be removed completely from a service. Risks will always exist. The probability of it happening depends on the context. And for every risk, a strategy can be drawn to identify the course of action. The four most used actions are as follows:

1. *Risk avoidance*: In some cases, risks can be avoided or removed from the system. Either a risk can be removed or the probability of it happening can be negated. Example: The risk of infrastructure and connectivity uncertainties of service staff can be avoided by cancelling the work from home policy.

2. *Risk transfer*: Where risks cannot be avoided, try to transfer it to a different party. Example: When you rent a car, it is possible that a minor windshield crack might result while traveling on motorways. Instead of coughing up outrageous sums to the rental company, you could buy excess insurance and transfer the risks of a windshield crack or any other damages to the insurance company. By paying a small amount, you are no longer liable for the damages and you have successfully transferred the risks to the insurance company.

3. *Risk mitigation*: For an identified risk, it is possible
    to find a solution to counter it when it materializes.
    Example: Although servers are stable, there is always
    a risk one might freeze or crash. The application that
    is hosted on it will become unavailable. To mitigate
    this risk, you can either load balance the server
    between multiple servers or build a blue-green auto
    failover mechanism for a passive server to take over
    in case of active server failure.

4. *Risk acceptance*: Suppose a risk cannot be
    mitigated or avoided, and no other party is ready
    for transferring it to them; you are left with no
    choice but to accept it. When the risk materializes,
    you will be ready to face the music. Example:
    The government announcing a lockdown of all
    businesses due to pandemics is unprecedented.
    Although disaster management mechanisms exist,
    such a global crisis does not spare any plans in
    place. In such cases, companies accept the risk and
    face the consequences.

Utility and Warranty

ITIL has something to offer to IT professionals from all technical and
management areas. The concepts of utility and warranty are dear for those
who are geeks by nature and academics at heart. ITIL derives heavily
from digital electronics, so if you can read the circuit, you will pretty much
understand the logic. Figure 3-3 diagrams the logic of the utility and
warranty of ITIL.

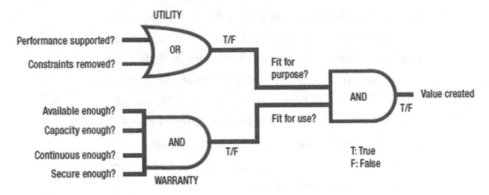

Figure 3-3. *Utility and warranty logic diagram*

Value is created from a service. To break it down further, let us say that it creates value only if it is fit for the purpose and fit for the use. Most of the time, these terms are used and abused in IT organizations without anyone knowing the actual meaning of them. So, let us try to understand what these two terms actually mean. Figure 3-4 presents a diagram of this concept.

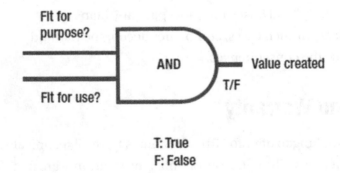

Figure 3-4. *Value creation logic gate*

Fit for purpose refers to a service's functionality. Does the service come with all the features and functions that it is supposed to carry? Does the service meet all the functional requirements? If yes, then one of the inputs into the AND gate will be True, and that takes us one step closer to creating value. A mobile service provider's core service is to provide the ability to talk over cellular phones. If this is achieved, then we can consider it fit for purpose.

On the other hand, fit for use refers to the ability to make use of the service functionality. Through the service functionality, you are given the capability to achieve certain outcomes. But can you make use of the service? If you can, this input to the AND gate will be True. If fit for purpose is also True, then you create value. If any one of the inputs is False, then value cannot be created. It's like having a mobile network and a capable mobile instrument but lacking sufficient bandwidth to allow you to slot your calls through. It's like having a top-notch, state-of-the-art television set but no electricity to run it.

Creating value is represented through an AND gate. Refer to Table 3-1 to help you understand when the value is created.

Table 3-1. *Value Creation Matrix*

Fit for Purpose	Fit for Use	Value Created?
TRUE	TRUE	YES
TRUE	FALSE	NO
FALSE	FALSE	NO
FALSE	TRUE	NO

Utility of a Service

ITIL Definition of Utility of a Service

The utility is the functionality offered by a product or a service to meet a particular need.

The logic diagram in Figure 3-5 shows an OR gate for the utility part of a service.

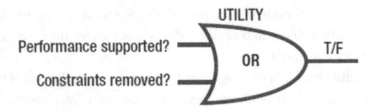

Figure 3-5. *Utility of a service*

For a service to be fit for purpose, it needs to meet any one (or both) of the following criteria:

1. Performance supported

2. Constraints removed

These criteria are represented through an OR gate, and Table 3-2 provides the conditions when the service would be fit for purpose.

Table 3-2. *Conditions for a Service to be Fit for Purpose*

Performance Supported?	Constraints Removed?	Fit for Purpose?
TRUE	TRUE	YES
TRUE	FALSE	YES
FALSE	FALSE	NO
FALSE	TRUE	YES

For a service to create value, it needs to meet certain criteria. One such case is its performance. A service must inherently improve the performance of the business outcomes that the customer desires. For example, a mobile phone service must provide the customer efficiency to enable better communication.

The second criterion for which fit for purpose is applicable is the constraints that can be removed through the service. If the service can remove barricades for a customer, it might fulfill the terms of the service m being fit for the purpose. The mobile service provider, by providing the ability to make calls while you golf, removes the constraints that usually would exist if you had to stop midgame, head back to your office, and make the call. In this instance, the constraints have been removed through the service the mobile phone offers.

For a service to be fit for purpose, it should boost performance or remove the constraints. If it can do both, even better.

Warranty of a Service

<u>ITIL Definition of Warranty of a Service</u>

Warranty provides assurance that a product or a service will meet its agreed requirements.

Warranty comprises of four parts:

1. Is the service available when needed?

2. Is there sufficient capacity available?

3. Is the service continuous?

4. Is the service secure?

All four criteria must be met for the service to be fit for use. This is represented through an AND diagram, as shown in Figure 3-6.

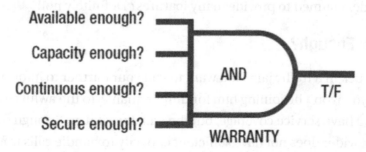

Figure 3-6. *Warranty of a service*

Table 3-3 provides the criteria for ensuring that the service is fit for use. It is not complete for all permutations and combinations. The AND gate provides a FALSE output whenever any of the inputs are FALSE.

Table 3-3. *Conditions for a Service to be Fit for Use*

Available Enough?	Capacity Enough?	Continuous Enough?	Secure Enough?	Fit for Use?
TRUE	TRUE	TRUE	TRUE	YES
TRUE	TRUE	TRUE	FALSE	NO
TRUE	TRUE	FALSE	TRUE	NO
TRUE	FALSE	TRUE	TRUE	NO
FALSE	TRUE	TRUE	TRUE	NO

The following illustrations provide examples for each criterion that needs to be met for the service to be fit for use.

Available Enough?

You subscribe to a cell phone service and pay a premium for that service. You are now heading out on holiday. When you reach your resort, you are flabbergasted to see that the mobile service provider does not have coverage inside the resort. Is the service providing you any value, although the provider claimed to provide many features? Definitely not!

Capacity Enough?

You are stuck in a traffic jam. You want to call your partner to inform him that you won't be joining him for dinner, thanks to the awful city traffic. You have service coverage, but the call does not go through. The service provider does not have sufficient capacity to handle calls from that particular cell tower. Even though there is coverage, if you are not able to make calls, is the service adding value? Nope.

Continuous Enough?

You are in the midst of the telephone round of an interview for a company based overseas. The call drops every few minutes, distracting you from the ideas you want to state and thereby causing you to lose your train of thought. The service has coverage and sufficient capacity, but is it giving you the value you perceive? Heck no!

Secure Enough?

You are calling your human resources department to discuss the appraisal your manager has given you. How would you feel if the conversation you are having from the confines of your home, with the HR person on a different continent, is accessible over the cloud by your manager? Is the service giving you value? You know the answer.

Note   When we do service assessments, we typically look at the various aspects of service utility and service warranty and the risks that they are exposed to. Of course, the costs of a service are also considered during assessments.

To sum up from these examples, for the cell phone service warranty conditions to be met, the service must be available, have sufficient capacity, must be continuous, and must be secure. With any one of these elements not in place, the cell phone service is not fit for use and does not add value.

Exam Tip   If you are not comfortable with logic gates and tables, from an examination standpoint, you are still safe. On the exam, your knowledge on the value creation formula will not be tested. But rather, the elements that make up a service and the meanings around a service being fit for purpose and fit for use are put up for scrutiny.

Exam Tip   From this section (Value), you can expect a minimum of two questions and a maximum of three questions to appear in your ITIL Foundation Certification exam.

Service Offerings

Like a platter of dishes on a menu card, a service provider has a list of service offerings that is made available to customers. The service offerings are designed to provide options for a customer, keep the service provider's service range attractive, and most importantly, it is meant to cater to all quarters of the customer's needs.

The service offerings are essentially built on top of the service provider's products by playing around with permutations and combinations of add-ons, accesses, and the level of support. So in essence, the service has to have a decent product to set as a base, and to build services atop it. For example, web streaming services such as Netflix and Amazon Prime are built on the product that streams videos. Using this as a core product, they offer multiple options for customers to choose from.

ITIL Definition of a Service Offering

A formal description of one or more services, designed to address the needs of a target consumer group.

Service offerings can be broadly based on the following divisions:

1. The service provider's products can be sold to the customer as goods, meaning it's a one-time transaction where the goods are transferred from the service provider to the customer. When the transfer takes place, the responsibility of the upkeep of the

product falls into the lap of the customer. Take, for example, when you purchase a laptop: the moment the product is handed over to you, you become responsible for how it's maintained and used.

This option soon loses momentum, as the service provider has potentially seen the end of a service relationship and there is nothing holding the customer back. Take another example of car sales. It is becoming more and more apparent that dealerships are giving lucrative options to customers to lease a car rather than buying it outright.

2. The second type of an offering is where the service provider provides access to customers to the service resources to be used under certain stated agreements. The management of the services still remains with the service provider, but the customer is free to use it under a set of terms and limitations.

    Netflix and Amazon Prime are classic examples. The streaming services own the digital content and they allow customers to watch it anytime for a monthly fee. Likewise, the car leasing agreement is a type of subscription service where the customer shells out periodic costs for using the car. The customer is also relieved of servicing and other expensive responsibilities. By opting for it, the customer enjoys the car at a small fraction of a cost that is paid periodically (monthly generally) and does not have to worry about maintaining it. On the flip side, the customer will never become the (proud) owner of the automobile.

Using the same product, different variants of services can be offered by a service provider to embellish the service list. Using the same example, Netflix offers their entire list of streaming offerings in standard definition, which is the cheapest service offering, followed by HD and UHD at a higher price. Amazon Prime, apart from offering videos for streaming, offers movies and TV shows to rent and also to buy at a one-time price. Providing variants is beneficial for the service provider to aim at different customer sectors with focused content and add-ons. It is beneficial for customers because they only pay for what they need and not for all the bells and whistles that they don't make use of.

3. The last in the list of service offerings are service actions. They are the maintenance bit of the service offerings, such as providing product and warranty support.

   Almost all products and services sold today come bagged with support and warranty. Without the added service actions, the product (goods) or service is not as valuable. Most service providers add the costs pertaining to service actions in the overall goods and services price to ensure that the customer does not feel the burden of purchasing service support and warranty separately.

   The service support and warranty too come in variants. A customer could buy basic support where he ends up never talking to another human on the other side or pay more for phone support and even a field engineer to visit the home. Warranty likewise can be extended over additional periods of time for an extra cost.

Exam Tip   The best way to understand the different types of service offerings is through the illustrations that I have offered. To reiterate, the first is purchasing a product such as a laptop, second is subscription based such as Netflix, and finally the third is service support and warranty.

Service Relationships

A service cannot flourish if it is developed in one organization and used by another. Service can only improve and meet the desired outcomes if it is a joint effort between the two entities. We have called this value getting co-created between the service provider and service consumer. For this value generation joint venture to happen, there must be trust between the two entities. The trust is built through a formidable partnership or service relationship where the service consumer is transparent about the needs, wants, and the constraints that are in place.

On the other hand, the service provider too comes clean on what is possible, what can be possible, and the challenges at hand. Through this absolute crystalline transparency, the service relationship between the service provider and service consumer strengthens and mutually benefits both organizations in working toward each other's successes—more so from a service consumer's perspective.

ITIL Definition of Service Relationships

A cooperation between a service provider and service consumer. Service relationships include service provision, service consumption, and service relationship management.

Service Provision

The service provider provisions services. In this section, I will list out the responsibilities of a service provider in service provisioning.

The following list is not comprehensive, but from an examination standpoint it is sufficient and complete:

- A service provider manages all the resources that are used in the delivery of services. This could include infrastructure, software, and facilities. Management of resources refers to the configuration management and the lifecycle of these assets.

- Example: Netflix is responsible for maintaining a catalog of its content, managing the infrastructure that is used to host the content, the software behind it, the people who maintain it, and everything else that goes into the making of the video streaming service. The service provider is wholly responsible for this.

- Based on the agreement with the customer, the service provider must provide accesses and has to ensure that the accesses remain active throughout the agreement term.

- Example: Netflix has the responsibility to provide access to their video content based on the subscription that a customer chooses.

- The service provider needs to keep a finger on the service's pulse to check its performance and whether it is meeting the outcomes that the customer intends. The service provider also has to ensure that the service is improving on a regular basis and does not become stagnant.

- Example: Netflix collects all the statistics that it can gather through its software and web interface. It knows which of its video content is popular and in which geography. This information is pertinent for the company to make business decisions—whether to axe or renew shows and the genre of content a majority would prefer. From a continuous improvement perspective, Netflix has to feed its customers with new content every week, improve the speeds through its content delivery networks, and improve the software's navigation and cataloging system if it is to keep its flock together. Today there are several such services and Netflix does not have the luxury of taking its customers for granted.

- Service actions such as service support must be made an inherent part of the service (based on the service agreement, that is). This could include email, phone, and chat support options. In case of goods procurement, it could also come with warranty and returning of goods.

- The makeup of a service company is seen through the lens of its support. So any service provider that is in the business of service management needs to ensure that the service provided is top of the line. Good service actions will lead to continued business from its customers and good word of mouth will give them more sales.

- Finally, the service provider is responsible for the supply (delivery) of the goods that are purchased by the customer. It is possible that the service provider might charge delivery charges from the customers. Yet, the responsibility of delivering it to the customer lies with the service provider.

Service Consumption

Only when the service provider offers the service, and it's mutually agreed with the customer, does the service consumption begin. On the receiving side of a service, the following responsibilities can be expected:

- The service consumer/customer is expected to ensure that the resources necessary for users to enjoy the service are made available. For instance, let's go with the Netflix example where the service provider offers millions of video content choices and the user from his end needs to ensure at a minimum that a working Internet and a smart TV/cell phone/computer is in place to enjoy the service.

- When the service offered does not work as expected or if a new request needs to be placed, the service consumer is expected to utilize the service actions part of the service to get the request fulfilled or to get the service restored.

- If dealing with goods, after the service provider ships out the goods, they need to be received to complete the service transaction. This is similar to receiving a package from Amazon.

Service Relationship Model

At the beginning of this section I spoke about service relationship. These are the activities that can be performed together for co-creating value and for both parties to be able to gain benefits from the business transaction.

The world of service management is convoluted. A service provider of a service ends up being a service consumer of another service. This could happen in many to many relationships. At any given point in time, all of us as individuals or as organizations act as service providers to other individuals or organizations or end up being service consumers from other individuals or organizations. This is depicted in Figure 3-7.

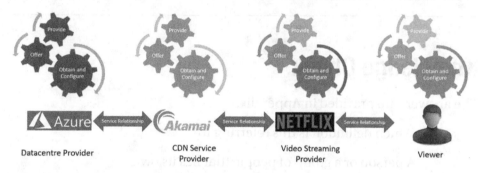

Figure 3-7. *Service relationship model*

Each of the set of gears refers to the cog wheels that make a service happen, either in provision or consumption. Let us start from the right with the illustration that I have used so far on this topic—Netflix service for video streaming. The viewer is a service consumer in this example, and has a service relationship with Netflix as a video streaming provider.

While Netflix plays service provider to the viewer, it consumes content delivery network services offered by Akamai. In this relationship, Netflix is a service consumer while Akamai is a service provider.

Moving on, Akamai consumes services from Microsoft Azure for its datacenter needs. So in this relationship, Akamai, which played service provider to Netflix, is putting on the hat of a service consumer and Microsoft Azure as a service provider. It is also possible that the viewer is a DevOps consultant who is hired by Microsoft to conduct a feasibility check. If this is the case, then Microsoft Azure becomes a service consumer for the viewer who becomes a service provider.

Exam Tip   From this section (Service Offerings and Service Relationships), you can expect one question to appear in your ITIL Foundation Certification exam.

Knowledge Check

The answers are provided in Appendix.

3-1.   Which definition is this referring to?

A person or a group of people that has its own functions with responsibilities, authorities, and relationships to achieve its objectives.

A. Sponsor

B. Service Provider

C. Organization

D. Customer

3-2.   Which of the following factors matter for a service to be fit for purpose?

A. Warranty

B. Utility

C. Value

D. Continuity

3-3.   Who am I if I am transparent about my needs, wants, and the constraints that are in place?

A. Service Provider

B. Service Consumer

C. Service Organization

D. Service Requester

3-4.   Which of these are related to results for a stakeholder?

A. Output

B. Risks

C. Outcome

D. Warranty

3-5.   Which of these is not an example of a service offering?

A. Providing access to service provider's resources

B. Goods receivable

C. Service actions like raising incidents

D. Amount of money spent on a specific activity

CHAPTER 4

Holistic Approach to Service Management: Four Dimensions

Service management is not linear. While there are multiple aspects and components that go into the making of a service, there are several others on the consumption side. Both these sets of components have to find true north and collaborate to create value. These various components that make and consume IT services are put together in a model called four dimensions of service management.

This chapter explores the four dimensions/quadrants of service management, and the buck doesn't stop with these four quadrants. There are several other external factors that influence delivery and consumption. We are going to examine them with a hawkish eye and drill down to the nuances.

Exam Tip   The four dimensions of service management account for two questions on the ITIL Foundation examination.

© Abhinav Krishna Kaiser 2021
A. K. Kaiser, *Become ITIL® 4 Foundation Certified in 7 Days*,
https://doi.org/10.1007/978-1-4842-6361-7_4

The Four Dimensions

Balance is essential in everything we do. A classic example is a diet that is based on balance. Almost all nutritionists would tell you to have certain food groups in every meal. Although carbohydrates are more feared these days than fat, they are still necessary to give you the energy you need to operate through the day. Proteins are the building blocks for growth and repair of your body tissues. Vegetables contain various vitamins, minerals, fiber, and antioxidants that contribute towards a healthy metabolism. So, the advice would be to consume all of them in moderation. This is the secret to a body that's both healthy and attractive. Plus, you will want processed foods such as chocolates and desserts that are mostly fat, but they satiate your mental cravings.

Likewise, in the service management field, services are much like us. They need all the constituent components for their growth and health. Development in one area and neglect in the rest will introduce instability that will take the service further away from reaching its objectives. Similar to different food groups for a healthy diet, there are four dimensions that are identified as constituent components of a service. They are:

1. Organization and people

2. Information and technology

3. Suppliers and partners

4. Value streams and processes

The four dimensions must work in unison in creating value for the customer in the most effective manner and in an efficient way. This is illustrated in Figure 4-1.

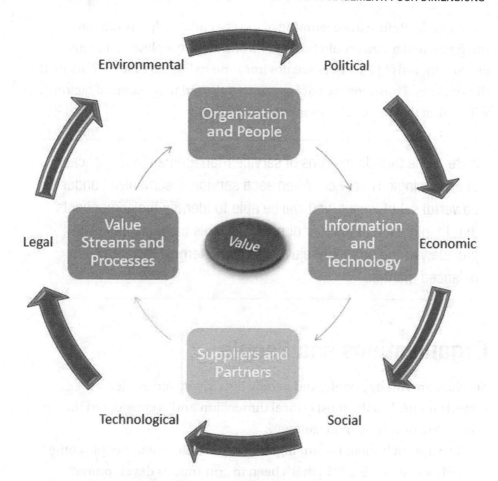

Figure 4-1. *Four dimensions of service management*

The four dimensions, although indicated as four separate entities working towards a common cause, are not as distinct and separate as it seems. There is plenty of gray area between the dimensions or aspects that utilizes multiple dimensions. For example, partners and suppliers can be part of a value stream, which necessitates looking at both these dimensions under a single view rather than distinct.

The next point to note is that IT services do not operate in a vacuum chamber. They operate in an environment where changes are rapid and inescapable. Before the beginning of the year 2020, who would have imagined that a virus could bring the world to a complete halt in just about 3 months? IT services are not immune to factors that are outside the dimensions. These contextual factors are referred to as external factors. We will look at this in detail later in this chapter.

Note   The four dimensions of service management are applicable to every single IT service. When each service is scrutinized under a powerful set of lenses, you will be able to identify the components that fit into each of the four dimensions. This categorization will provide you the ammo to rejuvenate and energize the areas in a balanced manner.

Organizations and People

Services are run by people, and people are driven and guided by organizations. It is the most critical dimension and is considered the first dimension of service management.

The area of human resourcing that organizations and people come under is a vast playing field that's been in continuous development for ages and will be in the same stage for years and centuries to come. Understanding human psychology and decoding the needs is an emerging field. From the service management's dimension perspective, we are specifically interested in the following aspects:

- Organization structures
- Culture
- Roles and responsibilities
- Leadership

Bird's-Eye View of Organization Structures

Organizations come in various shapes, structures, and volumes. We have oceanic companies like the IBMs and Wipros that are spread across the continents and have hundreds and thousands of employees working for them and for their customers. And then we have startup companies where the entire strength of the company could be in single digits and, if lucky, double. Between the startups and global corporations, you have a wide gamut of organizations varying in size and structure.

Every organization chooses a structure that works for it. There is no right or wrong structure. In fact, almost all the organizations change their structure based on changing atmosphere and circumstances.

The toast of the current trend is for a horizontal structure where an organization does not build a lasagna type layered organization. Rather, it builds a flat organization that has minimal layers and the bottom-placed employee has unhindered access to the top man. This is common in most startup organizations and has become synonymous with organizations that practice Agile principles.

As I mentioned earlier, nothing is simple and straightforward. While this flat structure might work in an organization that has tens of employees on its payroll, for a giant like IBM it is practically not possible. A 350,000 people company cannot have a flat organization. It simply isn't feasible. They opt for several layers to ensure that the structure caters to effective and efficient delivery of services. The vertically structured organizations build layers based on the leadership, management, and delivery responsibilities.

Exam Tip   While flat structured organizations tend to be Agile, the vertically structured organizations are process driven. The processes ensure that the service is delivered on time and within the set stipulations. You can expect a question on the structure of organizations in your exam.

Flat organizations are simple, and the structure does its job in transparent communication; in essence, everybody in the organization will have a pretty good idea of what everybody else is doing.

Vertical organizations are siloed. Every silo has its own set of responsibilities and deliveries, and people within a silo are expected to practice transparent communication. However, the challenge arises from the exact placement of the structure. How will the organization be structured? Will people with similar skills be placed in silos? So, during service delivery or product development, do they come together under a matrix organized structure? These are some of the tough questions that leaders must find answers for before determining the structural complexes.

As we touched base on in Chapter 2, a DevOps structure tries to break the silos as we know them and it brings people around the product that is being developed and managed. In essence, bringing people connected with products into a team is a silo in itself, a silo that houses various skill sets rather than a specialty. While silos in themselves aren't bad, the DevOps structure gives the maximum opportunity to create value through team structures. In fact, most organizations today are moving away from their traditional structures and into a DevOps structure.

Not Just Structures, Culture Too!

It's reasonable and necessary to change an organization's structures to ensure maximum effectiveness and efficiency and minimize conflicts. But that alone cannot do the magic. The underlying culture that an organization imbues matters a whole lot more than the structure.

Culture is about the organization's psychology. Is the organization intolerant about flouting ethics? Is the organization respectful of the wishes and desires of employees from a career perspective? Is the organization transparent in its decision making? Does the organization promote open communication? These are some of the questions that could determine the culture of an organization, and this eventually is going to determine the value that it generates for its customers. Because you are not going to have happy and fulfilled employees with a culture that doesn't support them and their aspirations, to put it simply.

Note DevOps promotes the culture of shared responsibilities and blamelessness. Through these cultural traits, the aspiration is to build a team that collaborates and works as a single unit rather than silos with conflicting goals and objectives.

How is a culture formed? It is not something like structure where I could change it overnight using a Visio program. Culture trickles from the top into the various parts of the organization. The leaders have to imbue the cultural aspects of an organization, start promoting it with their subordinates, and expect their subordinates to take the message down to their subordinates. The leaders have to share the vision and the goals with the rest of the organization. There is no easier way to build desired culture in an organization. It is tough and arduous work that requires preaching through following. The area of organizational change management delves into these aspects of culture building.

People Roles and their Responsibilities

Without a doubt, we must acknowledge that people make services happen. Without people, no matter how many activities we automate, it does not match up to what people can do. The people resource therefore must be preserved, protected, and nurtured. The organizational structures and cultures are the foundations that are to be in place before making people responsible for certain areas of activity.

"People" includes those in leadership positions as well as the employees in lower rungs of management and individual contribution.

It includes administrative functions that enable employees working for services such as human resources, procurement, and administration among others.

Choosing the right people is a tough nut to crack. I haven't known an organization that has got all its ducks in a row. They are always hunting for the right person and trying to chop, change, and experiment with options.

Organizations must get their leaders right, sooner rather than later. These leaders will be entrusted to start choosing the people in their teams, the people who deliver and the people who can make a difference in this game of value generation. Choosing leaders is absolutely critical!

After leaders pick their teams, they need to spell out their roles and responsibilities. They need to ensure that the person's aspirations, skills, and interests are considered while drawing the roles and the activities the person is made responsible for. In flat organizations, roles don't mean too much because of the reduced competition, and responsibilities too are generally not restricted to a single area of study. For example, a technical head may also be expected to manage procurements and sales. So, roles may not matter too much in flatter organizations, but they definitely do in vertical organizations. The level of competition is significantly higher, and the span of responsibilities will be quite narrow. A Unix administrator may not do much other than Unix administration in a global corporation. Therefore, it is quite likely that this employee looks for avenues that promise more action.

Managing career aspirations is a tough ask, and it must be managed without an excuse. People who work in a particular field will get bored with what they do, and their boredom will become visible in their work products at one point or another. Before getting to this point, an employee's aspirations must be understood and supporting actions must be taken. For example, continuous learning is one of the key items for most people who work in IT. Almost everybody likes to learn new skills and take their career forward, so the organization's culture must be built to support its employees in their future endeavors.

When we talk about people in this dimension, the scope is all people who are involved in the service delivery and value creation. It could be people from the customer organization who are playing the role of a product owner; it could be the engineers from a supplier organization; or it could even be the person involved in the sales area. We carry everyone along on the journey.

Exam Tip   Roles and responsibilities is a big topic, and the sky is the limit when we talk about what can be learned. From the examination perspective, it is important to note that identifying roles and their responsibilities is a critical task that is performed in service management.

I started my career in the ITIL area, with operations first and then as a consultant. My interest in the subject led me to higher positions, more responsibilities, and a chance to develop frameworks based on the customer's requirements. While I did more of it, I became adept at seeing the world beyond ITIL. Through a bit of luck, I moved into the Agile and DevOps field, and have discharged several roles including a scrum master, Agile project manager, program manager, DevOps consultant, and DevOps architect. Although I am an accomplished DevOps architect in my organization, I have not stopped learning. I have been studying newer technologies and adapting methodologies to fit the DevOps scheme for COTS (Commercial Off The Shelf) products. By keeping myself busy in learning and growing in my field, I have always felt that I am in the career of choice where the horizon for growing and learning is expanding by the day.

Leadership Matters

They say that a leader is as good as the team is. This is true, but it's a two-way street. An inspired leader can turn the fortunes of a team, an organization, or even a nation. It is paramount that the person leading people knows true north—the objectives of value creation.

There are several styles of leadership and all the ways take us to a common destination. It is not important which style a leader embodies, but it is important that a leader is in place to lead the team. The objective of this section is not to go into the details of leadership. There are several texts available on the topic. I used this section specifically to make aware the importance of leadership in the organization and people dimension of service management.

All Roads Lead to Value

So far in this book, no matter what I have touched upon, I have landed in one form or another on the importance of value. With the delivery of services, a service provider delivers value. It is this that drives a service provider in creating the product, the service, and everything built around it. Without value, there is nothing.

So it is absolutely imperative that everybody involved is oriented toward true north—the value that is being created. This can be made possible by percolating a clear understanding of which actions lead to value delivery for the customer, and how everybody involved can work in a collaborative manner aimed with a single objective. It could be through the team coming around the service in a DevOps team fashion or through a focused approach of delivery. There is no particular way of achieving value; but whatever the identified way, it needs to be accomplished as a single unit.

Information and Technology

Information and technology are used together generally in the information age. There isn't anything wrong with it; however, we must understand that both are distinct.

Information refers to the knowledge that we have gathered, the wisdom of experience, the data and everything else that goes with it. Technology on the other hand is the electronics and coding that makes our lives simpler. Be it the servers, the data center, the mobile phones, or the cloud infrastructure, they all fall into the technology space. Advancements in technology include automation, blockchain, artificial intelligence, and machine learning. The information and technology are used in conjunction, because the information is used on top of the technological components. For example, an asset inventory is used on top of an asset management database, which is a piece of software that helps in managing the data including retrieval with ease.

Focusing on the topic of information and technology dimension in service management, it can be applied to two areas:

1. IT for actual services (enjoyed by customers/users)

2. IT for service management (enabler for service providers and service consumers)

IT for Actual Services

Information and technology are leveraged to deliver IT services to customers. The dimension goes into the depths of information used during the course of creating, using, and managing IT services. This can be done both at the side of a service provider and a service consumer.

In the Netflix video streaming service, the IT of this service includes the servers, the content delivery network, and the video streaming technology. These are the various IT components that directly have a bearing on the IT service.

IT for Service Management

Information and technology for service management are those sets of informational and technological components that support the service provider and the service consumer to enable the IT for their users.

Continuing with the Netflix example, the company manages an inventory of video titles, an inventory of the software and hardware that is used to host the IT service, along with relationships. Furthermore, the service provider will leverage workflow management for obtaining approvals (as in service requests and change requests) or it could be a ticketing system to record incidents. All these systems and the service management information that resides on them are not used by the user. This information is used to improve the service, to ensure that the service runs unimpeded and the user gets the best of experience. Imagine how a user feels if the movie buffers every couple of minutes. Although the CDN provides the data to the user, there could be a problem that is raised on the service management to identify the root cause of the buffering. The solution coming out of it when deployed is value added for the user, because it aims to fix the buffering issue. This is a simplistic example of how IT for service management aids/supports/enables an IT service.

Note

IT for Services   Information and technology aspects that directly influence an IT service.

Note

IT for Service Management   Information and technology aspects that influences the management of IT services by the service provider and service consumer organization. This does not impact a service directly. Example: If a ticketing system is broken, the ability to log an incident is impacted, which delays the restoration of an IT service— indirectly impacting the IT service.

Considerations for Information

Information is power. In the hands of a wrong entity, it has the consequences of completely wiping out businesses and competition. It is therefore of utmost importance that information be handled with care and with a framework that ringfences it from misuses.

While designing information management, the information architect must consider various aspects such as:

1. Service providers must identify the different types of information that are needed to deliver the services and for service management. The spectrum of information must be carefully picked to ensure that the information gathered is just about enough and does not end up being overheads. Netflix during registration takes down our name, geography, email address, and credit card details. These details will help in the delivery of video streaming services for its users.

2. How is the information stored? Is there enough encryption in place to protect it from misuse? We have heard from time to time of several breaches that have made sensitive information public.

103

The consequences can potentially bankrupt companies and put individuals at risk. So, securing information is of critical importance.

3. How does a service provider manage the information? Information changes from time to time. How is it updated in their systems? For example, when a credit card on record expires, how do users get to update it? Is it on their portal or does an agent call to get the details? We have both instances and both work. The question is whether we have sufficient security, especially when a human is involved in the process.

4. When a user decides to stop using a service, what happens to the user's information? Is it archived or wiped clean?

5. Regulatory compliance is another dimension of managing information. There are regulations such as the General Data Protection Regulation (GDPR) for organizations based out of the EU that give users the right to choose how their personal data is leveraged. Likewise, there are multiple regulations in place across geographies and in various industries that specify information regulations. Compliance with them must go into the design of information management.

6. Most importantly, today it is by choice that information resides on a particular system. Other systems through interfaces and integrations seek the needed information. For example, let's say that Netflix stores customers' payment information on a

SAP system. During renewals, the invoicing system will pull the customer's payment information, charge it, and then disposes of the information. Such exchanges of data are quite common. So, the following criteria must be put in place for the information in play:

a. Is the information sought relevant?

b. Is the information sought available?

c. Is the information reliable?

d. Is the information accessible (permissions)?

e. Is the information on record accurate?

f. Can the information be retrieved in a timely fashion?

Considerations for Technology

Turning our focus to technology, there are more questions to ponder about.

1. It is quite rare that companies start from scratch. So, does the technology chosen gel well with the architecture that's in place? This is a question that prods capital investment to flow in the case of major architectural changes. For companies starting fresh, they can opt for anything under the sun and they would end up OK, but this is generally an unlikely case. Because even they would build on something that is already there rather than start from nothing. A news portal might opt for Wordpress as its content management system over something like Drupal, which is losing out heavily compared with 20 years back when it ruled the market.

2. What is the future of the chosen technology? I
    would be wary of choosing something that just hit
    the market. What if it cannot sustain and if it has
    major security flaws? So, it's important to choose a
    technology that has a future, at least as much as the
    experts can foresee. For example, if you had chosen
    Google Plus as a choice of social networking for your
    organization, you would have regretted the decision
    because the product is no longer supported.

3. Strategy is crucial with technology. Does your
    organization's strategy match with the technology
    decision? I know of organizations that seek to keep
    IT expenditures minimum and opt for open source.
    So for such organizations, going for Office 365 may
    not be the best option. They might opt for Google
    for Business combined with Chromebooks and the
    entire fleet of Google products to cut down on costs.

4. Every service provider organization has its own
    strong suits. Some have a host of architects who
    are doyens of Amazon Web Services. For this
    organization to opt for Microsoft Azure suite would
    be counterproductive. They must *put their mouths
    where the money is.*

5. Is the chosen technology secure enough to store the
    service-related information? Are there regulations in
    place that are met by the chosen technology?

6. Automation is essential today. Every company is
    looking at ways of reducing IT costs, and automation
    has been a reliable vehicle to offload mundane
    activities. The chosen technology must accelerate

employing automation. Most modern technologies do. It is unlikely that an organization might opt for mainframes today, which offer most resistance to automation.

7. An aspect of technology that is most desired is expandability. If I opt for a particular technology for implementing a functionality, I don't want to be restricted to opting for a different technology for a feature that I might introduce 2 years down the line. The identified technology must offer enough choices of flexibility in adaptation and a road map for the future imprinted.

8. With all the good things that technologies bring to the table, there is also their baggage. What are the risks and constraints that a technology introduces to a service? This is a critical aspect to consider before the decision is made. The decision also exposes the risk appetite of organizations that are willing to take chances for certain attractive features that a technology might offer.

Exam Tip   Any of the considerations put forth under information and technology might turn up in the examination. Therefore, it is imperative that you understand the meaning behind the consideration rather than the actual questions that I have put out. It is possible that the questions I have posed are not comprehensive. You must be in a place to judge whether a particular aspect of information or technology poses a direct benefit or contradiction for the impending decision to be made.

Partners and Suppliers

The third dimension of service management is the partners and suppliers. While the earlier two dimensions looked inward, this one is looking at external dependencies. We live in a world where cooperation and collaboration have become the norm between companies rather than an added advantage. No company can aim to provide services or products to its customers without taking help from other companies. The other companies could be in the form of a raw material supplier, network provider, or human resource contractor. The days of negotiations to win and to get the best possible deal are behind us. As a customer, we don't just want to get the best deal possible but also ensure that the relationship with the supplier is consistent and continuous. For this, it is imperative that the deal is a win-win situation. Due to this delicate balance, ITIL has identified partners and suppliers as one of the pillars/dimensions on which its service management is built.

Differentiating Partners and Suppliers

When I started my study on service management through ITIL V2, we understood who a supplier is. The roles and responsibilities were clear, and we knew how to deal with them. Then organizations started to tie up with others and started calling it a partnership. Through the prism of ITIL V2's supplier management process, the partnership between companies was nothing but a glorified customer enrolling for services/products from a supplier. So why call them a partner?

As I mentioned earlier, the relationship between companies is critical, and in this century of fast-paced growth, companies need to tie in thick relationships if they want to survive and thrive. Partnership, in essence, is essentially a customer-supplier relationship. However, a partner is given more privileges than a supplier, is trusted, and often gets a seat at the table during some level of decision making. Value is truly getting co-created between partners, and such companies often tend to share goals, culture, and business environment.

The strategy of organizations is to build partnerships with other companies that are responsible for the delivery of critical services and products. Companies sign generic agreements rather than specific ones, come up with goals together, and often try to be as flexible as possible with the other.

Most organizations today have a partnership with Microsoft because several laptops and servers they run are powered by Windows and other Microsoft software. These companies often get to install as many licenses of software as they want and retrospectively let Microsoft know of the numbers; and because of the partnership, they are entitled to a heavily discounted price. For Microsoft, the partnership brings in more business and can influence the organization into moving the non-Microsoft services and products toward their realm. For the organization, priority support, quick enablement of licenses, and a reasonable cost for the services and products is very much acceptable. This is a win-win situation.

What about a supplier? How do we differentiate them? The same organization relies on a stationery mart for all its stationery supplies. They provide the order based on their needs, and the goods get supplied. The transaction ends with the payment and delivery cycle. There is no need for a partnership, as there are a hundred other merchants willing to provide the same stationery sets and at a similar price. So this goods supplier is just a supplier and nothing more.

This applies even in our daily lives. For example, I buy heavily from Amazon. To me, I pick what I need and pay for it. When the item is delivered to my doorstep, the transaction ends. Amazon is not critical, as I can get a similar service from at least half a dozen vendors. However, their Prime membership changes the sense of it from being a supplier to a partnership, not in the true sense but in spirit. Being a Prime member, I get access to their deals 30 minutes before others. Although this is trivial, it gives me a sense of privilege and importance that through this Prime membership, I can possibly count them as a partner.

Note

Partners – Built on trust and mutual need of critical services/ products. Long-term commitment. Road map based.

Note

Suppliers – Clear separation of roles and transaction based. Driven by contract for delivery of goods and services.

Organization Strategy for Opting for Partners and Suppliers

An organization might choose to go in for a partnership or hunt for a supplier for a variety of reasons. This section investigates some common reasons for making this decision:

1. Remember the classic decision-making process involving buy or build in the software industry. Likewise, a strategic decision needs to be made by the company if they are going to build everything, or outsource it from another company because it isn't their core area. Why would a bank want to maintain its own IT department if it can outsource to IT majors who can manage it efficiently for them?

2. Costs definitely play a role in the decision. If I can run my own IT department and spend 50% less compared with outsourcing, then I would be inclined to hire the best of talents and run my own IT shop.

3. What if IT people prefer to join IT companies only for the depth and variety of work it can offer? Even if a bank wants to hire good people, they may not get them easily. This could be one of the major factors for outsourcing.

4. There could be substantive trends in the industry to do it one way or another. Let's follow the herd and be safe!

5. Legal and regulatory requirements could possibly turn the heat toward outsourcing. All these are risks and essentially, by outsourcing, an organization is transferring the risk to the partner/supplier.

Introducing Service Integration and Management

In the area of service management, the popularity of Service Integration and Management (SIAM) is second to ITIL. This is a framework that's been in vogue for a couple of decades and is recently making waves in the IT industry.

I mentioned earlier that organizations tend to have several partners and suppliers who are tied up with them for various goods and services. Managing the suppliers and partners requires finesse and management skills that are an expertise of their own. Organizations get into a partnership agreement with partners who can act as service integrators. A service integration acts as an interface between a customer organization and partners and suppliers. All strategic, tactical, and transactions activities pass through the service integrator layer. This layer can either be a third party (partner) or it can be an internal division within the customer organization. No matter where they sit, their role is to ensure that all partners and suppliers are effectively managed.

SIAM is a framework built on the foundation of service integration and service integrators. It goes into the various processes, practices, and best practices in dealing with partners and suppliers from the perspective of a service integrator. I encourage you to take this course up after you complete the ITIL 4 Foundation certification.

Value Streams and Processes

The fourth dimension includes the value streams and processes. It is by no means the least important because of its placement. Other dimensions have to be understood if this dimension needs to deciphered.

In this dimension, the other three dimensions are put together and sewn into a coordinated set of steps to co-create value. Service management elements such as processes, procedures, work activities, workflows, and controls are defined through this dimension.

The difference between a value stream and a process is significant. A process exists to transform the inputs into defined and predictable outputs. It does not inherently go into unwanted process steps and inefficiencies. As long as the desired output is obtained, the process' objective is met. A value stream goes a layer deeper. It is like a process but only in appearance. Underneath, it keeps a sharp eye on the various activities within a process that generate waste, with an aim to eliminate the waste and improve the productivity of the value stream, which in turn creates more value and at a faster rate.

Deciphering Value Streams

The term operating model refers to the set of activities that an organization undertakes. In service management, the operating model is aimed at creating value and the activities defined are aimed toward effective and efficient management of products and services. This is called an ITIL service value chain. More specifically speaking, the set of patterns within the service value chain that is aimed at creating value is called a value stream.

ITIL Definition of Value Streams

A series of steps an organization undertakes to create and deliver products and services to consumers.

Consider a set of activities that you could possibly perform in an organization. These activities will be performed in a certain pattern, and there are several patterns that could be drawn. These patterns are service value chains. The key patterns that can be identified to deliver value are called value streams.

As an example, if you were to visit a barber on a Saturday morning, the rush is generally high so you might have to wait a while for your turn. After the queue in front of you subsides, the barber asks for your preference and, based on that, cuts your hair. After the cut, he removes the cape and the hair and gives you a light brush before you make your way to the counter to pay for the service. All the steps that you took, you did so for value creation. With the barber who is the service provider, you were able to create value by getting a smart haircut. These activities that led to the value generation are a value stream. There are several wastes that we can identify in this value stream, such as the wait time and the vacuuming that the barber must do after you leave. The objective is to do more of the activities that deliver value and less of those that don't. So, to generate more value, reducing wait time or eliminating it is a definite way of doing that, and perhaps an automated vacuum cleaner can eliminate the manual cleaning activities.

In essence, generating value is a two-step process. First, we identify the opportunities to optimize the value stream. Then we automate wherever possible—generally activities that do not involve human cognizance. An illustration is provided in Figure 4-2. The activities in red are the waste generating activities that need to be reduced or if possible eliminated.

Figure 4-2. *Illustration of a service value stream*

An organization consists of several such value streams. The objective of value streams is to identify them—especially the activities that generate waste—and minimize or eliminate them. By reducing waste efficiently, we have effectively performed continuous improvement for the product/service that is in play. The second way to generate more value or to perform continuous improvement is to make the value generating activities more efficient and effective. This can be done using automation that decreases the turnaround time and the defect rate owing to human error.

Simplifying Processes

A process is similar to a value stream, but the objective is rather to get a desired output based on a predictable input.

ITIL Definition of a Process

A set of interrelated or interacting activities that transform inputs into outputs. A process takes one or more defined inputs and turns them into defined outputs. Processes define the sequence of actions and their dependencies.

Processes are buttressed with procedures, templates, and other similar artifacts.

You could envision a process as a set of activities that you need to perform, one after another, to achieve something. Each activity that you perform sets the precedent for the next one, and then the next. The objective of a process is to achieve an output that is along the expected lines and as desired.

114

Here's an example to make the concept simple and digestible. A process is very similar to a recipe for cooking a dish. In a recipe, you have several steps that you need to follow, as instructed, to get the dish you desire.

Let's look at the recipe for an egg omelet. It goes something like this:

- Step 1: Break a couple of eggs into a bowl.

- Step 2: Whisk it until it becomes fluffy.

- Step 3: Add salt and pepper to the mixture.

- Step 4: Heat a nonstick frying pan, and melt some butter until it foams.

- Step 5: Pour the egg mixture onto the pan, and tilt the pan until it covers the base.

- Step 6: Cook for a minute or two, and flip the omelet and cook it for a minute more.

- Step 7: Serve the omelet hot with toasted bread.

You need to follow the steps to the tee to get a good egg omelet. You cannot interchange any two steps to get the same output. In IT language, this is the process to make an egg omelet.

The main aspect of a process is the interconnectivity between the individual steps, and all the steps work collectively toward a common goal, a common objective that is desired.

When we use processes in ITIL effectively for products and services, we can find answers to a number of questions. These include identifying the delivery model of a service, identifying how a service works, identifying the value streams, and defining the roles and responsibilities of various parties.

PESTLE

Note   External factors influencing services and products are outside the scope of ITIL Foundation examination. I will still prod you to read this section, as these factors are practical and matter in work. If you are short of time, skip this section for now and return to it at your leisure.

The four dimensions are essential for designing and operating products and services. However, this does not happen in a vacuum. There are six external factors that are listed in Figure 4-1 that influence products and services either positively or negatively. Care should be taken to identify the positive influences and risks from negative potentials.

The six external factors that are identified in the study of four dimensions of service management go with the acronym PESTLE, and they are:

1. Political

2. Economic

3. Social

4. Technological

5. Legal

6. Environmental

Political Factors

Products and services are not immune to political actions of the organization or the state. A change in leadership and changes in legislation will affect how a service or a product is designed and run. Take, for example, the situation of Covid-19, where the crisis has led to a lockdown across multiple countries. This is a legislation that must be followed by all parties. The services that are offered go through changes to adapt to the changing conditions. I bank with HSBC and when I reach their call center, they announce that their agents are working from home and I could possibly hear pet dogs and kids in the background. Then they continue by saying that digital encryption is in place for agents to access sensitive information from their homes.

This is not normal. The external political factor has forced organizations to make alternative arrangements. This situation of an oncoming disaster would not have been a surprise entity, but rather service organizations are well prepared for such situations and even do a trial regularly.

Economical Factors

The economy is the lifeblood of running services, as they theoretically run perpetually. A certain amount is budgeted based on various factors and the political and economic conditions determine if the budgeted amount is sufficient or not.

Continuing with the same example, economy has fallen to unprecedented levels. This will force organizations to effect cost cuts across various segments of the services. With a smaller budget, the services are still expected to run, perhaps with lower efficiency. Staying with HSBC, normally the call I place will be picked up in less than a minute; the last time I called them, I hung up after waiting for more than ten minutes. I am certain that the agent strength has been culled since the Covid-19 inception.

Social Factors

They say that every ten years the generation changes. Where that matters in products and services is in the area of necessaries, needs, and wants. As the social climate changes, services and products must change with the times—without exceptions. Organizations that do not change wither away over a period of time, as their products and services would generally be treated as obsolete and people would look for shiny new things. Nokia is a classic example of missing the train multiple times when the cell phone boom involving touch screens came into vogue.

Technological Factors

Advancements in technology positively impact products and services. So it is imperative that organizations build an appetite for technical upgrades, which translates to budgeting more funds. In some cases they affect negatively if organizations don't travel in sync with the technology.

Consider the example of Blockbuster, the company that championed the movie and TV show rental business. Come streaming, they didn't keep up and now they are closed forever.

Legal Factors

Products and services are delivered within the ambit of legal boundaries. The law of the land has to be implemented without exceptions, and the rules change from time to time. That's the beauty of legality. Organizations must be flexible and adaptable enough to change with it.

Introduction of the GDPR in 2018 impacted all web channels that stored user data, which is a good majority. All digital channels had to make changes to websites to meet the regulation's demands.

Environmental Factors

Who would have imagined that environment can be a factor influencing services and products? Yes, they play a role. As environments change, the demands from users change too.

Users are respectful of nature these days and prefer to purchase services and products that are organic and serve toward the greater good. This will make companies rethink the way their products are produced and serviced.

Knowledge Check

The answers are provided in Appendix.

4-1.   Which service management dimension focuses on efficiency and cutting down waste?

A. Organization and people

B. Information and technology

C. Partners and suppliers

D. Value streams and processes

4-2.   Which service management dimension focuses on how the staff in a supplier organization is organized?

A. Organization and people

B. Information and technology

C. Partners and suppliers

D. Value streams and processes

4-3. Which service management dimension focuses on culture?

    A. Organization and people

    B. Information and technology

    C. Partners and suppliers

    D. Value streams and processes

4-4. Which of these are not considered under the information and technology dimension?

    A. Information managed by the services

    B. Supporting information and knowledge needed to deliver and manage the services

    C. Generic delivery model for the service

    D. Information and knowledge assets' protection and management

4-5. Which of the options accurately reflect the difference between a partner and a supplier?

    A. Clear separation of roles

    B. Partners maintain knowledge bases.

    C. Suppliers are managed by partners.

    D. Partners are managed by suppliers.

DAY 3

Approximate Study Time: 1 hour and 47 minutes

Chapter 5 - 41 minutes
Chapter 6 - 60 minutes
Chapter 7 - 6 minutes

On day 3 we study the most important topic in ITIL: the service value system and the service value chain. The topics covered on this day are the guiding principles of ITIL and form the basis for the rest of the framework.

CHAPTER 5

Value Creation with Service Value System

ITIL has stood for creating value through services. In ITIL V3, all aspects of service management were seen through the lens of value. It is no different in ITIL 4. In fact, value takes center stage with an entire chapter and multiple concepts revolving around it. What is different is that value is getting the right level of emphasis through a system that is built to deliver it.

This is a chapter focused on the service value system (SVS) and the service value chain (SVC), the engines that bring together and help co-create value. Further, we will explore the guiding principles that were first introduced in the ITIL V3 Practitioner certification course. These concepts are tied together with the concepts of opportunities, demands, and the importance of governance to ensure smooth sailing.

Exam Tip This is an important chapter from the examination standpoint. You can expect to find nine questions from this chapter alone, which can potentially take you through to a third of the marks needed to pass the examination.

© Abhinav Krishna Kaiser 2021
A. K. Kaiser, *Become ITIL® 4 Foundation Certified in 7 Days*,
https://doi.org/10.1007/978-1-4842-6361-7_5

Introducing Service Value System

I wrote about the value being co-created between a service provider and a customer. I also mentioned how services can no longer be delivered by a single organization. It needs other organizations, and the service integrates with various services and products to deliver value.

Let's focus one level deeper. For creating value, an organization, say a service provider organization, needs to have several components and elements to move in harmony to make it happen. For example, the organization would need the power of technology coupled with able people who can architect and build it. To bring these people onboard and others as necessary, you need a hiring function and to take good care of them, a human resources function. Plus, you need the finance departments to pay the salaries among other financial duties. I am just skimming the surface and have identified so many sets of functions that need to work in harmony to deliver value.

Another example that we all can relate to is the working of a car. A car has a zillion parts (or so it seems) and every single one of them is needed for its smooth running. Fuel is needed to power the engine, and the engine converts the fuel energy through combustion into mechanical motion. A battery is required to initiate the engine to start the combustible process. This mechanical motion is fed to the wheels through the mechanism of gears and axles. The wheels themselves need the rubber for a smooth ride and traction. While these are the internal dynamics, you need a controlling mechanism that is managed by a driver who controls the direction of motion using a steering wheel and the power through the combination of a clutch, accelerator, and gearbox. Yes, these are at the simplest level I can explain how a car runs and I am not even getting to the add-ons such as lights, wipers, mirrors, seats, and air conditioning. There are so many other features that modern cars possess that I have no idea where to start and end. My point is that all these parts that I made note of have to work in a particular way for the car to move in the desired direction and speed.

Considering transportation as a service, then the synchronous mechanism of a car that I described is the SVS. It is a system of works that brings together various discrete components into a single homogenous entity that delivers value.

For simplicity, I can break this down further into two streams that together define the SVS:

1. Discrete components that work together in unison

2. Organized scheme of things that brings together the discrete components; think of it as the policies, processes, and procedures.

Exam Tip   On the topic of a service value system, you can expect to get at least one question (equivalent to one mark) on your ITIL foundation exam. The question will be based on your ability to recall and recognize concepts.

ITIL Definition of Service Value System

The ITIL SVS describes how all the components and activities of the organization work together as a system to enable value creation.

The structure of an SVS is shown in Figure 5-1. It consists of the following components:

1. Opportunity and Demand as inputs

2. Value as the output

3. Service Value Chain at the center

4. Governance and Practices around it

5. Guiding Principles and Continual Improvement wrapping it all up

It is the various resources and assets within an organization that tie these discrete components together. Remember that an organization will contain various silos. By using various permutations and combinations of these organizational resources, we can generate value; this is possible through some tight coordination and integration.

It is also true that not all organizations are the same. You have some traditional organizations that can be rigid regarding the flexibility with which they can be manipulated to achieve value. And then there are the startups that change like a chameleon. The bottom line is that the organization's culture, flexibility, and adaptability will set the tone for creating value.

The components of the SVS are discussed in detail later in this chapter except for guiding principles in Chapter 6; continual improvement, which is explained in Chapter 10; and practices in Chapters 7 through 14. We have already discussed value in Chapter 3.

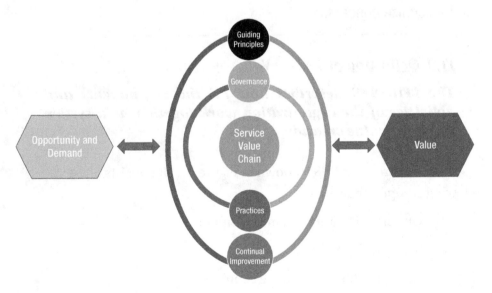

Figure 5-1. *Service value system*

Note   Alternately, you can define service value system as a set of things working together as parts of a mechanism or an interconnecting network to create value through products and services.

Opportunity and Demand

Any business that is undertaken is done so on the back of available opportunities. Without identifying them, going into business is like shooting oneself in the foot. Think about your neighborhood restaurant. Do you think they started the restaurant without doing some research on their potential customers, their competition, and other possibilities? The opportunities give rise to businesses and this is also true with products and services.

New products and services are introduced and brought into the market because there is significant knowledge of the opportunities that are in place. With cell phone connections coming in at an affordable cost in the early 2000s, cell phone manufacturers saw an opportunity and developed new phones and released a new one every so often. They latched onto the opportunity created in the market (facilitated by the government) to become relevant and rule it.

ITIL Definition of Opportunity

Opportunity represents options or possibilities to add value for stakeholders or otherwise improve the organization.

ITIL's definition of an opportunity looks from the perspective of creating value through products and services. Opportunities are not limited to creating and maintaining a new product or a service, but could also be for improving a service or any other aspect of an organization that can lead to a rise in value.

While service providers offer services, they get into a position where they can read the pulse of a customer and can sense other opportunities. These opportunities could be extending the existing services to newer areas or offering adjacent services, or enabling service add-ons that can offer further value to customers.

An aspect that goes hand in hand with opportunity or supplements it is the demand. An opportunity could open up for a service provider to offer products and services. However, without demand for it, it's doomed to fail. So when an opportunity is identified, the corresponding demand is identified, which is revealed during the market research and study that are undertaken.

Chevrolet in India having been successful for decades decided to source their cars from China through their subsidiary company SAIL. They sensed an opportunity to cut down the production costs and maybe pass on some of these savings to customers. However, the demand for Chinese cars in India was not as they had anticipated. The demand was low and their decision was irreversible. This meant that the car giant had to exit the car market in India.

ITIL Definition of Demand

Demand represents the need or desire for products and services from internal and external customers.

Understanding demand for products and services is essential. Companies must ensure that they find out the true need and, with the knowledge of opportunities available, offer products and services that are fit for purpose and fit for use (value).

> **Note**   Internal customers are from the same organization as the service provider. External customers are outside of it. The difference between internal and external customers is merely measured in terms of finances. External customers pay real money, and hence their importance is at a high. Internal customers, on the other hand, are an obligation, something that organization must tend to and cannot live without.
>
> The internal IT team charges the internal business units notionally. No real money gets transferred between the business units and the IT team but is noted only in the ledgers. It is like taking money out of your left pocket and depositing it into your right pocket.

Governance

The governance is an integral part of the SVS and it is at the core, meaning it processes the opportunities and demands coming through and has a major say in the value that is getting delivered. So, let us understand what governance is all about.

> **Note**   Although governance is part of the service value system, it is not in the scope of the ITIL Foundation examination. I still encourage you to read this section, as it is practical and matters in work. If you are short of time, skip this section for now and return to it at your leisure.

Governance is about providing direction to an organization, a project, or a country. Governments provide the necessary direction through legislations for countries. At an organization level, we have governance bodies that are set up to provide direction in the definition and enforcement of policies. In projects, governance bodies include key representatives from the customer, service provider, and suppliers, along with sponsors and others who are accountable for the outcome. Products and services too are created similar to projects or on the back of them, and have a governance body to provide direction.

Governance is part of the SVS through the processes and activities for managing services. This governance should conform to organization level governance, which is the primary governance body to ensure evaluation, direction, and monitoring of various activities. Every product or service will have a governance body that is set up to ensure that value is being created and delivered to the customer. The directions put forth by the service/product governance will be based on the organizational principles and policies. The governing body will have a high-level view of all activities that create value and those that are overheads; and more importantly, the ambit of continuous improvement comes under governance as well.

Service Value Chain

The service value chain (SVC) is at the core of the service value system (SVS). The SVS (Figure 5-1) is essential for taking in demands and converting them into value for the customer through products and services. To generate this value, the critical engine that puts things into motion is the SVC.

Exam Tip   On the topic of the service value chain, you can expect to get at least one question (equivalent to one mark) on your ITIL foundation exam. The question will test your understanding of the service value chain and your ability to use that understanding to answer the question.

The activities of SVC are illustrated in Figure 5-2.

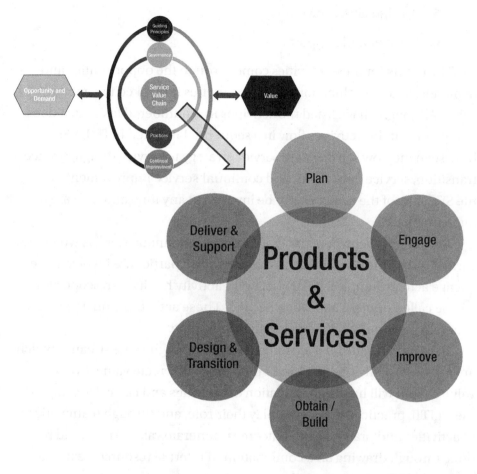

Figure 5-2. *Service value chain*

The SVC, which is bound by the guiding principles, governance, practices, and continual improvement, has six activities associated with it:

1. Plan

2. Engage

3. Improve

4. Obtain/Build

5. Design and Transition

6. Deliver and Support

The inputs for these activities come through the opportunities and demands, and a combination of these activities is invoked to generate value. Although I have listed the activities in a numbered fashion, it does not mean that the activities flow in a sequential manner. In ITIL V3, we have seen the flow starting with service strategy to service design, service transition, service operations, and continual service improvement. In the SVC, any of the activities can be invoked at any time and they are all interconnected.

Any requirement/demand that involves a planning exercise would be carried out by the plan activity. Whenever third parties are involved, the engage activity jumps in. Likewise, every activity has its own scope and will be called upon as and when needed. These activities work together to generate the required outcomes and create value.

Generating value for a customer is done through value streams, which are a series of activities that intake demands and create value. Every value stream will have a combination of activities and can call on any of the 34 ITIL practices to jump in, play their role, and through teamwork of activities and practices and outcomes, generate value. This could be done through drawing on a combination of internal resources, external resources, ITIL practices, skills, and competencies.

Let us consider an example where a new employee joins an organization, which is illustrated in Figure 5-3.

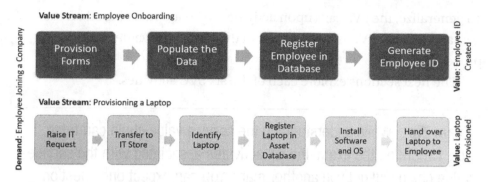

Figure 5-3. *Service value stream illustration*

There are two value streams that have been illustrated for the scenario where a new employee joins an organization.

The first value stream is registering the employee (employee onboarding) into the enterprise database, along with filling out various forms and signing nondisclosure agreements and other necessary documents. In this value stream, the first activity would be to provide the forms for the employee to fill out; second is to validate if everything is alright; and finally, accept the changes and generate employee number. The outcome is the employee ID that gets generated at the end of the process. This is value for both the employee and the organization.

The second value stream is provisioning a laptop for the newly joined employee. An IT request is raised for a new laptop, the IT store picks up the request and identifies a laptop from the store, they register the asset in the asset database, and hand over the laptop to the technical team to install the necessary operating system and the software. Once all the installations are complete, the laptop is handed over to the user. The outcome is provisioning a laptop to the employee, which needless to say is value being created for both the employee and the organization.

Each of these value streams works through a combination of activities: the input being the demand (employee joining a company) and the outcomes/value being created at the end of the value stream.

To generalize, the SVS calls upon activities to create value based on the demand and the SVC is at the center of the SVS in the value creation process.

The next sections explore each of the six SVC activities.

Exam Tip   While understanding the service value chain can fetch you 1 mark on the exam, the six activities associated with the service value chain will get you another mark. You can expect one question based on the six activities listed (as follows) on your ITIL foundation exam. The question will test your understanding and your ability to use the understanding in answering the question.

Plan

The plan activity in the SVC represents the phase or set of activities concerned with identifying strategies for the service provider organization and to make plans accordingly. If you are familiar with ITIL V3, this activity is like the Service Strategy phase. The major difference is the waterfall model in V3 and a parallel approach in ITIL 4. You can call on any of the activities at any juncture, and it need not flow like it did earlier, starting with the strategy phase.

The plan activity exists to ensure that all parties involved in the value co-creation share a common vision (or mutually agreeable ones) and agree on a road map with a good understanding of the status and future steps. This is not only applicable to new products and services alone but also to the improvement initiatives. The planning activity is not restricted to the value stream alone but also stretches to four dimensions, services, and products.

The various inputs and outputs are illustrated in Figure 5-4. This by no means is comprehensive but is put forth to provide an understanding of the role of the activity.

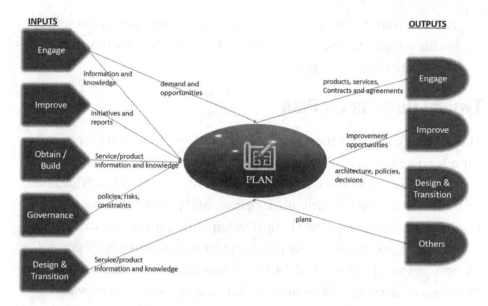

Figure 5-4. *Plan activity inputs and outputs under service value chain*

Typical Inputs for Plan

If you are in the business of drawing up strategies, you know that information around the customer demand, the opportunities that are available, the competition, and other market related information are most needed. These will come from the Engage activity from within the SVC. Remember that the Engage activity deals with all external parties for the service provider.

The identified improvement opportunities along with the status of improvements in pipeline and the current performance levels will help in making plans for the existing products and services. This will come from the Improve activity within the SVC.

The various changes that are done to the product/service (through change requests) are fed back to the Plan activity by the Obtain/Build and Design and Transition activities from within the SVC.

The governance layer of the SVS draws up the boundaries through the applicable policies to be considered and identifies the requirements, risks, and constraints that are in play.

Typical Outputs for Plan

The primary output for the plan activity will be to create and propose various strategic, tactical, and operational plans for the organization.

Based on the identified strategies and plans, the activity provides the architectural decisions, portfolio decisions, and policies that are put forth from the strategic perspective to the Design and Transition activity.

Further, the Engage activity gets the information and details around the services and products and the various contracts and agreements that need to be signed between third parties and the service provider organization.

The feedback loop works in a cyclical way with the Improve activity. The plan activity, based on its knowledge and overview, can identify improvement initiatives as well.

Engage

The activity in the SVC that deals with third parties, both within and outside the organization, is the Engage activity. The activity is entrusted with understanding the needs of not only the customers but also all involved stakeholders, and with maintaining a healthy relationship with them.

In the erstwhile ITIL, we did not have a phase per se, but this activity was carried out by the business relationship management and service level management processes.

The various inputs and outputs are illustrated in Figure 5-5. This by no means is comprehensive but is put forth to provide an understanding of the role of the activity.

In a world that is highly interconnected, this activity plays the role of a fulcrum to ensure that all stakeholders stay harmonious in relationship to the common vision and goals set forth. It must as well ensure that the pulse of stakeholders, be it customers or a regulation body, is monitored from time to time.

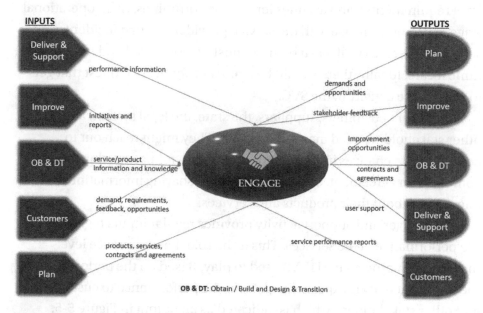

Figure 5-5. *Engage activity inputs and outputs under service value chain*

Typical Inputs for Engage

You can see in Figure 5-5 that the Engage activity has several inputs, which is expected in an industry that relies on several other third parties to provide enabling and supporting services.

The most critical input comes from customers in the form of feedback for the products and services rendered. Customers can be both internal and external. The skill is not just accepting the feedback but to discern it. Every feedback must be responded to on merit, and the activity must ensure that appropriate actions are taken. You will also find in the figure an output going into Improve activity. This is on the back of stakeholder feedback. Other inputs that can be expected from customers could be changes in the demand, change of requirements (or detailing out the high-level requirements), and avenues for new opportunities. At an operational stage, customers engage with the service provider through incidents and service requests as well. Each of these must be prioritized and treated with utmost care. Ideally, there should be a practice for every request that gets to the Engage activity in the SVC.

Apart from customers, suppliers, the state, the legal system, and other stakeholders need managing as well. They might reach out to communicate changes in regulation, exploration for partnership, for coming to an agreement, or they could just be sharing information and knowledge about their products and services.

The Deliver and Support activity provides regular inputs regarding the performance of the services. This is the role that the service level management process in ITIL V3 used to play. Based on the performance, the Engage activity is expected to present the performance to customers and other stakeholders, which is indicated as an output in Figure 5-5.

Further, the Improve activity provides information around the various improvement initiatives that are being undertaken in the organization along with the stage of development and timelines.

Obtain/Build and Design and Transition activities provide information and knowledge around the services and products. This is necessary to keep the activity abreast of the product and service changes.

Under the Plan activity, we looked at the output to the Engage activity, which is shown as an input.

Typical Outputs for Engage

Apart from relaying the feedback from stakeholders to the Improve activity, there could be opportunities identified for improvement in services and products that are passed on as well.

New demands and opportunities coming from stakeholders need to be put through the cycle of strategizing and planning, and this is done as an output to the Plan activity.

The inputs received from operational stages are fed as an output to the Deliver and Support activity after processing it with the set standard operating procedures.

Any requirements to build a new system or developmental inputs are fed to the Obtain/Build activity. To go with this, changes to contracts and agreements need to be sent out to this activity along with the Design and Transition activity, which is entrusted with the information surrounding product and service requirements. The Design and Transition activity uses this information to come up with the architectural designs, implementation plans, and deployments.

In the spirit of visibility and transparency, the Engage activity shares information around third parties, their services and products, and the knowledge gathered across the value stream.

Improve

The Improve activity in the SVC exists to effect continual improvement across the value streams, four dimensions, products, services, and all other service management areas.

The Improve activity in ITIL V3 was the Continual Service Improvement phase, which stretched across the other four phases.

An illustration of the inputs and outputs of the Improve activity is shown in Figure 5-6.

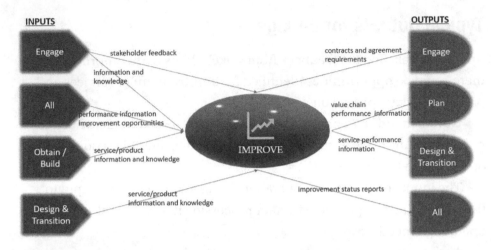

Figure 5-6. *Improve activity inputs and outputs under service value chain*

Typical Inputs for Improve

One of the key responsibilities for the Improve activity is to ensure that all parts of service management are on an improvement trajectory. To process and bring about improvements, the Improve activity is fed with various improvement opportunities that are identified across the system and also with the product/service performance information. This information is used as a baseline and as a measurement factor to bring about and prove the improvements that are brought about in the system.

To effectively improve the service or a product, the Improve activity requires inputs from customers and other stakeholders, which it gets from the Engage activity, along with the knowledge around third-party services and their associated components.

Obtain/Build and Design and Transition activities provide information and knowledge around the services and products. This is necessary to keep the activity abreast of product and service changes.

Typical Outputs for Improve

Typically, the Improve activity is expected to report on the improvement initiatives across the streams and parts of the organizations.

The Plan activity is particularly interested in understanding the various activities' performance in the SVC. This is measured and delivered to the Plan activity.

Based on the improvements in the systems, if there are any changes that are to be expected in services and products, then the related agreements and contracts too need a change. This information is fed to the Engage activity.

The performance information surrounding the services is provided to Design and Transition, as they have a stake in this information to alter the architecture and designs accordingly.

Design and Transition

Design and Transition is the next activity in the SVC. Its main purpose is to ensure that the designs and the transition road maps are in line with the overall plans set forth. From an activity perspective, it exists to ensure that the products and services are designed and transitioned to meet the customer requirements in terms of quality, costs, and time to market.

This activity is similar to the service design phase in ITIL V3 that was responsible for the overall design of a service. There are some parts of the service transition phase that have been embedded in the Design and Transition activity.

An illustration of the inputs and outputs of the Design and Transition activity is shown in Figure 5-7.

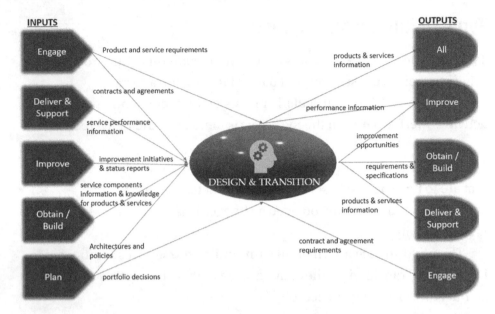

Figure 5-7. *Design and transition activity inputs and outputs under service value chain*

Typical Inputs for Design and Transition

Designs are typically drawn when the requirements are in place. These requirements come to the Design and Transition activity through the Engage activity. Apart from this, the contracts and agreements from suppliers and partners who support and enable the product and service creation are also fed through the Engage activity.

The designs are drawn within the boundaries set by the Plan activity—read as the strategic boundaries. This includes the list of products and service portfolios that have been agreed in the Plan activity, and the corresponding architectures and enterprise policies that are relevant during design and transition planning.

The Improve activity feeds information around the various improvement initiatives that are active, along with the results of the earlier performance initiatives. The purpose of feeding these to Design and

Transition is to meet the objectives of these initiatives through improved designs. The performance information after applying improvements is fed back to the Improve activity along with other identified improvement opportunities.

The performance of services from the operations (Deliver and Support) and also from improvement initiatives is an input to the activity, as this data is used as a baseline for bettering the designs. This also acts as a feedback for the Design and Transition activity, as it measures up to the service level targets that have been set.

Understanding of the existing service components is obtained through Obtain/Build. This information will typically help in reusing, optimizing, and scaling up as needed. The Obtain/Build activity also provides information around products and services and the changes that they have been through. It could include specifications, known errors, and other operational data. This information is pertinent to enable effective design decisions.

Typical Outputs for Design and Transition

Design and Transition is an activity that plays a crucial role across the SVC. It is one of the main sources of information pertaining to products and services. Say, for example, the Plan activity needs this information because it can potentially influence the existing and future strategies and road maps. Obtain/Build would need this information to develop the product or a service. It needs to be passed on to Deliver and Support, as this is pertinent information for supporting the product or the service.

The Engage activity acts as a conduit for the contracts and agreements that are identified from a design perspective. It could be contracting with a new vendor for an identified design or partnering up with an automation company to meet certain goals.

The various improvement opportunities along with the performance information identified by the Design and Transition activity are fed to the

Improve activity for managing the improvement initiatives to closure. The shortcomings identified in this activity are fed to the Improve activity in anticipation of finding a permanent solution for them.

As we build new products and services, the identified requirements and specifications from a design and transition perspective are inputted to the Obtain/Build activity. This data will be used by the Obtain/Build activity to procure components such as servers, software licenses, and resources, among others.

Obtain/Build

Obtain/Build is the next value chain activity, which deals with mobilizing the right kind of resources that are needed to deliver value to customers through products and services, and to develop products and services. It is an activity that is entrusted with ensuring that all necessary service components that fit the bill are made available before the service delivery can begin delivering value. For example, service components such as infrastructure, people, software licenses, and automation, among others, may be necessary for developing a product or a service. Ensuring that these resources are in place is one of the jobs of the Obtain/Build activity. Once these are in place, the next objective is to build it before the next value chain activity—Deliver and Support—can take over.

Securing and procuring resources is new to the ITIL framework. The focus thus far has been on identifying the different types of assets and resources that were needed to run a service successfully. How these resources would be obtained was primarily kept outside the scope. It was expected that procurement and human resource processes would step in and deliver. With ITIL 4, these activities have been formalized. The activity around development of services was carried out by the service transition phase.

The various inputs and outputs to Obtain/Build activity from other SVC activities is illustrated in Figure 5-8.

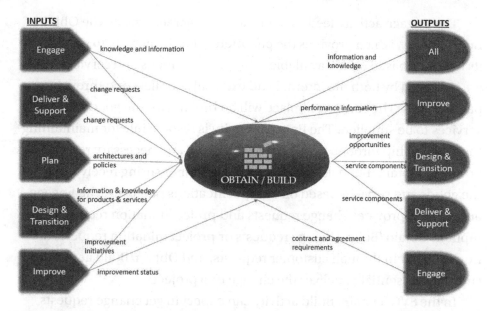

Figure 5-8. *Obtain/Build activity inputs and outputs under service value chain*

Typical Inputs for Obtain/Build

In other value chain activities, we have seen that the output of Plan—architectures and policies—is consumed by other value chain activities. Obtain/Build also consumes it, as the information is used in obtaining and building as per the specifications.

Requirements and specifications come from the Design and Transition activity. This is essentially the designs that have been developed by the activity. This information is used by the Obtain/Build activity to procure and mobilize resources. After the resources have been mobilized, products and services are developed based on the designs.

Knowledge and information of new or changed services is an input that comes through from Design and Transition activity. Any new services or changes to the existing one require new resources to develop and deliver them.

The Engage activity feeds in contracts and agreements to the Obtain/ Build activity, which provides the parameters for the activity to conduct its business based on the available third parties. Goods and services are delivered by both the internal and external suppliers and through partnerships. The contract in place will be binding for the goods and services to be supplied. The Engage activity is responsible for maintaining the relationship through which the information and necessary resources flow, and Obtain/Build activity is responsible for ensuring receiving of the goods and services based on the specifications put forth. The Engage activity also provides change requests and project initiation requests as an input to Obtain/Build. Change requests or project initiation requests are normally put in through customer requests, and Obtain/Build activity's support is essential to deliver the change or a project.

In the SVC, Obtain/Build activity can expect to get change requests from Deliver and Support activity as well. Based on the change requests, changes are needed to be done that require additional resources/people, and a project team may be needed to do the actual development before the end product is fed back to the Deliver and Support activity. Example: If a transition of an operating system is identified, let' say a project team is involved to deliver it. The project team operates in the Obtain/Build activity. To carry out this activity, which is a result of a change request, people with the right skill sets need to be hired, infrastructure needs to be provisioned for the new operating system, and the operating system licenses need procuring as well. Once the resources are in place, the operating system upgrades are carried out and tested. When satisfied, the finished product is handed to Delivery and Support for maintenance and operational work.

The Improve activity is interested in bettering products and services. From its perspective, the improvement initiatives and statuses are provided to Obtain/Build to materialize the identified improvement initiatives.

146

Typical Outputs for Obtain/Build

From the Obtain/Build activity, we should expect to see outputs that are typically services, products, modified services, modified products, and various individual components that make up these products and services.

The service components, which include all the knowledge about the service, are fed to the Design and Transition activity to enable a smooth transition into Deliver and Support activity. Staying with the same example as earlier, after the operating system upgrades are done, the finished product is handed to Design and Transition to plan and deploy it into production. After the deployment, the responsibilities to manage the services and the service components lie with Deliver and Support. In a related example, if the Obtain/Build activity was to procure and configure a switch, and if it can be replaced without the aid of a full blown transition plan, it gets delivered directly to the Deliver and Support activity.

Staying with service components, the knowledge and information about these services are consumed by all other SVC activities and are a primary output of the Obtain/Build activity. If anything is modified or built anew, every activity needs to know how to carry out their respective responsibilities such as Engage for engaging third parties when the contracts need changing, to the Improve activity for setting a new baseline.

Deliver and Support

The Deliver and Support activity pertains to operations and maintenance of services. The purpose is to maintain the service status quo and to ensure that the services deliver as per the specifications and designs that are put in place. Importantly, all stakeholders must be able to obtain value and meet their expectations.

Let us further explore two terms that are used here: deliver and support. Deliver pertains to the service that is delivered, the capability that is extended to users and customers. Support comes into play when the service does not function as expected, or when changes (service requests) are requested that enhance the service experience.

Deliver and Support hires a majority of people in the IT industry. For every person in development, you can expect eight to ten people hired in the operations area. This is due to the perpetuity nature of operations. While projects have a limited time period, operations run as long as the products and services are supported. However, in DevOps, the lines become blurred and the gulf between the two is reduced somewhat, because you tend to have a continuous development lifecycle and share resources between both development and operational activities.

The various inputs and outputs to the Deliver and Support activity from other SVC activities are illustrated in Figure 5-9.

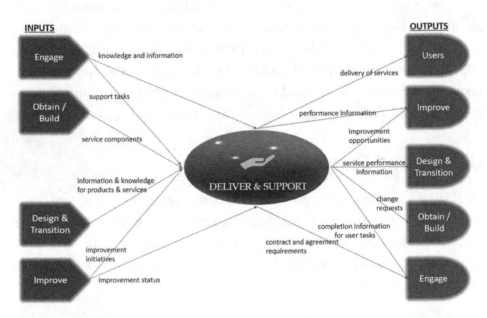

Figure 5-9. *Deliver and Support activity inputs and outputs under service value chain*

Typical Inputs for Deliver and Support

Deliver and Support is an activity that ensures that services are maintained and any anomalies are duly taken care of. The inputs to this activity therefore will mainly come from the user community in the form of incidents and service requests. These service requests get to the Deliver and Support activity through the Engage activity. Remember that users talk to Deliver and Support through the Engage activity.

Apart from the support requests, the various contracts and agreements and knowledge and information around third-party components are fed through the Engage activity. This information is vital to upkeep of services.

In the Obtain/Build activity we looked at how the flow of services that are built gets transitioned through the Design and Transition activity. The input that comes through the Design and Transition activity is the information and knowledge about products and services that have been transitioned—the information that is necessary to keep the services in status quo and the knowledge to perform break-fix activities. The Obtain/Build activity also feeds in the information around service components, which helps in providing support to end users.

Improvement initiatives, plans, and statuses of ongoing improvement activities come through the Improve activity.

Typical Outputs for Deliver and Support

The longest and continuously running activity, Deliver and Support, acts as an input system to multiple activities within the value chain and to the users.

The services that are delivered and the support that is extended through incidents and service requests are the primary outputs to customers and the user community. While you support users, the Engage activity, which provides the inputs to support users, needs to be informed of its progress. Say for example that a user raises an incident stating that the printer in the bay is not working. The Deliver and Support activity resolves the printer problem and sends out a notification through the Engage activity to the user that the printer is now working.

Further, any changes needed to the contracts and agreements go back to the Engage activity as well.

Apart from the support task statuses, the Engage activity will also receive performance information that indicates the service levels that have been agreed for the service. This information is fed to the Improve activity as well, which acts as an input to identify improvement initiatives.

The Deliver and Support activity too contributes to improvements by identifying improvement opportunities and inputting this information to the Improve activity to take further action. Generally, this would work in two ways. First, surveys are sent out to customers and users seeking their feedback on the service and support. These inputs could be collated and analyzed to identify improvement opportunities. Second, the IT staff working in Deliver and Support knows the services like the back of their hand because they deal with them quite closely and find themselves in a position to identify opportunities for improvements. All these improvement tips are like gold dust to any service provider.

The Design and Transition activity requires feedback on their designs and transitions that have been put in place. This feedback comes in the form of service performance information from Deliver and Support. Examples of service performance information include availability reports, capacity reports, and network bandwidth reports.

Changes to services are quite common during operations. They could come in the form of replacing and reconfiguring infrastructure or making changes to the network or software. Such activities are handled by Obtain/Build, and this information comes through the Deliver and Support activity.

Knowledge Check

The answers are provided in Appendix.

5-1. Which of the following does not figure in the service value system components?

A. Guiding Principles

B. Four Dimensions

C. Practices

D. Continual Improvement

5-2. Which of the following accurately represent the definition of opportunities?

A. Represents options or possibilities to add value for stakeholders or otherwise improve the organization

B. Provides demand information for creation of value to the service value system

C. Provides the option to add resources and assets to meet the demand coming through from sponsors

D. Represents the various value options that can be presented to the customer in order that it can be co-created

5-3. Which of the following activities deals with stakeholders?

A. Engage

B. Deliver and Support

C. Customer Relationship Management

D. Business Relationship Management

5-4.   The primary function of Obtain/Build is:

   A. Obtain resources and build plans

   B. Develop project plans and implement it

   C. Secure resources and develop services

   D. Secure products and build services

5-5.   Which of the following is not an output for the Deliver and Support activity?

   A. Obtain/Build

   B. Users

   C. Plan

   D. Design and Transition

CHAPTER 6

Influencing Through Guiding Principles

Think about guiding principles as a set of boundaries that are drawn. You can play within these boundaries and, at no cost, cross them. Well, to rephrase it, these are more like recommendations and not rules or policies that you are bound by. The nonprescriptive nature of ITIL is perhaps one of its strongest suits, and it continues the legacy with the guiding principles.

The concept of guiding principles is in fact new to ITIL. It started much later in 2016 with the ITIL Practitioner certification. To start with it had nine guiding principles, and in ITIL 4 there are seven. This does not imply that the list has been trimmed down. The principles have been revamped from the outset, expanded, and some of the principles are combined to make the list comprehensive and still not cumbersome.

The seven guiding principles of ITIL are as follows:

1. Focus on Value

2. Start Where You Are

3. Progress Iteratively with Feedback

4. Collaborate and Promote Visibility

5. Think and Work Holistically

6. Keep it Simple and Practical

7. Optimize and Automate

For the sake of printing out and remembering the guiding principles, I have also included it in a cyclical form in Figure 6-1.

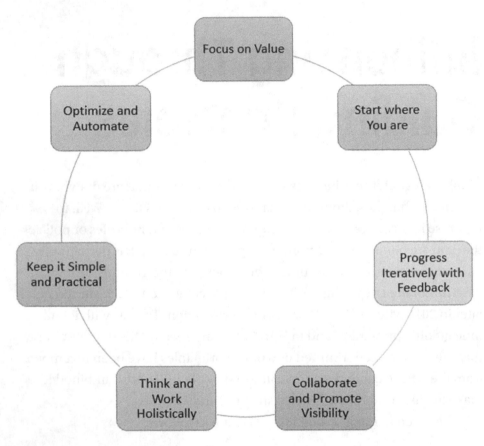

Figure 6-1. *Guiding principles*

Exam Tip   The guiding principles are the most important topic on the ITIL foundation exam from the number of marks that it can carry. You can expect to get five questions on your ITIL foundation exam—that is 12.5 percent of the total questions. The questions will test your understanding, and you will be required to apply your understanding for answering the questions. Therefore, I have delved deep into this topic to ensure your maximum probability of success.

ITIL Definition of Guiding Principle

A recommendation that guides an organization in all circumstances.

In my opinion, these guiding principles are not restricted to ITIL and service management alone. You can apply them to any industry and it would be true. In other words, they are universal and more importantly, practical. Every one of them is common sense and yet needs to be reminded at every step of the way.

In several ways, ITIL's guiding principles follow the Agile manifesto. For example, *working software over comprehensive documentation* is a classic example of where we lay emphasis on things that embellish but not the core value. Guiding principles Focus on Value and Keep it Simple and Practical gel well with it. Likewise, *responding to change over following a plan* is embodied with Progress Iteratively with Feedback.

Note   Agile manifesto states (not in scope for ITIL Foundation exam):

Individuals and interactions over processes and tools

Working software over comprehensive documentation

Customer collaboration over contract negotiation

Responding to change over following a plan

Every organization implements service management in its own way. There are several other frameworks and methodologies in use. Organizations will choose to combine and mix different methodologies and frameworks to come up with a customized framework that works for them. The guiding principles ensure that they allow enough room for these frameworks to combine and synergize. It is important to note that the guiding principles work toward creating value for the customer and help improve products and services on a continual basis.

Agile methodology provides guidance for how projects are to be run in an Agile manner, which promotes flexibility and dynamism. Value is generated through meeting changing customers' needs. DevOps goes one step further by acting as a superset for development and operations. While development processes are managed through Agile, operations are done through ITIL. Merging the two frameworks/methodologies is not seamless. When you have a common team working on both, you are bound to have conflicts, like how you prioritize one over the other. It is in such situations that overarching guiding principles would come into play in providing direction. For the example of prioritization, keep creating value as true north. Then, you weigh the various development and operation items against the value they create, work on an item that generates the most value, then move down the list. Of course, I have diluted the scenario quite a bit. You will have other factors in play, and the product owner will act as the value determiner. Similarly, for other frameworks such as Prince, Lean, COBIT, and others, you could apply the same set of principles to bring them under a common north star.

An organization should not pick and choose the guiding principles that are applicable to them, because all of them come as a box set and it makes practical sense to practice them. However, not all guiding principles are applicable in all circumstances and scenarios. An organization should identify the guiding principles relevant for the scenario and use it (them) judiciously.

Exam Tip   Identifying the seven guiding principles is important. However, what is more important is the context in which each guiding principle is brought into action.

Focus on Value

The entire ITIL is built around creating value to the customer. So, a guiding principle that specifically says *focus on value* is overemphasizing, is it not? Not really. This guiding principle, the first of the seven, gives a definite boundary, steps, and direction toward focusing on what is most important to our consumers and customers.

ITIL Definition of Focus on Value Guiding Principle

All activities conducted by the organization should link back, directly or indirectly, to value for itself, its customers, and other stakeholders.

A service provider exists not to provide services to customers but to provide value through services. How does a service provider achieve this? As per the ITIL definition, the service that is offered must be dissected in terms of its deliverables. Each of these deliverables must be mapped to the service consumption and the business processes at the customer's end. Through this exercise, a service provider will be in an ideal situation to measure if the services offered are generating value, and if more value can be generated by tweaking services and in the process can create value for themselves along with other stakeholders involved through the value generation lifecycle.

Picking the Netflix example, the video streaming service provides ample value to customers who like to be entertained and who want to pass boredom by doing this. They gather data from their customers on the genre, the language, and the age ratings that are streamed by their customers. This information is used to recommend other available shows to customers and to fund new shows that are on similar lines as the demand indicates. This exercise of Netflix gathering data and using it wisely is an example of generating more value for the customer. In the process, Netflix too creates value through the content it produces, which could lead to additional customers signing up. Other stakeholders like the production companies, story writers, and actors also become part of the value generation and create value for themselves through video production.

Value generation can be typically fulfilled using the four-step process:

1. Understanding the service consumer

2. Understanding the service consumer's perspective

3. Obtaining feedback from the customer

4. Applying the learnings

Understanding the Service Consumer

Value generation 101 dictates that you know the person who is going to enjoy your service. Unless you understand the consumer's desires, tastes, needs, and necessities, you cannot aim to deliver a service that makes them happy. A service consumer is generally happy if the service generates value and can deliver its intended purposes.

A Mexican restaurant that wants to open in a neighborhood studies the surroundings before setting up their enterprise. Depending on the class of people and the ethnicities, they decide on whether to open shop. This restaurant is likely to run well in a neighborhood that has ethnicities that prefer spicy food, such as Indians. A typical Chinese neighborhood would prefer something closer to Asian than western, for example.

Apart from the service consumers themselves, a service provider must look toward understanding the other stakeholders in play, like sponsors who will be funding the service, the customers, and others, as necessary.

Understanding the Service Consumer's Perspectives

Knowing the consumer is information. Getting to know consumers and their needs in depth is knowledge. The service provider must aspire to go in depth—not just getting objective answers to questions but to truly understand them by going into the perspectives. This would typically be answering the 6Ws – who, what, where, when, why, and how.

From a service management perspective, this translates to a service provider understanding:

1. Why the consumer uses this service?

2. How does the service generate value?

3. Who uses it?

4. Where and when is it used?

5. What is achieved through the services?

6. What are the financial limitations for the customer?

7. What risks are involved that can be foreseen?

Remember that value has a lot to do with perception. You might be brilliant at offering fiber-based broadband Internet service. But if your brand has a negative perception, customers may go elsewhere. So, it is essential in the value generation process to measure value through the eyes of the customer rather than mere numbers. Second, the perception of value does not always remain constant. A beautiful vacation spot in Scotland could have zero visitors in the times of a pandemic, for example.

Finally, costs and risks play a significant role whether a customer chooses a service provider or not. Customers may not opt for cheap services for fear that their quality may be substandard, and opt for something reasonable and fair instead.

Obtaining Feedback from Customer

Feedback is like gold dust in the service industry. With the changing perceptions of value to a customer, keeping up with them is a challenge for service providers. So, they try and obtain feedback from their customers on various factors. Try and map this to the 1,001 emails you receive from your service provider seeking 2 minutes of your time. Clicking on this link in the email will take you to a survey that's aimed at understanding your potentially changing perceptions.

The feedback mainly tries to understand the customer experience (CX), which is also referred to as user experience (UX). CX is defined as the product of interactions between an organization and a customer over a period, with respect to products and services. This experience/feedback will provide information about how a customer feels about the product/service and the organization providing it.

As I mentioned in the previous step, it's a game of perceptions. CX is based on how a customer feels about a service. For the same service, you will have one set of customers who might love it and an equal measure who might hate it. Take the example of a movie. You have certain critics who are extremely critical and others who hail with big praises. When you look across the spectrum, you will find customer experience expressed in various shades of gray. A service provider organization in such a situation would look at the majority perception, and if the popular feedback is to make certain changes, they will definitely opt to do so.

Applying the Principles/Learnings

What is the point of conducting surveys, taking feedback, and spending tons if you are not going to use the knowledge to make changes to products and services? It's like a fisherman taking all the trouble to go into the deep sea and catching a fish only to throw it back into the sea.

The following four steps are recommended to apply the principles:

1. Understand the customer, the customer expectations, and perceptions.

2. Collect feedback on the service from customers, consumers, and other related stakeholders. Feedback should be obtained across the period when the consumers enjoy the service.

3. The service provider's staff to be made aware of the customers' interests, their likes, and dislikes. Further train the staff on improving customer experience.

4. Value creation should be done at every step of the service, especially during operations. It is in the operational stages when users interact the most with the service provider staff. So, this is a critical interaction that directly affects value generation. During other project phases such as initiation, design, and improvement, ensure that the customer is factored into co-creating value.

5. People from the service provider staff and the customer organization must be stakeholders in the value generation process during any improvement activities undertaken. Make transparent what value means, how it is measured, and how the parties come together in creating it.

Exam Tip   Understand the theme associated with value like focusing on the consumer/customer and their perceptions, feedback, and acting on it. It is like the PDCA cycle. On the exam, you can expect questions that will test your understanding of how value is created.

Start Where You Are

Think about body transformation. To look like a Greek god, you can only start from the current state of your body and start your regimen toward transforming your body. You cannot just say let's scrap this body and start afresh. It does sound ludicrous doesn't it? Yes, it does and for a reason.

Many a time, when organizations jump into transformation exercises or even where they need to get to point B from point A, it is exciting and tempting for those involved to start everything anew. Without the overheads of the current state, the architects would be able to build anything they want and design masterpieces. In reality, it doesn't work this way. To start something from scratch, you need huge capital, and not only financials. It takes more time to get to point B starting afresh and, most importantly, getting used to the new ways of working will never be a smooth ride. Finally, there could be a solid base today that we totally ignore for the sake of excitement.

In this principle, we encourage starting from where we are rather than starting all over. We look at reusing the basic core rather than laying a new foundation. And we define a process to make this judgement call.

Note   More than once I have mentioned that the present and the future is in the DevOps space. For a traditional development and service management organization to switch over to DevOps is a massive challenge. Implementation of DevOps happens in phases, where we try and reuse components of the existing processes and integrate them into the holistic methodology. By doing this, users, staff, and other stakeholders do not feel alienated from the existing processes and resist the new ones.

Assess the Current State

Before you make a call on changing anything, it is worthwhile to see where you are currently. It may not be an arduous road to the intended target if you start with what you have. Or it may be better to scrap everything and start with a blank slate. The answer to either of these options can be obtained if the current state is assessed objectively.

It is often the case that we set out to change something by creating it afresh, and the current state assessment is done merely as an academic exercise; then it is quite possible that we will end up with assessment results that point toward starting afresh. Conversely, if you are bent toward building on top of what you have, the assessment will be colored in the way intended.

Therefore, it is crucial that the assessment carried out is unbiased and is purely seen through the eyes of objectivity. The assessor must therefore put on the hat of an inquisitive child that questions every single move, to identify the motive and to get a true sense of reality.

The true sense of reality can be obtained through measuring. Measurements too can be colored through interpretation. So, it is recommended that the measurement parameters are laid bare, with no ambiguity, and measurements are taken from the source and automated wherever possible.

Measure Everything

When I started my journey on a body transformation, the first thing that my trainer asked me was if I owned a measuring tape and a scale. He emphasized that the baselines need to be measured before we start the journey, and we needed to keep measuring and recording the measurements every single week. How else can we know that something is working unless it is measured?

In service management, several metrics are gathered and key performance indicators (KPIs) are tracked. However, where some of the organizations can possibly go wrong is by measuring the wrong numbers.

Going back to outputs and outcomes: track outcomes, not the outputs. The service desk is often pegged with a KPI known as first time right, which puts the onus on the agent to resolve the issue while the caller stays on the line and not have to put the ticket on hold or pass it to a colleague. To accomplish this KPI, the agent might try to close out the call with an incomplete resolution leading to a desired output but not necessarily a favorable outcome. This will most likely leave a bad taste in the customer's mouth and the outcome of the service does not generate value in any sense. Instead of measuring the first time right parameter, measure if the customer had to call back again to report the same issue; measure if the customer feels that the solution provided is complete; and measure mainly from the customer's perspective. This will give the true sense of measurements that gives the organization a taste of reality.

Note   Goodhart's law is apt for this situation and it states: *when a measure becomes a target, it ceases to be a good measure.*

Applying the Principles/Learnings

With a good understanding of the current state of affairs backed by measurements that give a well-rounded reality, you will be in a fairly good position to decide to opt for overhaul or build/renovate over the existing state.

Reiterating and putting the principle to practice, the approach you are likely to undertake will resemble the four steps indicated in Figure 6-2.

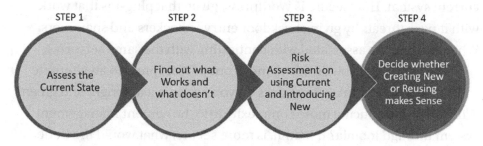

Figure 6-2. *Applying the principle of start where you are*

Consider an example of a website that needs to be modernized, and certain new analytics features and shopping cart are to be added.

Step 1

You would do an assessment of the different elements of the website, such as the content management system that runs the website, the data, the coding technology, and the flexibility to integrate with other tools that you might want to introduce.

While you do this, you will not stop with just the website; you might go into assessing the server it is hosted on, the performance throughput, and security.

At the end of this exercise, you will have a good handle on what you are dealing with. The next step is to turn this information into knowledge.

Step 2

Now it is time to create two categories: what is working and what isn't. Remember the saying: if it ain't broke, don't fix it.

Your website is running on Wordpress, one of the best content management systems. The theme that you are running is old and buggy. The website is hosted on a server that is shared with other users, which is causing performance issues. The same aspect might feature on your security list too. When it comes to integrating shopping carts, there are plenty of plug-ins that offer ready integration.

Step 3

Put on the hat of a risk manager and start assessing the risks with the current system. How secure is Wordpress, given that plug-ins that work with it pose threats by giving backdoor entry to hackers and spammers. What are the risks associated with continuing with the same server?

Next up, what if you decide to move out of Wordpress to an alternate solution such as Joomla? What risks do you see or is it all bright and green? Will you be introducing more complexity into the content management system through Joomla? If Joomla is more secure, what would the trade-offs be between an easy to use and maintain software like Wordpress and complex and secure Joomla. Plus, there are risks of higher expenses by using Joomla due to its complexity.

Your risk assessment exercise would draw out all these questions, which gives a stable platform for decision making.

Step 4

As a website owner, I need to make a decision based on the information gathered in steps 1, 2, and 3. I don't want the costs to go out of bounds. Pertaining to security, I am told by the risk manager there are ways to secure Wordpress websites. So reusing Wordpress would help me stay in the familiar zone for making website updates and the miniscule configuration changes that I make from time to time. I decide to stick with Wordpress.

The server is a concern, and I decide to move to AWS on a server that is exclusive to me. This takes care of the performance issues, and I am told that performance can be bettered on the fly by adding resources to the server dynamically.

In any case, going for a new website design was always going to happen. This will be done as a Wordpress theme.

This principle can be applied to products, services, processes, practices, team structure, or any other part of the organization and service value system.

Note   It is extremely uncommon that products, services, or practices get overhauled without reusing what is already there. Even in transformation exercises, we reuse what is already there and start building on top of it.

Progress Iteratively with Feedback

The third principle relates directly to the Agile project management framework, where the work is broken down into individual chunks and is delivered in several iterations. DevOps being a superset of Agile builds on the principle of iterations that are defined by feedback.

The concept of Agile delivery, as the name goes, is built on the premise that the requirements change and a project undertaken with a traditional approach fails to create value, as the perception of value (requirements) changes by the time it is delivered. To avoid this gulf between value and delivery, project management transformed into delivering in several iterations, and each successive iteration would consider the changing requirements and the feedback received from the involved stakeholders.

Today, most IT projects are built in an Agile model and are highly successful because the projects are no longer projects—they revolve around products. Along with the DevOps methodology, product management has replaced project management.

Product management involves building improvements and maintaining the product. Improvements can come in multiple facets – be it changes to the product or service, or the underlying technological environment, processes, practices, and other elements that go into the making of a product or a service.

In the past, under the release management process, we used two techniques to deploy releases: big bang and phased approaches. In big bang, the release was deployed in a single iteration, while a phased approach considered multiple iterations and was aimed at studying the first iteration before proceeding to the next. However, the previous ITIL iteration was designed to work in a waterfall model where the entire requirements are first gathered, designed, built, implemented, and then maintained.

Importance of Feedback

As the saying goes: "feedback is the breakfast of champions." If a product or a service must remain relevant in the market today, it needs to rely on customer feedback and must evolve dynamically.

The role of feedback must be upheld to the highest order and at every stage of the service delivered. Feedback should be requested and customers must be persuaded to provide feedback. Unless the service provider knows what the customer is thinking, they will never have an accurate understanding of the wants and needs, which translates to value being delivered, which further leads to continuation of the business relationship. So, the burden of identifying when, where, and how to obtain feedback from the customer solely rests on the service provider's shoulders.

A mature feedback process can expect to gather:

1. Perception of the user of the product/service

2. Perception of the customer of the product/service

3. Upcoming requirements (demand)

4. Understanding of the value chain deficiencies

5. Information around customers' relationships with their partners, suppliers, and service providers

Let's say you are building a role-playing game using the Agile framework. In the first iteration, you construct the worlds where the players are going to fight for dominion. The customer (or could be delegates) get a feel for the environment and provide their feedback. Their feedback is considered for development in the next iteration along with designing of characters. At the end of iteration two, the customer says he is happy with the environment, but the characters are not coming out strong—they seem rather puny. In iteration three, you fix the characters. This is how the feedback is used in Agile projects to deliver what the customer wants, where the customer becomes a part of the journey rather than just acceptance at the end of it all.

Note   Not all feedback is gold. You get chaff as well. So, it is important that the feedback is studied, and measured against the product you are designing. If the feedback makes sense, then go ahead and use it. Otherwise, let the customer know along with the rationale.

Feedback Feeding Iterations

Iterations are like mini projects. The entire sequence of development and testing takes place within an iteration. Most importantly, iterations are time boxed, meaning there is a definite time frame for when iterations start and when they end. Unless notified, one iteration follows another and then the next. These iterations are referred to as sprints in the Agile framework. This is illustrated in Figure 6-3.

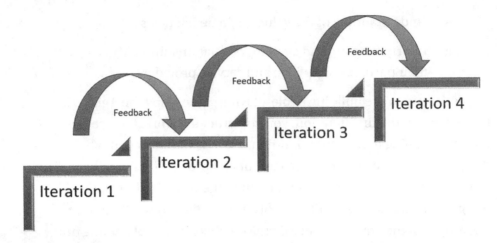

Figure 6-3. *Feedback feeding iteration*

So, although iteration through Agile gives great flexibility, there are constraints that decide which piece of work gets accepted into an iteration; generally it is not recommended that new pieces of work get accepted into an iteration midway. Also, the team is going to pick only so much work that is proportional to the capacity available. Flexibility does not mean that the resources working on the project would endure night and day and stretch beyond their means to deliver more than they can manage.

In the game development example, typically at the end of a sprint a demo session is held for the customer. The customer is expected to participate and provide feedback. The feedback is immediately considered, analyzed, and the customer is asked to prioritize working on the feedback or other open items. Based on the customer's directions on prioritization, the team works on the requirements in the next iteration. In essence, feedback fuels iterations and has a definite bearing on the development that happens in every iteration. So, it is essential that the service provider obtains feedback and reverts to the customer quickly to ensure the power of feedback in iteration is not lost.

While Agile is the way today and the way forward, it does not guarantee successes all the time. There are times when the service provider's team may not succeed in delivering what they promised. The ability of the service provider to learn from mistakes and adapt at breakneck speed to the shortcomings will be definitive. It is about failing fast and learning from the experience. Only then will the quality of the outcome stand in shining armor.

Applying the Principles/Learnings

There are some techniques that the power of iterations and feedback brings to the table. One of the most used is the minimum viable product (MVP). In this, the product/service that you have conceived is built with the minimal possible configuration, and at times a subset of the final product/service. By investing a fraction of resources and efforts, the feedback received from the MVP is valuable for planning and execution of the final delivery.

Say you are building an online banking system. Any such system will have several functionalities like account statements, transfers, and standing instructions, among others. Instead of planning to build all the functionalities, you pick the most basic one: account statements. Develop it and then seek feedback from the customers. In fact, many organizations build an MVP product and invite end users to test it and give them their feedback. In this case, normal bank customers would use it as they would the existing online banking system and would provide their views. Based on the feedback, the product development can alter the course, make corrections, and move in a direction to meet what customers like the best.

> **Note**   Using iterations does not imply that the development
> happens at a quicker pace. Iterations and MVP also do not imply
> that incomplete or half-baked products are released into the market.
> A product can be broken down into several pieces of individual
> functionalities. In iterations, individual functionalities are identified to
> be developed in a time boxed period. Specifically, in MVP, the minimum
> set of functionalities required to characterize the product is included.

While we recommend working in iterations fed by feedback inputs, we should not lose sight of the end product that has been visualized. In other words, do not stray away from the final objective that you need to achieve. It is possible that working in iterations puts on blinders to the teams involved, which is not entirely wrong. Therefore, a customer representative, a project team member called the product owner is in place to keep tabs on the progress in relationship to the final product delivery.

There are many traps that the development team can fall into. One of the common traps is to develop once and develop right; a good amount of analysis goes in before the development can begin. At times, the analysis is so deep and in detail, the team in charge of it would not know where to stop their analysis and this concept is called *analysis paralysis*. To avoid this, every activity that the team undertakes needs to be time boxed, including the non–core-developmental efforts.

Collaborate and Promote Visibility

Collaboration, cooperation, and visibility are some of the key factors that drive Agile and DevOps methodologies. Especially in DevOps, without team members and teams collaborating, the thought of a single team coming together for the success of a product is unthinkable. Likewise, the work that is done must be transparent to the customer. The customer needs to be involved in day to day activities. Hence the need for the product owner to be a part of the development team. The days of service provider organization being a black box are over. Welcome to the world where customers and service providers collaborate, share, and become partners in creating value and success.

In the past, the concept of work was highly siloed, and we had people sitting in various teams that mastered a particular skill set. They were brought together for the execution of a project, and when the project concluded they went back to their caves. This is a matrix type of an organization. Even today many organizations swear by it, although they claim to run products in a DevOps methodology. Silos promote division and do not share knowledge. Containing information and knowledge will hinder the process of decision making, which impacts the entire organization.

Collaboration Partners

The days of a single service provider or complete in-house delivery are over. Multiple service providers must work together toward a single product delivery. For example, an application could have a company working on the development side of things, another organization supporting it, and yet another organization taking care of its interfaces. In such a scenario, there are bound to certain trade secrets that organizations would want to keep under wraps. However, doing so will only harm the customer because it results in poor delivery, delayed resolution, and increased rework. So, do the organizations shun their differences and their unique selling propositions for the betterment of the customer? The answer could be yes in certain situations. The situation could be when multiple service providers are working on the same piece of code or a shared technology. For example, the service provider working on support could benefit from the coding efforts of another service provider. But consider the bigger picture. Every company will have something to give and something to take. So, while they might end up opening their arms in sharing their skill sets, they might gain in a different area. After all, the other service providers were chosen because of their prowess in their respective areas.

Another collaboration opportunity is between the service provider and the customer. Customers are often kept outside the project, as they are expected only to provide requirements and accept delivery. At least this was how it used to be, but now things are changing with customers engaging at every level of the delivery including initiation and planning. While sharing between service providers is acceptable with a pinch of salt, when it comes to customers it is not that easy. Service providers do not naturally feel comfortable to invite the devil into their homes. They want to avoid questions that might pertain to capacity, ways of working, and the technologies employed. The customer could end up being a constraint rather than a buttress. Once again, these thoughts are archaic, because not only is the service provider's mindset changing, the customer's is too. Both work toward a common goal. If one fails, the other does too. The blame game does not end up with one or the other winning. It hurts them both.

The game of collaboration between a service provider and a customer must be played with specific rules. The customer becomes part of the team and is responsible for prioritizing the backlog items and clarifying the requirements. The development team and the customer come together daily to share updates, including those where they are stuck. This necessarily removes the surprise element from the equation. When the sprint ends, the demo that the product owner witnesses is not something like a movie premiere seen for the first time. They would have witnessed its growth from day 1, and the demo is an event where the delivery gets accepted and further feedback is given, which helps during the rest of the delivery process.

Two aspects are important: the service provider would want the customer to be open to providing feedback, and the customer should share their feedback openly without hesitation. If any of the feedback is bad or wrong, so be it; it will not take away the importance of being a customer. The development team will use what is important and discard the rest.

Means of Communication

The world is flat—not literally though! Customers, service providers, and other stakeholders sitting in a single location is as rare as hen's teeth. DevOps calls for collaboration, and this is possible through frequent conversations and visibility of work. Being remote does not really bode well for collaboration, does it? Well, we have the technology to make up for it.

Tools such as MS Teams, Slack, and Google Meet feature high on the list and promote collaboration. Video calling, group chats, and boards for sharing information (like we do on Facebook) are some of the common features that enable information sharing with the familiarity of sitting across the table. The service provider and the customer must ensure such tools are made the platform for all communications and should move away from other forms. In the programs I manage, it is an unwritten rule that emails are used where formality is called for. Otherwise, all forms of communications—between peers, between the service team and the customer, between the service team and suppliers—are done through a collaboration tool. No emails are used unless approvals are sought for legal and auditing purposes.

For improvements to happen, the role of feedback is at the center. This communication takes place through customers who talk to the service providers, generally speaking. But what about the general users who don't get a chance to voice their opinion and feedback? To get their feedback, surveys and studies are conducted to gather feedback. Based on the general perception and feedback, contact is made with users to get clarifications if needed, and improvement action undertaken.

Expanding Visibility

The various initiatives and activities that are taken up are not always known to the various layers in an organization. It stops at a certain management level and does not trickle down. This lack of visibility plagues most organizations today and is a leading hindrance factor to creating team spirit and invigorating loyalty. Leaders must spread the message of what the organization is doing, especially in product/service development and improvement initiatives. This information should percolate along with the reason for doing it in the first place and how it points to true north: the organization's vision and mission goals. Most importantly, this is not a one-time effort. Such communications should be periodic, and the means matter too.

The next area where lack of visibility is common is in product/service development where the customers feel that after getting the requirements, the development team seems to have disappeared. Poor visibility on work progress will set in panic for the customer because without it, there is no guarantee that the product/service will be delivered on time and as per the specifications. The customer may feel that the work entrusted to the service provider is not important to the organization if they do not showcase the work on a regular basis. Therefore, it is important to keep communication going through continual visibility of work progress. Agile provides the best framework to meet the visibility and communication goals.

Think about the domino effect. Poor visibility will impact decision making as well. How can the decision makers provide direction if they have little clue as to how their ship is moving? Therefore, it is crucial for a product or service team that is working on a new product/service or improving one to ensure that open communication and proper visibility are the norm in their organization.

Applying the Principles/Learnings

The principle of collaboration and promoting visibility has multiple facets of learning. The most important of them all is visibility of work across an organization and visibility of work progress to customers and decision makers. Plaguing decision making is perhaps the biggest sin one can make in a corporate setting.

In the world of remote working, the emphasis is on collaboration for successful deliveries. First and foremost, this cannot be achieved if organizations opt for silos. The DevOps model is also a silo in a sense, but it is a silo that's built around a product/service that provides value to a customer and this is how we must move forward. Keep the customer as the focus and integrate the teams around the customer.

Communication is another key aspect, which according to some studies makes up 65 to 75 percent of the overall project time. So, it is imperative that we get this right. Identify the right types of communication and communicate periodically to the right people. Seek feedback and use it wisely.

I say use it wisely because not all feedback is useful. We need to embrace the good ones and ditch the rest. A common misinterpretation is that collaboration equals consensus. This is not true. Consensus is one way of leading but is not the only way. There are times it does not work. A good leader should be able to choose one type of leadership over the other. For example, we pick an exercise to identify the right technology for a product that we are going to develop. Such a decision should be left to the experts, such as solution architects. Carrying out a consensus activity with the entire team is foolish.

Note   There are different types of leadership. The popular ones are: leadership by example, where leaders set the pace; authoritarian leadership, where the leader makes decisions on his/her own judgement; leadership by coercion, where the leader moves the team toward his/her decision; and leadership by consensus or democracy, where the team's opinions are given weight in making decisions. No one leadership is good or bad. We need to use different types of leadership in various scenarios. A good leader will know when to wield each of these styles.

Think and Work Holistically

No product or service stands alone to deliver value. It needs to be connected to other services to fulfill all objectives. Take any example that you could think of, IT or not. More and more we are realizing that all things are connected. If any of the leading countries takes a dip, economies and markets around the world follow the dip. For months and years to come, there will be all kinds of problems with supply, demand, and other trades. An everyday product like the Windows operating system cannot operate alone. Try disconnecting it from the Internet and the default applications. Do you find it useful without the Internet and other applications like Office, Chrome, and others? The idea is to think of a connected world and think holistically rather than in isolation. The Windows product development does not think with blinders on when they make changes to the product. They think about the impact it is going to have to the hardware it sits on and the seamless integration with software manufactured by other organizations, to say the least. Likewise, whenever you plan and execute activities surrounding products or services, do not think small, but cover your scope from one end of the spectrum to the other.

Do your suppliers know what changes you are bringing about to the services? Are your customers in alignment with the proposed design changes of the product that they use and integrate with their enterprise toolset? This is the direction that we need to undertake and come to terms with. We might hold all the cards and yet we might have to make decisions and lead in a consultative approach.

Applying the Principles/Learnings

A database such as a configuration management database (CMDB) identifies and documents the integrations and dependencies. Such a picture needs to be drawn for every product/service for us to be able to define the road map with the right set of stakeholders.

One way of defining products and services is through the number of integrations that they come built with. The more integrations, the more complexity, because making any changes would require visibility to all stakeholders and concurrence too. Even if the involved technology and coding could be simple and straightforward, the complexity grows with the integrations. This is one of the primary reasons for middleware products to be considered most complex, and every change requires plenty of forward thinking and planning.

To manage complex integrations or any number of integrations for that matter, collaboration and providing visibility (guiding principle #4) is the key. Without which, managing products or services would be next to a nightmare. Along with this, you need to have an agreed set of principles, processes, and practices so that everybody in the value chain talks the same language and points toward true north.

The more complexity, the more hands needed to manage it, and this could potentially end up with human-induced errors. No matter how brilliant we are, we err, and the panacea is automation. Any work that is repetitive and does not require human cognizance can be easily automated. There is more on this topic in guiding principle #7.

Keep it Simple and Practical

Minimalism is a theme that has been picking up pace since the Second World War. The concept is to do the minimal set of things necessary. In all areas of life such as arts, films, architecture, and even in technology, it has become the new norm. It follows the principle of doing the minimum number of things to achieve the objective as long as it is within the set bounds and is practical.

Keeping things on a leash to achieve the objectives in a minimal way is not alien to IT and IT management frameworks. The Lean transformation framework, which is strongly associated with Agile, guides optimizing the resources, people, efforts, and energy of your organization toward creating value for the customer.

The sixth guiding principle—*keep it simple and practical*—also embodies the principles of Lean, and the guidance is around keeping things minimalistic and pragmatic.

The outcome that we want to achieve is important. The outcome could be a derivative of a product, service, or a process. If the outcome can be achieved in fewer steps, and remain compliant to organizational and state policies, then this leads to achieving this guiding principle. This could be done either through removing wastes, automating activities (guiding principle #7), and/or doing away with bureaucracies.

We all know that keeping things simple and practical is the best way of achieving outcomes. Yet we falter in our efforts. The most common reason is to add controls at every step of the way, the management's decision to micromanage activities and to mimic traditional practices.

What to Shelve, What to Keep

This is an interesting decision, isn't it? When there are several process activities, several services with varying crosslines, the identification of the activities and services that are sheer waste is not visible like neon in the dark. A detailed analytical exercise must be undertaken, especially if the services and processes have overbearing dependencies, to identify the fault lines. We can carry out an activity similar to the business impact analysis, where every activity is analyzed from all possible angles to identify the impact to the business, to the service provider, and to other involved parties.

During design it is natural to add activities to review other activities in a bid to get the outcome right. The number of reviews or controls added make up the bulk. This is still not the problem, as it can be achieved (practically). The problem is when it goes beyond the call of reason—when the process activity reviews or controls become an overhead. Is there a way to make things flow smoothly with validations that can be done automatically? Yes, there are always ways, and the objective of an effective service management design is to find this way.

If a government wants to track cash transactions to ensure that all taxes are paid and all financial activities that are carried out are legal, then they need to set up a number of 'control towers,' processes and practices to monitor. What if they reduce the currency in the system and mandate online payments as the norm, even for trivial amounts? This would change the culture of a system, where people would automatically start transacting online, giving the government ample data to track illegal activities through technology.

Note   BIA is an analysis methodology in ITIL V3 that helps in identifying critical IT services for the customer's organization. This tool helps to spell out all possible impacts when services go down. For example, I am an author, and work full time writing books, articles, and blogs. If I were to lose Internet service, I would:

1. Not meet my writing targets

2. Not make money writing, which is a financial loss

3. Not meet my legal obligations, as I fail on my SLAs

4. Lose readership base, which puts me at a competitive disadvantage over my peers

In this example, I have broken down the impacts of losing a critical IT service. The first three items on the list are black and white, and they are often referred to as hard impacts. The last in the list, losing readership base, is a soft impact, as it is my perception of the impact and it cannot be quantified as I did with the others. To summarize, BIA deals with both the hard and soft impacts of the customer if he potentially loses IT services.

Enablers to Simplicity and Pragmatism

Staying with the same example, if the government wants 100 percent compliance then they must ensure that the system is enabled and free from conflicts. The online banking transfers must be free even for small amounts. Residents must be enabled with free Internet for carrying out banking activities. If these are in place, people will feel enabled to follow the rules that are in place and it is a win-win situation. Let us consider otherwise. If banks charge a certain miniscule percentage on every transaction, why would anybody want to transfer online if they could just do a cash transaction? Who would like to lose money just to keep the government informed of their financial activity? Without free Internet for banking activities, residents will have a way out to not be compliant.

The design that is put in place must look at the inputs, players, triggers, and outcomes holistically and find a solution that is conflict free. You do not want to introduce conflicts, which is a surefire way of ensuring failure.

Picking an IT service management example this time, change management is a classic example of governance playing ball with operations. There are approval processes to ensure changes can go into the system. If you are tasked with a design to expedite changes, you would propose a standard change management process whereby the changes are preapproved and can be carried out during the agreed terms and conditions. Having just a standard change management process is not sufficient; there are too many loopholes and conflicts. How do you ensure that it is compliant? Sure, an audit is one way, but it's too reactive and the hit rate is too small. How about embedding the change management process with some automation, such as providing write/modify accesses to servers only when a change is registered with the server configuration item mapped to it, along with the change window. Only during the change window does the server allow its configuration to be changed. This is just the tip of an iceberg; a lot more can be conceived and achieved on the back of this idea to ensure that unauthorized changes do not get executed.

Applying the Principles/Learnings

The minimalistic lifestyle is popular for a reason. It gives people fewer things to worry about and increases the happiness quotient. How? It removes the complexities in life that otherwise would take considerable efforts to maintain. Apply the same principle to service management as well. Keep things simple and run proof of concepts to ensure it is practical.

The easiest way to achieve it is by doing a business impact analysis (as I stated—and not the traditional one). For every activity, find out how it is adding value, and whether it is taking you closer to the outcome or not. If it is either taking you away from the goal or standing still, then it is a waste that you can well afford to lose.

The days of bureaucracy are over. Approvals and oversight must find alternatives that involve automation and simplification. Remember that there is always a better and simpler way to achieve things; you just need to think consciously about finding it.

Optimize and Automate

The final guiding principle is around fine tuning and cranking the service management system to deliver in full force: *optimize and automate*. When this principle is applied, the product, service, or processes are already in place. It is a matter of making it more effective and efficient, and not about the functionality itself. Optimization deals with the effectiveness of removing wastes from the system and introducing activities or modifying existing ones toward bettering the outcome.

Automation, on the other hand, deals with efficiencies that are gained by using technology. Automation removes human intervention and ensures that the activities entrusted to it are completed successfully to a tee. Does it mean that humans are not involved in automation? Absolutely not. During execution, yes, the machines take over. However, the design and build of automation is done by people who identify the activities, define the inputs, design the work processes, and put in checks and balances to ensure that the automation can be relied upon. What we achieve through automation is speed (efficiency gain) and negation of human errors. While humans are prone to making errors, machines do as programmed—you program once and you can execute it a million times and get the same output every single time. However, there is a limitation on the kind of activities that can be automated. Only activities that are repetitive in nature—where the nature of inputs, work processes, and outputs are concerned—can be done by the machines. Other activities that require human cognizance cannot be automated, at least for now. There are artificial intelligence engines built by organizations that are trying to emulate human brains, though it is not conclusive that they can replace them completely.

These days all industries employ automation. It is necessary no matter how many human resources we have, because certain activities such as monitoring infrastructure or self-healing are better done by the machines than us; we are too slow and may lack the focus to keep an eye on things every second.

Why does the principle combine optimization and automation together? They seem to be distinct activities you might say! Not really. For the cycle of optimization to complete, it needs to end with automation. In other words, first we must optimize and then automate, as indicated in Figure 6-4.

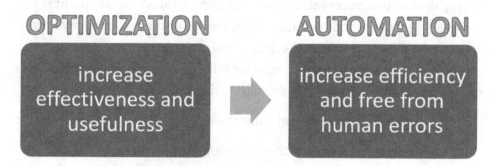

Figure 6-4. *Optimization and automation*

Optimization Practices

Any work processes that we can think of can be optimized. Think about the day to day processes and workflows that we deal with. Even after optimizing them, you can perhaps still find more opportunities to optimize. Example: When we go grocery shopping, we normally grab a shopping cart and walk the aisles picking up stuff that we want. In the end, we stand in line at the cashier's desk where the cashier scans every single item, bags them, and then we pay. We put the bags back in the cart and take it to our cars and then to our homes. The first level of optimization can be what most grocery shops in the UK call smart shopping. A scanner is given to shoppers when we start walking through the aisles. As we pick up products, we scan them and bag the products directly. At the end, there is a kiosk where we scan the code from the scanner and make the payment ourselves. As the products are already bagged, we take the carts to our cars and then to our homes. The next level of optimization could be doing online shopping and paying for it. We select something called *click and collect*, which allows us to get to the grocery store at a certain time and all the products that we have paid for are bagged. Imagine the time saved; at least for me, this is about 2 hours saved per week. Online shopping along with delivery can be the next optimized level, where the driving time to the grocery store and back can be saved too. My point is that every process, workflow, and service can be optimized as many times as needed—if there is sufficient capital, zeal, and ideas.

Carrying out optimization somewhat follows the continual service improvement (CSI) process that existed during the ITIL V3 days:

- Agree on the scope of optimization

- Analyze the areas which are in scope

- Measure the baseline for future comparison

- Agree with stakeholders on the road map

- Ensure all stakeholders are involved in the process and gather their inputs

- Execute improvements in an iterative manner

- Keep track of the metrics that define the optimization success

- Compare metrics with baseline to obtain the level of optimization achieved

Automation Practices

As is the case of optimization, automation too can be applied to most of the areas. The only constraint could be the application of technology into the particular area. Say if you are dealing with a work process that involves interviewing others, then possibly automation would have a limited role. However, even there, automation can be used for initial screening of resumes and to run assessment exams for all candidates.

In the area of DevOps, we use automation heavily: including continuous integration, continuous delivery and deployment, automation/continuous testing, monitoring, self-healing, configuration management, and cloud management, among others.

Applying the Principles/Learnings

Reiterating the learnings in this principle:

- As indicated in Figure 6-4, it is a good practice to optimize first and then to automate, to ensure that the automation carried out does not exemplify and increase the complexity required for automation on nonoptimized work processes.

- Measure everything. The only way you can decide whether an optimization has worked is through the metrics.

- When it comes to technology, there will certainly be dependence on capital. The best way to counter it is to start with technologies that are already employed. Once they bear fruit, capital could flow easily.

- All optimization and automation activities should be carried out in iterations, along with the feedback received from previous iterations (principle #3).

Knowledge Check

The answers are provided in Appendix.

6-1. You are a service management consultant hired
      by a company to investigate the reasons for their
      customer's dissatisfactions. Upon investigating, you
      find out that the customer's needs are not met. To fix
      things, which of these principles would you start with?

   A.   Think and Work Holistically

   B.   Start Where You Are

   C.   Keep it Simple and Practical

   D.   Progress Iteratively with Feedback

6-2. You are an internal service management consultant
      hired by a project running in DevOps mode. There
      is a need to increase the operating margin of the
      project. You find out that the processes are complex
      and there are plenty of bureaucratic practices.
      Which guiding principle would be best suitable in
      this circumstance?

   A.   Optimize and Automate

   B.   Collaborate and Promote Visibility

   C.   Keep it Simple and Practical

   D.   Start Where You Are

6-3. You run a project that has multiple work streams.
      The product is common but the work areas are
      different. For example, one work stream is on

enhancements, the other on reducing technical debt, and the third on support. Which of the guiding principles will be most beneficial?

    A.   Optimize and Automate

    B.   Keep it Simple and Practical

    C.   Progress Iteratively with Feedback

    D.   Collaborate and Promote Visibility

6-4. Your customer is not clear about what the final product should look like. He is wavering as the days go by. To not lose out on the competition, which guiding principle would serve in this situation?

    A.   Progress Iteratively with Feedback

    B.   Think and Work Holistically

    C.   Keep it Simple and Practical

    D.   Start Where You Are

6-5. Which of the following is the best definition of a guiding principle?

    A.   A recommendation that guides an organization to set up service management system

    B.   A guide to build products and services

    C.   A set of prescribed principles that provide direction to create value

    D.   A recommendation that guides an organization in all circumstances

CHAPTER 7

ITIL's Management of Practices

ITIL 4's masterstroke is to introduce practices in ITIL and do away with processes and functions. The problem was not so much that it was complex, but the underlying concepts and their overlay were often complicated; and to ITIL seekers, it was often a fairly lengthy learning curve.

ITIL's processes represented the series of activities and its workflow that was necessary to turn an input into an output. Functions were team structures that provided the resources for carrying out process activities. Practices and functions engaged in a matrix arrangement where processes called on different functions to carry out process activities. In the current ITIL, both the ITIL processes and functions are put together to work in unison as a practice.

A practice is defined as a set of organizational resources designed for performing work or accomplishing an objective. It is based on a set of organizational resources (four dimensions of service management; Chapter 4) that could be people, infrastructure, software, or processes, and all these resources are aligned/designed in order to achieve a specific objective. The keyword is a specific objective, and not general. If you put together a practice for making burgers, it does not put together anything other than burgers. If you want a burrito, then you need a different practice for it.

© Abhinav Krishna Kaiser 2021
A. K. Kaiser, *Become ITIL® 4 Foundation Certified in 7 Days*,
https://doi.org/10.1007/978-1-4842-6361-7_7

This is a chapter that introduces the category of practices and the individual practices that are a part of it. Details of practices that are in scope will be taken up in the rest of the chapters.

Category of Practices

Recall that practices are an integral part of the service value system (Chapter 5). Every practice supports multiple value chain activities, and it includes resources based on the four dimensions of IT service management.

ITIL practices are categorized broadly into three distinct parts:

1. General management practices

2. Service management practices

3. Technical management practices

Practices that are generic in nature that fall under the domain of general business management but could work with service management as well are categorized under general management practices.

Practices that are used primarily in the service management industry come under service management practices.

Technology practices find a home in service management through technology oriented organizations.

General Management Practices

General management practices, as the name indicates, are generic in nature. These practices are common across frameworks and methodologies.

ITIL Definition of General Management Practices

General management practices have been adopted and adapted for service management from general business management domains.

There are fourteen general management practices in ITIL:

1. Architecture management

2. Continual improvement

3. Information security management

4. Knowledge management

5. Measurement and reporting

6. Organizational change management

7. Portfolio management

8. Project management

9. Relationship management

10. Risk management

11. Service financial management

12. Strategy management

13. Supplier management

14. Workforce and talent management

In the course for the ITIL Foundation exam, the Continual Improvement, Information Security Management, Relationship Management, and Supplier Management practices are in scope.

Service Management Practices

Service management practices were bred in the stables of service management organizations such as IBM and HP. ITIL's processes were a collection of best practices from such organizations. As the activities followed turned into theoretical processes, ITIL became a de facto standard for service management. These processes have continued in a new avatar as practices in ITIL 4.

ITIL Definition of Service Management Practices

Service management practices have been developed in service management and ITSM industries.

There are seventeen service management practices in ITIL:

1. Availability management

2. Business analysis

3. Capacity and performance management

4. Change control

5. Incident management

6. IT asset management

7. Monitoring and event management

8. Problem management

9. Release management

10. Service catalogue management

11. Service configuration management

12. Service continuity management

13. Service design

14. Service desk

15. Service level management

16. Service request management

17. Service validation and testing

In the course for the ITIL Foundation exam, the change control, incident management, IT asset management, monitoring and event management, problem management, release management, service configuration management, service desk, service level management, and service request management practices are in scope.

Technical Management Practices

While the service management practices found birth in ITSM organizations, the technical management practices found their alma mater in organizations that are technology based. These practices provide the linkage between technical activities and workflow-related activities.

ITIL Definition of Technical Management Practices

Technical management practices have been adapted from technology management domains for service management purposes by expanding or shifting their focus from technology solutions to IT services.

There are three technical management practices:

1. Deployment management

2. Infrastructure and platform management

3. Software development and management

Deployment management is in the scope of this book.

Knowledge Check

The answers are provided in Appendix.

7-1.   Which of the following practices does not figure in
       the technical management practices?

   A. Deployment management

   B. Release and deployment management

   C. Infrastructure and platform management

   D. Software development and management

7-2.   Which of the following statements are true?

   A. Service management practices were bred in service
       management organizations and were adopted and adapted
       into ITIL.

   B. Service management practices were the best practices from
       the hospitality and service industry.

   C. Service management practices were developed by
       ITIL authors and were adapted and adopted by service
       management organizations.

   D. Service management practices were de facto standards in
       most organizations before they were documented as ITIL.

7-3.   Which of the following practices do not feature
       under general management practices?

   A. Portfolio management

   B. Programme management

   C. Project management

   D. Risk management

DAY 4

Day 4 starts with the study of ITIL practices, which help service providers manage external stakeholders: supplier and service management processes. Then we move on to practices related to enabling support: service configuration and IT asset management practices. The day ends with continual improvement practices (an element of the service value system).

CHAPTER 8

Practices to Manage Stakeholders

ITIL recognizes that services cannot be offered in isolation; they require plenty of continuous support to complete the delivery, and the support of external parties. These external parties could be customers, users, sponsors, suppliers, or other agencies that could hold a stake with legislation and other compliance parties.

Managing work activities within an organization removes the dependency on third parties, which is amply less complex than the tasks related to handling stakeholders. The practices that manage stakeholders will be discussed in this chapter. The practices that we are going to delve into are:

1. Relationship management

2. Supplier management

3. Service level management

Exam Tip You can expect between two to three questions to appear from this chapter.

© Abhinav Krishna Kaiser 2021
A. K. Kaiser, *Become ITIL® 4 Foundation Certified in 7 Days*,
https://doi.org/10.1007/978-1-4842-6361-7_8

Relationship Management

Not all stakeholders measure up equally in the scale of importance. Some could be like a lifeline for a service provider, while others could vary on a scale of importance. So, logic dictates that not all the stakeholders will be treated equally. Each of the stakeholders is engaged at a separate level to get the most value at every identified stage.

At a corporate level, we engage with stakeholders at a strategic, tactical, or operational level. Let us take an example of an IT company that uses MS Teams for collaboration. The company's success in delivering to their customers depends on how well their teams can collaborate with the other involved teams. So, MS Teams becomes all the more important; Microsoft will be treated as a strategic partner, and they would enter into agreements to ensure that the company gets the latest updates and product road maps visible well before other normal customers. The strategic relationship looks at a long-term relationship. The same IT company partners with a cab company to commute their employees to and from their homes. There is an agreement that the cab company retains the prices for the entire calendar year and also makes any number of vehicles available within the hour. This is a tactical relationship that helps the company look ahead in a medium term. Then there are operational transactions where the company procures or transacts on a case to case basis. For example, they could place an order for one thousand cartridges for their printers. There is no burden of relationship between the supplier and the company. It's transaction based. There need not be relationship managers meeting officials in the company from time to time exploring options to help further their businesses.

Relationship management deals with strategic and tactical levels of partnering and relationship building with stakeholders.

<u>***ITIL Definition of Relationship Management Practice***</u>

The purpose of the relationship management practice is to establish and nurture the links between the organization and its stakeholders at strategic and tactical levels.

Relationship Management Activities

Further, the practice exists to ensure that the relationships between stakeholders flower to become fruitful for all involved parties. Relationship management follows a lifecycle (as indicated in Figure 8-1) through the following stages:

1. Identification

2. Analysis

3. Monitoring

4. Continual Improvement

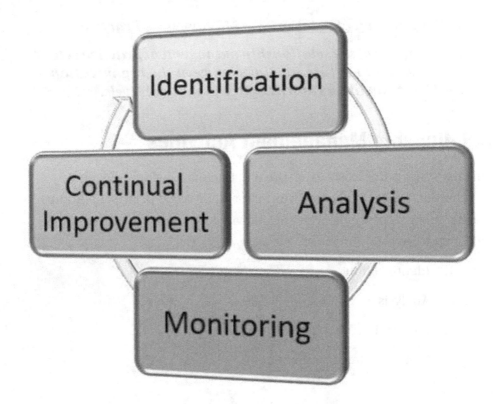

Figure 8-1. *Stages of relationship management*

Let us break down what the relationship management practice can achieve and why it needs to be a part of the ITIL framework. Value creation is the true north, and we have already established that value is not created alone but rather co-created between a joint venture between the service provider and the customer; this is mathematically illustrated in Figure 8-2. Since it's a joint exercise, there is that extra emphasis to get the relationship by increasing harmony and reducing conflicts. Only when all sets of parties sing the same tune does music begin.

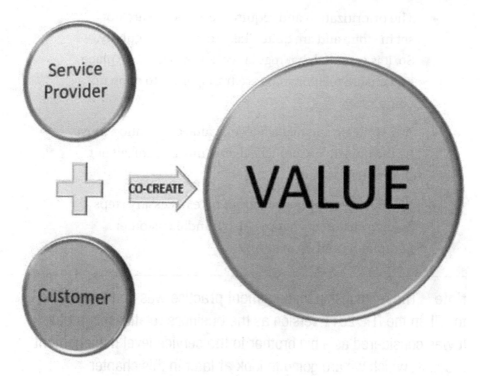

Figure 8-2. *Value co-creation formula*

The relationship management practice exists primarily for these purposes:

- The various stakeholders of products and services have their own set of requirements, and understanding it wholly and completely is essential. Plus, some requirements will be more important than the others, so it is important to understand the prioritization of the requirements as well.

- The prioritization and requirements per se are not
  set in stone and are quite likely to change regularly.
  So, it is essential that regular conversations take place
  and ensure relationships are transparent to open up
  completely.

- At a strategic and tactical level, value co-creation must
  be the objective. Conflicts, if any, must be sorted out—
  the earlier the better.

- Manage customer satisfaction; take necessary steps
  to keep customers happy. Also handle customer
  complaints and escalations.

Note   The relationship management practice was first introduced
to ITIL in the ITIL 2011 version as the business relationship process.
It was considered as a big brother to the service level management
process, which we are going to look at later in this chapter.

Engagement in Service Value Chain

We have established that the service value chain is the heart of the
service value system, and the activities within the service value chain
determine the value that is developed and delivered. With reference to
the relationship management practice, let us examine how the practice
engages with various activities within the service value chain in Table 8-1.

Table 8-1. *Relationship Management in SVC*

SVC Activity	Involvement	Details
Plan	High	Requirements are passed onto Plan for planning exercise. Keeps a finger on the pulse of the market trends, which determine strategic direction undertaken including portfolio decisions.
Design and Transition	High	Feedback from customers is passed on to Design and Transition, which improves the service and reduces the possible kinks.
Obtain/Build	Medium	This activity gets to hear the requirements from the horse's mouth, which reduces possible problems coming from misalignment from Plan activity.
Engage	High	Engage deals with third parties, and relationship management exists to build the bond with stakeholders.
Deliver and Support	Medium	Feedback on services is passed to the Deliver and Support activity.
Improve	High	Services are improved on the back of strong relationships with customers and other stakeholders and the open feedback received.

Supplier Management

Supplier management practice is one of the mature practices in the ITIL framework. Before I get into the practice details, the word *supplier* must be understood.

A customer obtains services from a service provider. The service provider likely will have other service providers servicing in the form of goods and services. These service providers from the perspective of a customer are called suppliers. In short, a service provider's service provider is referred to as a supplier. Outside of ITIL, suppliers are also referred to as vendors.

For example, a service provider providing email services to a customer requires servers and data centers. The companies that provide servers and data centers are referred to as suppliers. Technically, they may be service providers to the email service provider. Yet, from a customer standpoint, they are referred to as suppliers.

> ### ITIL Definition of Supplier Management Practice
>
> ***The purpose of the supplier management practice is to ensure that the organization's suppliers and their performances are managed appropriately to support the seamless provision of quality products and services.***

Supplier Management Activities

This is a vast practice and it manages several activities. The primary ones are as follows.

Supplier Strategy and Planning

The practice is expected to draw a strategy for identifying and planning the activities that the suppliers will manage. This strategy is drawn from the customer's requirements and the capabilities of the service provider.

The service provider will evaluate what parts of the service can be inherently offered and which ones are to be sourced from a supplier. Based on the analysis and decision making, suppliers are chosen and their engagement is planned.

Supplier Evaluation and Selection

The role of a supplier is up for grabs. Many prospective suppliers pitch their goods and services to the supplier management practice, which is tasked with evaluating and selecting suppliers. The evaluation and selection is normally done through a request for proposal process where the suppliers are technically evaluated first based on their response to a preset questionnaire. Then, among the shortlists, commercial factors come into play while selecting the supplier.

Contract Negotiations

The second round of selections involving commercial factors comes under the contract negotiations activity. While capable suppliers are shortlisted, the best among equals are determined based on commercial factors.

Contract negotiations happen at multiple levels, and it may not always happen at the beginning of a relationship. Contracts are reviewed on a periodic basis and rate negotiations carried out depending on the market circumstances.

Drawing up new contracts, renewing existing contracts, and terminating contracts are a result of this activity.

Supplier Categorization

Under relationship management practice, we looked at the practice working with strategic and tactical stakeholders. The supplier management practice is responsible for categorizing suppliers into three categories generally: strategic, tactical, and operational. The most important suppliers (strategic and tactical) will be additionally managed by the relationship management practice.

Managing Performance

The suppliers are not exempt from measuring their effectiveness and efficiencies. The service provider carries out regular performance checks to ensure that the supplier is holding up its end of the bargain. If the supplier falls short, this may be grounds for termination of their contract.

Before managing performance and during contract negotiations, KPIs and SLAs are agreed, and the terms of measurement too are defined.

Sourcing Strategies

An organization can choose a supplier strategy based on various circumstances among security, legal, and legislative aspects. The decision to choose one or the other is purely strategic in nature, and every company might choose to go in a different direction.

For example, if an application needs to be developed and supported, company X might choose to outsource the entire product development and support to another service provider including all the integration pieces. Company Y might choose to hand over the application development to one service provider and the support to another. Company Z might choose to split the application into multiple features and hand over each of the features' development and support to a different service provider. The thinking behind each of the decisions could come from:

1. We want one service provider to handle everything, which leads to single point of management coupled with optimum rates coming out of the collaboration that can be achieved.

2. Development is a different piece of cake from support. The expertise required is different as well. We need service providers who are leaders in their industry, so splitting development and support is the best option.

3. It is too risky to put all our eggs in one basket. We
    don't want any of the service providers to feel that
    they can hold us to ransom by managing all our
    services. So we split the application into multiple
    parts and hand it over to different organizations.
    We understand that the costs could escalate, but we
    are not an organization that's price sensitive for the
    development and management of this application.

Let us look at the different sourcing strategies that are employed.

Insourcing

Although insourcing is fast becoming extinct, there are companies
that want to do everything on their own. The products and services are
delivered within the same organization.

Outsourcing

The delivery of products and services is handed over to different
organizations. The tenets are the same as insourcing. Instead of an internal
organization providing services, it is handed over to an external one. This
has been quite popular over the last two and a half decades.

Single Sourcing

Single sourcing is like outsourcing, but all products and services are
handed over to a single service provider. In some cases, it could also be an
external service integrator managing multiple service providers on behalf
of the customer. Having a single supplier has its advantages in terms of
ease of collaboration, sharing of knowledge, and cost optimizations.

Multisourcing

The delivery of products and services is not handed over to one but to multiple organizations. The division of services could be on the lines of capability or geographic sense. For example, organizations that are supreme in SAP could get the SAP part of the application, an organization that is commercially reasonable could get the generic parts of the application, and infrastructure support could go to a company with relevant expertise. This way, the customer gets the best of all worlds. Managing multiple service providers is going to be a challenge though. This is mitigated by bringing a service integrator into the picture.

Engagement in Service Value Chain

Table 8-2. *Supplier Management in SVC*

SVC Activity	Involvement	Details
Plan	High	The sourcing strategy comes from the supplier management practice under Plan.
Design and Transition	High	The requirements, functional terms, and conditions are to be defined by the supplier management practice under this activity.
Obtain/Build	High	Service delivery from suppliers is directly and indirectly consumed in the Obtain/Build activity.
Engage	High	Supplier management practice manages suppliers and all their constituent activities in the Engage activity.
Deliver and Support	High	Performance management is carried out under this activity.
Improve	Medium	Along with suppliers, improvement opportunities are identified, tracked, and closed in this activity.

Service Level Management

The story so far from a stakeholder perspective is that the relationship management practice builds relationships, engages with customers at a strategic and tactical level, and deals with all other stakeholders. The supplier management practice focuses on all things suppliers. Engaging with stakeholders operationally has not been identified as a practice yet. The service level management practice fills this role.

ITIL Definition of Service Level Management

The purpose of the service level management practice is to set clear, business-based targets for service levels, and to ensure that delivery of services is properly assessed, monitored, and managed against these targets.

The service level management practice exists to ensure that the service levels are agreed between the customer and service provider organizations, and they are tracked. The whole objective is to provide the services at an expected level of performance and efficiency. Let us try to understand what service levels are first.

ITIL Definition of Service Level

One or more metrics that define expected or achieved service quality.

It is a measure of a service that is agreed upon and defined that is deemed minimum for a service to be fit for purpose and fit for use. For example, when you order a pizza from Domino's, the pizza company advertises that it will deliver within 30 minutes (in some geographies) or the pizza is free. The 30 minutes is a metric or a service level that is defined and tracked to ensure it is met. If it is not met, then the consequence in the IT world could be followed by penalties, which is equivalent to a free pizza if the delivery took longer than 30 minutes.

Primary Activities of Service Level Management

The following activities are carried out by the service level management in lieu of the services delivered to the customer:

1. Agree service levels with the customers that are binding. Example: availability levels, capacity levels, incident resolution timelines, etc.

2. The practice ensures that the service provider organization meets the agreed service levels. The practice has an oversight of the various service levels and although it may not directly manage service delivery teams, the service level management practice is accountable to meet the service levels. To do this, the practice monitors the service levels, collecting, analyzing, and reporting the service levels back to the customer.

3. Regular service reviews are performed, especially if the service levels are less than adequate, to identify the root cause and to ensure that corrective actions are put in place. If improvements are necessary, it feeds into the Improve activity in the service value chain.

4. Following up from the service review activity, the practice logs all the shortcomings and issues back to the customer and other stakeholders including internal management.

Remember that all the agreed service levels are against a service and not individual components of a service. For example, the service availability of an end to end service is measured. The individual servers that make up a service, although their individual availabilities are measured, do not come under the ambit of the service level management practice as long as the service is not impacted.

Service Level Agreements

ITIL Definition of Service Level Agreement

A documented agreement between a service provider and a customer that identifies both services required and the expected level of service.

The service levels that are agreed with the customers are put together in a document called a service level agreement (SLA). This document is generally appended to the contract document between the customer and the service provider. A good practice is to map the SLAs against the parameters of services that directly or indirectly impact business processes.

Note   Service level requirements (SLRs) are the set of expectations that the customer puts on the table with respect to IT services (or aspects of it). SLRs are aligned to business objectives and form the basis for negotiating and agreeing to service levels between the customer and the service provider.

To state a few examples of SLRs, the customer might ask for critical incidents to be resolved within the hour, might ask for changes to the systems to be implemented within a day, and might ask for 100 percent availability of Internet service. Not all SLRs are feasible, even by the top service providers. In fact, the cost of services tends to go up exponentially as the service level requirements hit a high percentage. So, the art of negotiation is to find the balance between the service levels and the cost of providing services.

Then there are some SLRs that are impossible to match, even by the best of service providers, perhaps implementing system changes within a day. Not all changes may be feasible given the timeline, as changes need to be developed, tested, and then deployed. It takes a lot of planning, coordinating, risk measures, and countermeasures. If the service provider signs off on an SLR stating that all changes would be implemented within a day, he would be setting himself up for a grand failure.

Here are some of the specifics that are included in the SLA document:

- A service catalog is a collection of all services that the service provider offers; it's like a restaurant take-out menu. So, when an SLA is defined, it must be referenced to the service catalog and not be arbitrary.

- There are a number of ways service levels can be defined and agreed. A service may have multiple facets and each of them could be a service level to be defined and tracked. Achieving all but one facet may look green on the outside, but the customer could be hurting based on a particular area where the service levels had dropped below expectations. Therefore, it is important to define service levels in conjunction with the context of the business. For example, if an Internet service provider provides over 99 percent availability of services in a period of a month, it may still not be sufficient if the Internet availability is not 100 percent during the processing of month-end activities. So, a good SLA document breaks it down into two sections or maybe three: one for month-end, one for general working hours, and the other for nonworking periods.

And the service provider can claim that all things are going well if the month-end and working hours service availability are in the green.

- The SLA must be drawn between the service provider and the customer. It is important, however, to ensure that on the business front, all relevant stakeholders agree to the levels and also are aligned on the service provider's organization. This is critical, because you want the service levels to match with the actual business processes; this is taken care of when the right business stakeholders are involved. Also, the expected service levels must be feasible to arrange from the service provider's side. So, it is imperative that the delivery organization along with the design team is involved before finalizing the agreements.

- I mentioned earlier that the SLA document is an addendum to the contract document. It is expected that the contract document is worded legally, but the SLA document must be devoid of all things legal. It must be put down in a simple and straightforward manner, and devoid of ambiguity. This will ensure that both the business and service provider understand what the agreement states after the lawyers are no longer involved. This will ensure maximum alignment between the parties.

Note   The Watermelon SLA Effect

You know that a watermelon is green in color. When you cut into it, the insides are red. A thing being green on the outside but red on the inside is a popular metaphor in the service management world.

Consider the example I quoted earlier about the Internet availability levels. Meeting 99.9 percent availability in a month is no mean achievement. And yet the customer is not happy. Why? Because the Internet failed 0.1 percent of the time during the last working day of the month, the period when the month-end jobs were getting processed. This 0.1 percent Internet failure contributed to various delays and the customer did not meet his targets.

The customer does not appreciate the Internet service even though it rates high on the availability scale. In other words, the SLA for Internet availability is green because the SLA states that a minimum of 99.5 percent is to be achieved. However, it is red from the customer's perspective because it failed them when it mattered. Just like a watermelon: green on the outside and red on the inside.

This is a common mistake that happens time and time again. Both parties must ensure that the right business parameters are considered, and SLAs are drawn to avoid the watermelon effect.

Engagement in Service Value Chain

For the activities in the service value chain, the service level management practice acts as an input and acts as the voice of the customer from an operational standpoint.

Table 8-3. *Service level management in SVC*

SVC Activity	Involvement	Details
Plan	High	Operational service performance influences the planning activity around services and service portfolios.
Design and Transition	Medium	Feedback on operational service performance will influence the designs of existing and future designs.
Obtain/Build	Medium	Obtain/Build will receive service levels for services and components, and the various reporting capabilities that are necessary.
Engage	High	Service levels will act as a critical input for engaging with various stakeholders and the core of service reviews.
Deliver and Support	Medium	Deliver and support will receive service levels that they need to keep up with.
Improve	Medium	Feedback received from customers will act as an input to Improve activity for initiating improvement activities.

Knowledge Check

The answers are provided in Appendix.

8-1.   Which of the following stages does not feature in the relationship management practice?

A.   Identification

B.   Analysis

C.   Monitoring

D.   Continuous delivery

8-2.   What is a supplier?

    A.   A supplier services the customer as a service provider for goods.

    B.   A supplier is generally a service provider for a service provider.

    C.   A supplier is contracted by the customer to manage the customer's service providers.

    D.   A supplier is engaged by a service provider to engage with the customer and offer services.

8-3.   Relationship management practice deals with the customer at what levels?

    A.   Strategic, tactical, and operational

    B.   Strategic and tactical

    C.   Tactical and operational

    D.   Strategic

8-4.   What is the objective of service level management?

    A.   The service level management practice exists to ensure that the supplier details are documented in the contract between the customer and service provider organizations, and the performance of suppliers is tracked.

    B.   The service level management practice exists to ensure that the service providers and suppliers agree on the service levels for the services offered to customers, and they are tracked.

    C.   The service level management practice exists to ensure that the customer agrees to the service levels that can be delivered by the service provider.

    D.   The service level management practice exists to ensure that the service levels are agreed between the customer and service provider organizations, and they are tracked.

8-5.   Which activity in the service value chain is responsible primarily for providing feedback from customers?

    A.   Deliver and Support

    B.   Obtain/Build

    C.   Engage

    D.   Plan

8-6.   Which of the following is not included in an SLA document?

    A.   Service levels

    B.   Service objectives

    C.   Metrics

    D.   Key performance indicators

CHAPTER 9

Practices to Enable Service Support

A service is essentially conceived, designed, built, and supported throughout its life cycle. Throughout the life cycle, two things happen: the services are supported, which necessarily means that services keep going as they should; and if anything breaks, then a break fix is applied. Then there are several changes that happen during its lifetime. Smaller modifications to a service are done on an ad hoc basis on the back of change management. Major changes undergo a continual improvement cycle. While all these activities are visible to stakeholders and highlight various achievements, there are silent players in the game that make it happen. These are the enablers that buttress the service support practices.

This chapter discusses the three support enabling practices that are quintessential for managing operations, running modifications, and implementing improvement initiatives. The practices that we are going to look into are:

1. Information security management

2. IT asset management

3. Service configuration management

© Abhinav Krishna Kaiser 2021
A. K. Kaiser, *Become ITIL® 4 Foundation Certified in 7 Days*,
https://doi.org/10.1007/978-1-4842-6361-7_9

Exam Tip   You can expect between one and two questions to appear from this chapter.

Information Security Management

Information security is one of the general management practices. It is an area that has held higher significance every passing day because the threats from hackers and malwares increase quite rapidly. No application or service is exempt from information security threats. In ITIL, information security is introduced in the design and is not an afterthought during the operational stages.

It is true that the lines between information security in ITIL and DevSecOps or Rugged DevOps have blurred somewhat. Although DevSecOps or Rugged DevOps define the boundaries for information security, the exclusivity of information management is retained in the ITIL framework. For example, Rugged DevOps could lay the boundaries for setting up services. While the interfaces to the service and to the outside world are managed through Rugged DevOps, the inner workings of the service are managed by ITIL. However, with DevSecOps, the DevOps processes collaborate with the ITIL information security practice to define and implement controls that manage the external interfaces as well as the data contained within.

> ### *ITIL Definition of Information Security Management Practice*
>
> *The purpose of the information security management practice is to protect the information needed by the organization to conduct its business.*

The definition of the information security practice is defined at a high level to take care of the data element within the service. The result is to ensure that the business that we serve does not get affected by the materializing of threats of information security.

Information security is achieved through the definition and implementation of various security controls, policies, processes, and work procedures. Primarily, it is three sets of activities that set the tone and leverage the definitions of the controls, policies, and processes:

1. Detection (monitoring)

2. Correction

3. Prevention

Various information security threats and risks must be defined and tools set up to detect them. Monitoring security threats is done on several data mediums such as monitoring emails, Internet pages, malwares, anomalies, data loss prevention, and intrusion. For each of these areas, there are several competitive tools that become robust by the day.

Many of the detection tools also play the correction part. Once they detect, they are able to self-correct the threat through a programmed sequence of correction procedures. When it comes to information security, time is of the essence. Threats must be identified and rectified in a timely manner to ensure that the viruses and intrusion attacks do not get the luxury of time to carry out their mission.

Prevention is the real cure that ensures that the identified threats are no longer an issue. It can be seen as a permanent solution. While corrective action provides a one-time fix, preventive action offers no chances for threats to take shape.

The question thus becomes about the balance that organizations must strike between the three sets of actions. The ideal situation is to prevent all threats, but in the process innovation gets stifled. An environment that restricts risk taking goes against the principle of Agile and DevOps. So, how should organizations decide on the balance that they need to strike? Well, that depends on their risk appetite and the chances they are willing to take in the name of experimentation and innovation.

Areas of Information Security

Information security is an ever expanding field of practice. With technology reaching new heights, information security areas is playing catch up with identifying and tightening controls for each of the technological aspects. There was a time when security was mainly concerned with viruses. Today, it has stretched to various angles such as phishing users, DDoS (distributed denial of service) attacks, MITM (man-in-the-middle) attacks, among the usual suspects such as malwares, adwares, spywares, and trojan horses.

Each of these information security threats target different systems, and their approach is different on what they target and how they go about it. All these threats can be explained through the information security quintet consisting of:

1. Confidentiality

2. Integrity

3. Availability

4. Authentication

5. Nonrepudiation

The quintet is illustrated in Figure 9-1.

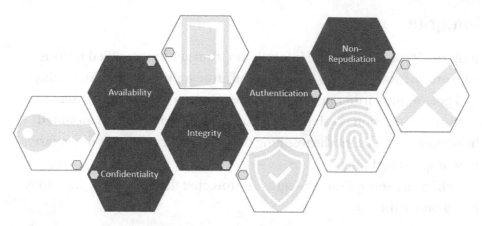

Figure 9-1. *Areas of information security*

Note   In ITIL V3, the information security triad (confidentiality, integrity, and availability) was considered. With the technological advancements, it is now a quintet. As we explore newer areas, the length and breadth of information security too will expand.

Confidentiality

Confidentiality is the protection of information from unauthorized access. In other words, only those with access to information are able to access it. Service providers and customers store information on servers, SharePoint application servers, and other file servers, and this data could contain sensitive business strategies, tactics, credit card information, or personal information of the end users. This information needs to be secured through methods known best to information security professionals, such as encryption and safeguarding.

To protect confidentiality, service providers must ensure that access controls exist along with rigor to ensure that the accessor can only do what is allowed. Further, information classification is necessary to protect secret and confidential information.

Integrity

Integrity is the protection of information from getting modified by those who are not authorized to do so. It tightly integrates with confidentiality and goes a step further in protecting the interests of all the involved parties. Information is valuable if it is accurate, and when it is modified by unauthorized users, the resulting data can pull companies down faster than a speeding bullet.

There are several ways integrity is protected these days, cryptography being one of them.

Availability

Availability ensures that the authorized parties have access to information when they need it. If you provide the right level of encryption through confidentiality and ensure integrity through cryptography, but fail to provide accessibility to those authorized, the whole exercise of securing information is counterproductive, right? The value from service comes from parties having the availability to access information when they desire to access it. Hackers have found a way to breach information security by blocking access to information through distributed denial of service (DDoS) attacks.

Several popular websites such as Facebook get hit by such attacks fairly regularly. In this sense, denial of access to information is a breach in achieving information security objectives.

Authentication

Authentication is the process of identifying the right entity to provide access to gateways and resources. It is an area that is quite vulnerable, as it is primarily used by users and protecting it would not just be in the hands of the service provider but with all users.

However, there are things that a service provider could do to ensure that the system authenticates with the right level of details. For example, a service provider could enforce a certain complexity of passwords. With more complex passwords, systems can be protected from brute attacks. These days, multifactor authentication has taken effect, with the password being followed by a one-time password sent to mobile phones or authenticators apps providing the additional layer of security. There are other means as well, such as fingerprint scanners and face recognition methods. The objective is to ensure that only the right person can authenticate and move past the system's threshold.

Nonrepudiation

Nonrepudiation is a fairly new-ish term. It refers to keeping timestamps, artifacts, and tracking to ensure that a certain action can be backed with ample proof. Let us consider an example: a user could subscribe to a daily newsletter. To ensure that the user accepts the agreement, the newsletter service sends an email out every day wherein certain information needs to be provided. The user will be asked to check a box to confirm if he agrees to receive an email daily. Plus, an email goes out to the user to confirm by clicking on a link. By following up with these actions, the user cannot claim in any court of law that the newsletter is spam sent without their consent. Other real-time examples could be the payment terms and agreements signed up on various websites and applications. Although no formal contract in the form of legal stamped papers are used, the digital agreements serve the same purpose.

With my publisher, I signed a contract through an online agreement service called Docusign, where the terms of the contract were laid out and I digitally signed on the terms put forth. The agreement that I have signed is valid in a court of law, and neither my publisher nor I could ever deny signing it because ample proofs are made available.

Engagement in Service Value Chain

You should expect information security management to play a significant role in every activity in the service value chain.

Table 9-1. *Information Security Management in SVC*

SVC Activity	Involvement	Details
Plan	High	Information security is not an afterthought. It has to be driven and considered from the planning stages.
Design and Transition	High	The design and transition activity must consider all the security aspects during the design of products and services, and appropriate controls must be defined. During transition, effective transfer of security controls is to be done to operations.
Obtain/Build	High	Based on the inputs from design, information security controls are to be translated into development of the products and services, including the outsourced components to suppliers.
Engage	High	Information security can be successful only if all involved stakeholders are part of requirements, design, development, and operations. The Engage activity must ensure that all parties are in sync on information security aspects.
Deliver and Support	High	The mechanisms built for monitoring security incidents should be prioritized. And, as an when security incidents are reported, they must be ably dealt with.
Improve	High	While improvement of services is imperative, security aspects have to go hand in hand with the proposed improvement initiatives.

IT Asset Management

Asset management is a general practice across industries. The practice refers to managing assets in various industries. For example, in the automobile industry, a car is made up of several components, and the car itself is a finished end product. Each of the individual parts and the car are referred to as assets. An asset is the lowest detail of a component that is tracked throughout its life cycle. Perhaps in the same company, they may track components like steering wheels and doors as assets but not the screws, rivets, and bushes that hold them together.

IT asset management practice manages assets in the IT industry, and more specifically in the industries that are run on the ITIL framework. Therefore, it has been categorized under service management practices and not general management practices.

ITIL Definition of IT Asset Management Practice

The purpose of the IT asset management practice is to plan and manage the full life cycle of all IT assets, to help the organization:

- *maximize value*

- *control costs*

- *manage risks*

- *support decision-making about purchase, re-use, retirement, and disposal of assets*

- *meet regulatory and contractual requirements*

The IT Asset Management practice is essential to ensure that the assets that contribute to a service are critical, and managing it is a backend activity that if not carried out seamlessly can cause disruptions. Take, for example, a server: its warranty information needs to be tracked and extended as necessary. When it reaches close to its end of life, it needs

229

replacing. All the requisite information for extending or replacing is contained with this practice. As the definition states, the decision making around purchase, reuse, retirement, and disposal is made possible through the asset management practice. Managing it well and effectively also reduces the risks surrounding IT assets.

Further, costs can be controlled by having an accurate inventory and an equally accurate estimate of the upcoming demand. If the organization knows what it has in store, then they will not go on a buying spree but rather use what they have. Likewise, buying or renting decisions can be made as and when needed, aided by the asset inventory information.

Finally, there are various standards like ISO 9001 and ISO 20000 that mandate that inventory information be maintained and retained to attenuate the risks that come with mismanagement of IT assets. Plus, there could be government regulations that can be met only through accurate asset inventories.

Well, we spoke of the value coming from the IT asset management practice. But what is this IT asset that we are talking about?

ITIL Definition of IT Asset

Any financially valuable component that can contribute to the delivery of an IT product or service.

Any component that contributes to products and services and that has a financial cost associated with it is an IT asset. Examples are servers, routers, switches, software, or smart watch. Why only financially valuable components, you might ask? Look at the latter part of the definition: components that contribute to the delivery of an IT product/service. There are IT components such as processes, policies, and frameworks that contribute toward a service and can be considered essential components. However, such components do not come under the purview of the IT asset management, as the life cycle differs, and the objective of the IT asset management is to oversee inventories that start with procurement and end with disposal.

A typical life cycle of an IT asset is illustrated in Figure 9-2. It starts with a planning exercise that includes estimation, forecasting, and getting demand-related information. This is followed by procuring the asset or building it, followed by its implementation. The IT asset is maintained and upgraded until it reaches its end of life, and upon reaching its end of life, it is retired and disposed of.

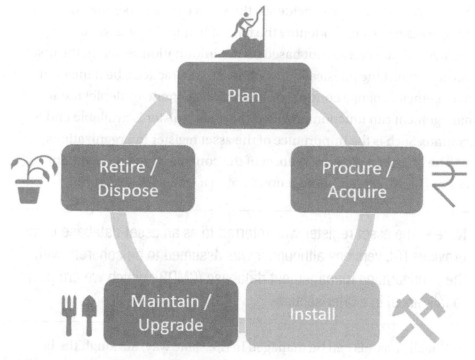

Figure 9-2. *Life cycle of an IT asset*

Exam Tip   The definition of an IT asset is one of the frequently asked questions on the ITIL foundation exam. The question will center on identifying the right definition from a list of choices. So, it is prudent for you to understand and memorize the definition verbatim.

Types of Asset Management

At the heart of IT asset management is a database that consists of all IT assets along with other pertinent information including its status. This is the asset register. If the organization would like to carry out an inventory check of their assets, their first and only point of inspection is the asset register. The basis for carrying out planning and acquisitions is the asset register. When users raise incidents, the service desk personnel look into the asset register to identify the type of laptop that is assigned to them. Audits are carried out based on the information stored in the asset register against the physical/software asset. All practices, be it incident management, change control, problem management, or deployment management can function provided the asset register is available and is accurate. Such is the importance of the asset register in organizations.

The IT asset register is a subset of the configuration management system (CMS)—either homogenously or in a federated structure.

Note   The asset register was referred to as an asset database in the previous ITIL versions although it was assumed to be coherent with the configuration management database (CMDB), which we are going to talk about in a later section.

Not all IT assets can be managed in the same way, although the life cycles of all IT assets are similar. The type of IT asset management is determined by the nature of the asset and its ownership. Broadly, asset management can be classified as follows:

1.   Hardware asset management

2.   Software asset management

3.   Client asset management

4.   Cloud-based asset management

Hardware Asset Management

Hardware asset management, as the name indicates, is the management of hardware assets: assets that are physical in nature. Example: racks, servers, switches, laptops, telephones, and IoT devices.

Maintaining hardware requires processes that are rugged, precise, and complete to ensure that all circumstances and scenarios are considered during its design. Managing hardware may not always be automated where they can be monitored. Many times, a physical inventory needs to be carried out. So it is essential that all hardware assets have a label that asserts a unique asset ID, to identify the asset in the asset register.

I was tasked with pulling together an inventory for a German manufacturing giant that was spread across 45 locations in India. While a majority of IT assets were on the network, there was a good proportion that was behind a firewall. And many more were in stores (and probably forgotten). For all the assets on the network, I was able to carry out an automated inventory through a Java program that we pushed to all systems. For those in stores and behind the network, I hired close to a hundred staff who went around searching for assets. It was like looking for a needle in a haystack. After this humongous exercise, based on the customer's internal financial records, the inventory that I carried out was just about 97 percent accurate, which was better than their expectation of 95 percent.

Software Asset Management

Software assets are a different beast. With software asset management, we manage the licenses, including freeware and trialware. Licenses come in multiple shapes and sizes: there are licenses that are tagged to assets, tagged to users, and concurrent licenses, among others. It is imperative that organizations are compliant at all times, as software publishers carry out regular audits, and penalties for noncompliance are quite severe (especially for CIOs).

233

A few challenges with software asset management are to maintain the software register where the licensed copies are stored, and access is controlled. Software licenses often go down the drain when hardware assets are decommissioned. So, tight processes must be wound around the hardware management processes to ensure that licenses do not get lost.

Client Asset Management

Client assets refer to assets that are handed to individuals, such as laptops, mobile phones, smart watches, and data loggers. The challenge comes from the danger of data loss that could result because of lax processes and information security controls. Sufficient controls need to be put in place to ensure that secret and confidential data does not get into the wrong hands.

Several techniques are employed, such as using BitLocker on laptops and carrying out remote wipes at the scent of repeated wrong authentication.

Cloud-Based Assets

Cloud assets are a different breed altogether. Typical hardware assets are no longer physical assets, and software too is generally bundled with the hardware. Management of cloud-based assets must consider various factors such as the dynamic nature of asset creation and deletion. At the click of a button, servers can be created and spun down through pipelines. How does one carry out IT asset management on assets that are dynamic in nature?

Well, in such circumstances, we employ configuration management. The cloud assets are managed through a configuration management (not service configuration) tool that maintains the data based on the servers that are spun and despun. Examples include Chef, Puppet, and Ansible.

Further, how do you identify specific costs to specific services when servers are shared across services? That is another challenge that the emergence of cloud in IT service management has thrown up, which is what makes ITIL and IT service management evergreen and interesting.

Engagement in Service Value Chain

Table 9-2. *Asset Management in SVC*

SVC Activity	Involvement	Details
Plan	Medium	Asset management practice maintains financial data, and planning activities leverage this data. It helps the organization manage costs and create value.
Design and Transition	High	IT asset statuses are determined based on the activities carried out by this activity.
Obtain/Build	High	This is an essential part of the asset management, as it has a direct correlation with asset procurement.
Engage	Low	Customers may at times seek information on the residual value of their IT assets.
Deliver and Support	Medium	The practice supports this activity by identifying the assets along with current statuses.
Improve	Low	Improve may consider the impact on IT assets by the recommended improvement initiatives.

Service Configuration Management

Most projects fail because of the lack of managing configurations and having total control over the various components that make a project tick. Service configuration management is the foundation upon which the entire project is built. Ignoring the foundation will logically see the walls and roofs of the project crumbling down in record time. The practice plays a significant role for systems made up of multiple components that are integrated with other systems and run on multiple dependencies. Sound familiar? Yes, almost all systems today are complex, owing to the need for integration and its respective data sources and data consumers. In such a complicated setup, it is imperative that systems are driven by configuration management, which is relied on heavily by projects.

ITIL's service configuration management practice (formerly service and asset configuration management) has matured over the years and has been powering the service industry for several years. The practice has been the spine for IT services over the years, and within ITIL the process has matured with each version. It is a practice that determines whether a service provider succeeds or not in delivering IT services and defines the breadth of the services offered.

Note   You will notice me using service configuration management and configuration management. They are one and the same. While service configuration management is the official practice name, generally the practice is referred to as configuration management.

ITIL Definition of Service Configuration Management

The purpose of the service configuration management practice is to ensure that accurate and reliable information about the configuration of services, and the CIs that support them, is available when and where it is needed. This includes information on how CIs are configured and the relationships between them.

Configuration management gives you a blueprint of IT services, the architecture underneath, and the dependencies. It provides an accurate reflection of the connected pieces and dependencies. It is this network of components that makes the service work. Having it in a form that's alive and accessible gives the ammunition to make changes to services with ease, identify business impact with minimal analysis, and resolve outages in a jiffy.

These are the tools that you need, to be a valid player in today's market where changes happen on the fly and customer wish lists change faster than the lifespan of mayflies. A project without accurate and dynamic configuration management is a living nightmare. Imagine making changes to one part of the system without understanding the impact they could cause on other dependent systems. This happens commonly in the software development industry. It is not uncommon that architects are baffled when they have certain dependencies and defects crop up through the regression of acceptance testing quite late in the development life cycle. This is a blunder of sorts because there is a good likelihood that software delivery might not happen as per the promised schedule, and if the development teams try to cram in fixes at the last minute, defects pop up. If only the architects had a working configuration management process in place, they could have identified everything that needed to be changed and could've avoided the negativity that emanates from failures.

Let us try and understand the term CI, which stands for configuration item.

ITIL Definition of Configuration Item

Any component that needs to be managed in order to deliver an IT service.

Exam Tip   The definition of a configuration item is one of the frequently asked questions on the ITIL foundation exam. The question will center on identifying the right definition from a list of choices. So, it is prudent for you to understand and memorize the definition in verbatim.

A CI is a fundamental component of a service that can be configured, tracked, accounted for, and controlled. For example, in an email server involving servers, routers, and MS Exchange applications, each server, router, switch, application, and firewall can be considered a CI. Why? Because these CIs can be tracked, controlled, accounted for, and audited.

You might ask me if a server is a CI or if the hard drive, memory, and other components inside a server are CIs. Who decides what can or cannot be a CI? This is a decision made by the configuration architect based on the nature of the service, its interfacing to other practices such as incident and change control, and most importantly the cost. For example, a server can be considered a CI. Conversely, each of the components of a server such as the processor, memory, and hard drives can be considered as CIs, which necessarily alludes to a lot more effort (and cost) in coming up with the configuration management and maintaining it. Therefore, generally the decision is left to the architect to make a judgment call on what level a CI should be considered. The general practice is to measure the value that is derived by delving deeper into the services for deriving CIs.

Every CI has several attributes attached to it. Attributes are various details that get recorded against a CI, such as owner, location, date of commission, status, and configuration. All these attributes are controlled through change control. This is the layer of control that ensures that the configuration management remains accurate and nobody can make changes to it without the approval and consent of the change control governance.

CMDB, CMS, and Service Model

Configuration management database (CMDB), configuration management system (CMS), and service models are inherent elements of the service configuration management practice.

Configuration Management Database

A CMDB is a repository containing all the CIs including their relationships. For example, in a CMDB, the dependency between the CIs can be defined through relationships such as "runs on" and "supported by."

Within the CMDB, you can have multiple services, the individual CIs, and their relationships. Most modern ITSM tools, such as ServiceNow and BMC Atrium, offer placeholders to record the upstream and downstream impacts. If you pick up a service and want to use it visually to see how CIs connect to one another, you will see an array of connections between the CIs. Using this visual image, other processes such as incident management can troubleshoot incidents with ease, and processes such as change management can identify upstream and downstream impacts with a click of a button. Imagine if this were not in place; the whole activity involving analysis and troubleshooting would be tough.

In an organization, you could have multiple CMDBs depending on the requirements, business structure, and customer obligations. For example, you can have a CMDB for business units A, B, and C; a CMDB separately for customer ABC; and yet another CMDB for internal infrastructure and software. There is no limit, as long as the logic makes sense to manage, control, and simplify matters.

Configuration Management System

The CMS is the super database that contains all the CMDBs and more in its ecosphere. It is the layer that integrates all the individual CMDBs along with other databases in the IT service management space, such as known error databases, incident records, problem records, service request records, change records, and release records.

ITIL Definition of Configuration Management System

A set of tools, data, and information that is used to support service configuration management.

Figure 9-3 provides an illustration of a CMS.

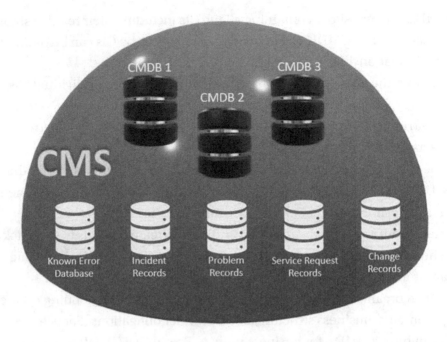

Figure 9-3. *Configuration management system (CMS)*

In this illustration, you have three different CMDBs sitting in it: one could be a SAP ecosystem, and the other two for different technology ecosystems. Remember that the individual CIs in the CMDB can possibly link to CIs that are in another CMDB. Example: A .net application that retrieves data from an SAP system. Also, in a CMS you have various other databases like the known error database (KEDB), incident records, problem records, service request records, and change records. The data within the CMS can get interlinked to support the service management practices. Suppose a server goes down and the corresponding CI gets mapped on an incident record. With a workaround put in, a problem record is raised and the same CI gets mapped in there. A permanent solution is identified, which requires the server configuration to be changed. A change record is raised and the server CI is mapped. Likewise, no matter what activity you perform within the service management space, they all come under the CMS.

Remember that there could be multiple CMDBs in an organization, and all the CMDBs and other databases will be part of a single CMS.

Service Model

A service model is also referred to as a service map. It is a graphical view of the CMDB that showcases the relationships between the interconnected CIs. A view of a service model is shown in Figure 9-4.

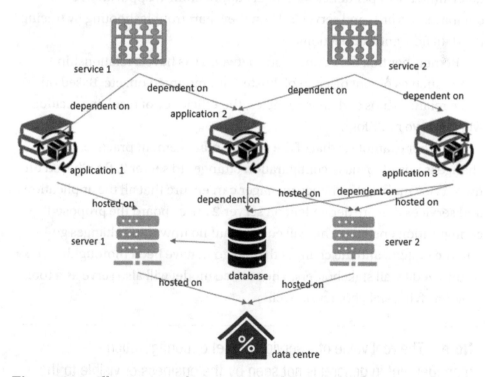

Figure 9-4. *Illustration of a service model*

In this simplistic example, there are 2 services that are powered by 3 applications. Applications 1 and 2 are required for service 1 to function, and applications 2 and 3 are required for service 2 to function. These applications are hosted on servers as shown in the figure: application 1 on server 1 and applications 2 and 3 on server 2. There is a database that is utilized by applications 2 and 3, and this database is hosted on server 1. Both the servers are hosted in a data center.

The value is not in representation of a CMDB in a graphical format; it lies in its application. If an incident is reported that service 1 is down, the incident management practice would look at the service model and determine the dependencies—namely application 1, application 2, database, server 1, and server 2. Then they start troubleshooting by tracing the data flow and connections.

Remember that the connections between CIs have a relationship name, such as parent of, child of, hosted on, mounted on, etc. Based on these relationships and dependencies, the efficiency of resolving incidents will improve multifold.

Another example is that of the change management practice. If a change is raised to make configuration changes to server 2, then based on the service model, the change manager can ensure that all the applications and services that are dependent on server 2 are onboard the proposed configuration changes. This will ensure that no unwanted changes go into the system, and the changes that do go in have been thoroughly scrutinized by all stakeholders. The service model will also serve as a tool for identifying stakeholders as well.

Note   The real value of a service model or configuration management in general is not seen by the business or visible to the outside world, but it is the engine that powers all other practices that services depend on.

Primary Activities of Service Configuration Management

Service configuration management activities have multiple phases, like identifying the relationships and the CIs, validating that the CIs and relationships are accurate, and leveraging the CMDB to provide reports for various purposes. Broadly, it's divided into four major activities.

1. First and foremost, the CIs have to be identified and populated in the CMDB. Their relationships with other CIs must be defined.

2. Changes are common, which means that the CIs in the CMDB change as and when a change is applied. The next process is to modify changes to the CI and the CMDB when changes are implemented.

3. Unauthorized changes are prevalent, which means that some changes could be performed outside the change management practice. Also, there is a possibility that the activity of identifying may not have been done with 100 percent accuracy. So, it is imperative for the service configuration management practice to conduct periodic validations across the CMDB. These validations could be done through technology and automation.

4. To formalize the validations, an auditor could be employed to perform checks against the CIs that are in the CMDB and against those that aren't. An auditor might walk into a datacenter and randomly choose a server from a rack and pull up its details in the CMDB. The details in the CMDB are compared with the physical CI. An auditor could also come powered with discovery tools that will help uncover CIs that are not in the CMDB or vice versa.

243

Engagement in Service Value Chain

Table 9-3. *Service Configuration Management in SVC*

SVC Activity	Involvement	Details
Plan	Low	The CMS could be leveraged during identifying and proposing changes to services.
Design and Transition	High	Design leverages on the CMS and also provides inputs based on design changes. Transition too is highly dependent on the CMS.
Obtain/Build	High	Generally, CIs are created on the back of the obtain/build activity.
Engage	Low	Third parties could leverage on the CMS to identify dependencies or provide impact information.
Deliver and Support	Medium	This activity, as explained earlier in service model, leverages on the CMS for achieving efficiencies and work completion.
Improve	Medium	Configuration management has evolved over the years, and it has become better because of the various improvements that have happened. Based on the needs of IT, the practice will evolve and adapt.

Knowledge Check

The answers are provided in Appendix.

9-1. Which of the following is the true purpose of information security management practice?

A. To protect the information needed by the organization to conduct its business

B. To protect the financial and regulatory information of the business

C. To ensure that the systems, information, and networks are adequately secured against security threats

D. To ensure that a security ring fence is built to protect the knowledge that the company holds in its repositories

9-2. Which of the following is the right definition of an IT asset?

A. An IT component that goes through the life cycle starting from procurement to disposal

B. A component that has a financial value and is owned by the service provider to provide services

C. An IT component that is required to deliver a service

D. Any financially valuable component that can contribute to the delivery of an IT product or service

9-3. What is the difference between CMDB and CMS?

A. CMS consists of all the physical systems, while CMDB is a database of IT assets.

B. CMDB has incident records, problem records, and others along with IT assets information; CMS contains multiple CMDBs.

C. CMS is a database of CIs and CMDB consists of multiple CMS.

D. CMDB is a database of CIs and CMS consists of multiple CMDBs.

9-4. What is the primary objective of a service model?

A. To provide a graphical representation of the CMDB that will help projects understand the architecture and make decisions related to planning and improvements

B. To provide a graphical representation of CIs and their relationships that will help the organizations identify the CIs whose relationships are not defined, thereby supporting the verification of the CMDB

C. To provide a graphical representation of the CMDB that will provide an overall architecture of the services, and this can be used for making architectural decisions

D. To provide a graphical representation of the CMDB in order to increase productivity, reduces outage times, and provide support for making decisions

9-5. Which of the following is the correct definition of a configuration item?

A. Any financially valuable component that can contribute to the delivery of an IT product or service

B. Any component that needs to be managed in
    order to deliver an IT service

C. Any component that delivers value to a
    customer through the efficiencies provided by
    the incident management practice

D. Any financially valuable component
    that needs to be managed by the service
    management practice

CHAPTER 10

Continual Improvement

Lou Holtz, the famous linebacker and coach, once said: "In this world, you are either growing or you are dying. So, get in motion and grow." This rings true in every aspect of life, work, and entertainment—more so in products and services. Name one product or a service that has remained the same without improvements or new features, and yet has ruled the market for decades. None. Maintaining status quo in ownership of products and services will get us nowhere but out of the market and out of users' minds. It is therefore an imposed necessity on product manufacturers and service providers to keep enhancing their offerings and to keep the boat moving toward newer shores. Think of products such as mobile phones, where a new phone is churned out every few months. This is not because the earlier ones have become obsolete, but to keep consumers interested and keep the ball rolling. In services, look at Internet service providers. Their services do not remain constant. They endeavor to increase speeds, make their networks more reliable, and offer several add-ons. Once again this is not because of a paucity of their services or products, but to ensure their survival, which hinges on improvements. In the ITIL world, continual improvement exists to keep the ball in motion, to ensure that all that is offered is being constantly bettered.

© Abhinav Krishna Kaiser 2021
A. K. Kaiser, *Become ITIL® 4 Foundation Certified in 7 Days*,
https://doi.org/10.1007/978-1-4842-6361-7_10

Continual Improvement in SVS

Continual improvement is part of the service value system. Let us revisit SVS in Figure 10-1.

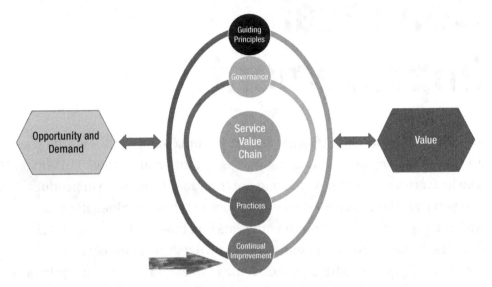

Figure 10-1. *Continual improvement in service value system*

In the SVS, continual improvement is one of the critical elements that helps generate value. Together with the guiding principles, continual improvement ensures that the service value chain has the right focus toward enhancing products and services. The improvements don't just happen directly to a product at an operational level, but are far ranging into tactical and strategic areas as well.

Continual improvement in the SVS comes in the following shapes in ITIL:

1.   The continual improvement model, which consists of seven steps that provide guidance on how improvements are to be initiated and managed throughout the life cycle

2. In the SVC we have talked about the Improve
    activity, which is tasked with the business of
    ensuring improvements to services.

3. Continual improvement is a practice as well under
    general practices. The practice provides guidance
    around its operational nature and gives wheels to
    the seven-step model.

Exam Tip   Continual improvement is an important topic from the
ITIL Foundation exam perspective. It is one of the few topics where
the depth of information understood matters for securing marks. You
can expect anywhere from three to five questions to appear from this
chapter.

Seven-Step Model

The seven-step model found its roots in Lean and moved into ITIL in its
ITIL V3 version. The model has been leveraged across organizations with
great success; the steps involved are logical; and it can be applied to any
area, be it manufacturing, finance, services, or life. Figure 10-2 shows the
seven-step model of continual improvement.

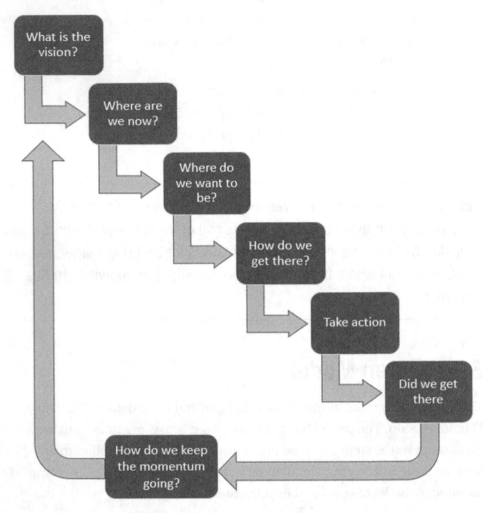

Figure 10-2. *Seven-step model of continual improvement*

Note   In ITIL V3, the seven-step model had only six steps (it was known as the continual improvement model). The missing step was step 5, take action, which was clubbed with how do we get there (step 4).

Each step means different contexts and hence different views and actions. The actions themselves will be defined based on the industry and type of improvement: strategic, tactical, or operational. However, what is consistent is the flow; the steps to be followed must follow one another, as illustrated in the model.

The model is all the more significant because it aligns to organizational vision and mission and plugs seamlessly into its business process flows. The results therefore are also in line with what the organization expects.

Every improvement action follows the seven-step model, and at any given time each of the improvements could be anywhere in the flow. For example, improvement for processes could be at step 2, an improvement for performance could be in step 5, and then another improvement for GUI could be starting out at step 1. In Agile terminology, the seven-step model for continual improvement is iterative in nature and fits like a hand in a glove with Agile methodology.

What Is the Vision?

Vision in the business context comprises the long-term goals and objectives for the organizations. Every business will therefore start with a vision, such as being a leader in mobile cell service with over 50 percent of the market share (and maybe spreading peace across the globe through spirituality and thoughtfulness).

Here's a real-life story about vision. McDonald's founder Ray Kroc was in a bar with a bunch of MBA students. He asked one of them: "What business do you think we are in?" The student duly replied: "You are in the business of selling hamburgers." Ray retorted: "I am selling hamburgers but that is not my business. My real business is real estate."

As a service provider organization, you must make sure that you understand your customer's vision. Unless you are in sync with it, you will start working toward, for example, selling hamburgers rather than the core business objectives.

The IT strategy must be based on the business vision, mission, goals, and objectives. This is the only way the service provider can understand and create value (through improvements) to the customer organization.

The first step of continual improvement primarily considers the vision/goals of the organization from the perspective of the business unit where the improvement is set to take place. For example, an oil and gas business unit will have its own vision. Any improvements planned under this unit will adhere to its vision rather than a generic one, because every business unit's goals and objectives are very specific (apart from increasing revenues and making profits). Second, the improvement itself will set out with its own objectives. Both the visions and objectives are considered in step 1.

Step 1 tries to achieve the following:

- Understand the high-level context and objectives to be met

- Proposed improvement is well defined and agreed by all involved stakeholders.

- Define all the roles that are involved in the improvement engagement and their role expectations

- Define the understanding of value that is generated through the proposed improvement

Where Are We Now?

Unless the present situation is known, it is impossible to measure the level of improvements applied at the end of the cycle. The key to success in meeting the end goal is to know the starting point. Think of it as a journey that you are undertaking. If my end goal is to reach central London, it is important to understand where I am right now. Only by knowing your current location will you be able to reach your destination.

To understand the current position, the starting point, the best tool to employ is an assessment. It needs to be performed to gather the current establishment, setup, and performances. Perform a dipstick check to obtain a snapshot view, which will be used as a baseline for future comparison.

The assessment must be based on all aspects of a service, such as culture, people, technology, processes, and so forth. Only when all aspects of a service are obtained will it be possible to perform an unbiased assessment of the current baseline, not based on conjecture.

We carry out assessments with the aid of objective measurements, meaning we measure parameters that can be measured and that provide a basis for future comparison. Measurements are not done based on subjective parameters like feel-good factors. The measurements undertaken act as a baseline. Although, I must admit, finding a baseline and measuring it is easier said than done. In reality, identifying parameters for future comparison is an arduous task that requires foresight into the improvements that are being put in.

Note   A baseline serves as a starting point and as a comparison value for the progress made through improvements.

Suppose you missed this step; you can still carry on with your improvement exercises, but you will not be able to measure improvements that you have undertaken. Take, for example, you want to improve the performance of a website. If you have not collected data before moving your website to a faster server, how do you know the extent or if the performance has improved at all? Maybe you could do it based on perception, but it's not objective and not as accurate.

Where Do We Want to Be

At this stage, we know what the organization is seeking, and we have figured out where we are standing. Now the challenge is to set a goal for the improvement exercise to take us from point A (where are we now) to point B (where do we want to be). But remember that in this step we are not concerned about how we are going to get there but merely identifying and firming up on the endpoint we intend to reach.

You might think that step 1 (what is the vision) and this step are one and the same. Not really. Step 1 is aspirational. Vision is set at a high level and is fairly ambiguous in nature—like being the number 1 burrito joint in the UK. How do you measure being number 1? Is it based on profits, revenue, or the number of burritos you sell? In what length of time would you aspire to be number 1? There are several other questions that can come out of a vision. However, with step 3 (where do we want to be) we define the goal in specific terms, with no ambiguity and with precise targets. For example, I want to be the number 1 burrito joint based on the number of burritos outlets across the United Kingdom in the next 2 years.

One way of finding the destination is to perform a gap analysis between steps 1 and 2. Based on the vision, which gives a general direction and the current position, the enormity of the gap is known. Based on that, the goal may be drawn not to reach the vision straightaway but in multiple iterations. For example, I may be starting out a burrito restaurant, and my vision is still being number 1 in 2 years. But I would rather walk before I run, so I set an intermediate goal of reaching the top 5 in a year's time.

In this step, the critical success factors (CSFs) and key performance indicators (KPIs) are also set. The set goals, CSFs, and KPIs must follow the SMART principle, which stands for specific, measurable, achievable, relevant, and timebound.

Any improvement action that is identified must come armed with the end goal. It must not be perpetual like "improve the turnaround time for incident resolution." Fine, this is a good initiative, but how does the team know that they have achieved the improvement objective. A better goal would be improving turnaround time by 15 percent faster than the current turnaround time. So in other words, this is a step that cannot be missed; if missed, the improvement action will never succeed because nobody would be in a position to declare the improvement action as having achieved its goals.

Note

<u>Critical Success Factors</u>

CSFs are something that must happen for the activity to succeed. For example, "safeguard ATM machines" is a CSF in the banking industry, more specifically in the money disbursal services that the bank offers its customers. So, for the money disbursal to happen successfully, it is critical that the ATM machines are safeguarded from thieves, skimmers, and hackers. It is a common occurrence in countries such as India, where ATM machines are wheeled away in the middle of the night. In African and American countries there have been countless cases of ATMs being rigged to capture the debit card information. To counteract this, the CSF mentioned in this example sets the direction.

<u>Key Performance Indicators</u>

Key performance indicators (KPIs) are the key components used to measure success. Simply put, they define the measure and the trends that make or break the output of a process or a project. As the name states, they are performance indicators, and they indicate whether the performance is on the expected lines or going downhill. In the IT service management industry, we use KPIs to measure the outcome of an IT service or a process.

Defining a KPI is an art driven by the maturity of an individual or the organization. It is of prime importance to identify individuals who can make a particular activity a stunning success or a lame duck. Identifying KPIs is not as easy as differentiating white from black, but rather it's like picking out iron filings from a heap of sand. You need to use a magnetic wand, which in this case is the diligence of a mature professional.

How Do We Get There?

When I get to step 4, I know where I am and where I want to be. The overall vision too is available for guidance. The *how do we get there* step focuses on the process of getting from point A to point B. Reaching point B can be done in a number of ways, so this step is responsible for identifying the best possible option under the given circumstances.

For example, a startup company with no product portfolio wishes to develop a video camera application. Based on their current position, they need to start from scratch and get to a fully working competitive application. Their vision gives them guidance on how the design should be done. The vision reads: "by all means, we use open source applications to build customized solutions." So, how the application will be developed has the basic boundaries drawn and objectives clearly set forth. In this step, the design of the aforesaid activity takes place.

If you fail to carry out this step, you will fail to meet your objective. In other words, the improvement activity fails to realize its intention.

Take Action

At this stage, step 5, the designs are available for the development to happen. The development can happen in any framework, be it waterfall or any of the Agile flavors. What matters to step 5 is that the improvement delivery takes shape based on the design coming in from step 4. As we are familiar in Agile, the requirements change all the time, and we need to swing from one post to the next in a quick manner. Similarly, improvement development too may have to change directions and pivot as needed, to realize the needs of the business and the organization.

Typical project management aspects of managing risks, measuring progress, stakeholder management, and other activities come into play. This is a critical step in the improvement journey.

Did We Get There?

While the busy bodies are focused on completing the work on hand in step 5, it is possible to lose sight of the target and become internally focused. That is when the iterative nature of Agile comes into good use by keeping a tight tab and verifying the end product against the requirements. Step 6, did we get there, is an activity that verifies if the improvement that has been delivered is fit for use and fit for purpose.

One cannot afford to miss this step, as the step keeps the improvement delivery project on track, focused on customer's requirements and acting as a guide throughout the journey.

This step-in principle declares an improvement either a success or a failure.

How Do We Keep the Momentum Going?

An improvement is like a train. It does not stop at one; there are several trains that come and go to a station. Likewise, improvements too cannot be done in isolation. There are always improvements to be done. There is no such thing as a perfect product or a perfect service. To keep the improvements going one after another, like trains arriving at a station, is a challenging task.

The process of collecting improvement ideas must keep kindling new fires in the eyes of the users and other stakeholders. The teams involved in the improvement activities must be inspired, focused, and motivated enough to define new improvements and make them possible. All this is possible only if the organization plays its cards right through able leadership, organizational change management, and knowledge management practices.

The worst that could happen is for the improvements to reverse and the service to go from average to bad. Well, it is quite possible that a service in status quo without improvements can go stale while it sits stagnant.

The other side of the coin is that carrying out improvements may not always be successful. There will be failures along the way. How does the leadership treat failure, how does the team handle it, and what will be the market implications? Various organizational practices must come together to address situations, especially when they go into a reverse gear. It is said that we learn more from our failures than our successes. So, able knowledge management practices must be in place to capture the learnings coming out of failures and to use this as ammunition to come out on the other side as a roaring success.

This is a step that should not be missed. If missed, then the future of the product or the service will be in doubt, as improvements alone can keep them alive.

Continual Improvement Practice

Continual improvement's second role in ITIL 4 is that of a practice. It comes under general management practices.

Note   Continual improvement practice is an important practice from an examination perspective. You are expected to understand the practice in depth (and not just the concepts).

The practice exists to keep up with the changing market and changing requirements, and to ensure that the products and services get the necessary improvements as and when needed.

ITIL Definition of Continual Improvement Practice

The purpose of the continual improvement practice is to align the organization's practices and services with changing business needs through the ongoing improvement of products, services, and practices, or any element involved in the management of products and services.

The practice does not just exist to identify and deliver improvements. Identifying improvements is not an activity that can happen in a conference room with a room of stakeholders. The *spark* needs to be ignited in people who are part of the organization, and for the people to come up with improvement opportunities, am appropriate culture needs to be inculcated. The continual improvement practice deals with the entire spectrum of people, process, and technology in coming up with improvements for products and services.

Key Activities of the Continual Improvement Practice

The key activities of the continual improvement practice are:

1. Building a culture of keeping an eye out for identifying improvement opportunities. You cannot just have a continual improvement team (like some companies do)

who do nothing but identify improvements. Coming up with improvements is not done in a vacuum, and it requires the staff to express freely and experiment without fearing repercussions. In short, everybody in an organization must work toward continual improvement. The top leadership in organizations must promote such a culture, which is coincidentally the backbone of DevOps culture as well.

2. Various ideas and suggestions are shared and discussed. This generally happens successfully at an informal level. To formalize it, there must be identified ways in which the people who have a spark get to register it before it escapes their brain cells. I used to work for Atos (formerly Atos Origin), and they had built a portal called FISH (fresh ideas start here) to capture and manage ideas. Every idea that was registered was read, promoted, and voted by employees of the organization. After securing a number of votes, the idea was reviewed and prioritized by a high-level committee and implemented if it met certain guidelines. The activity that every organization must look toward is a process for registering continual improvement ideas, and duly assessing and prioritizing them.

3. Identifying ideas and assessing them do not cost money. Prioritization is done because the money in the bank is usually limited and a certain budget is often set aside for improvements. Between thousands of improvement ideas, a select few should be chosen and a budget secured for their implementation. Next up, getting the time of resources who can realize the identified improvement.

4. After getting the money for improvement projects,
    a plan needs to be developed and the project
    delivered. How a project gets delivered depends
    on several factors, but the key activity is that the
    implementation gets done.

5. What determines if an implementation was indeed
    successful? Key performance indicators step
    in. They provide measurements and evaluation
    processes to understand if the parameters that were
    supposed to be addressed with the improvement
    have bettered or not, and if the end user is
    realizing more value than before. It's generally
    not straightforward, but if it is thought through
    well enough before the implementation, then
    monitoring, measuring, and evaluating should be
    easy enough.

6. The biggest and most challenging activity is to play
    the coordinator's role. Any improvement requires
    multiple parts of an organization coming together.
    Securing their time and parleying between varying
    ideas and getting things done is tough and requires
    special skillsets.

Continual Improvement Tools

Achieving constant improvements is arduous. Think of your own house,
wherein you are expected to keep making improvements every day.
Forget about living there peacefully; the task is to make some aspect of
your house better. For better or worse, doing things is the easier part.
Coming up with ideas on day 1 is easy, day 10 is OK, but day 100 will be
a tough nut to crack. I talked earlier about how the entire organization

263

must become a stakeholder in identifying improvements. Likewise, in the example of coming up with home improvement ideas, your family (including the extended ones along with friends and neighbors) must be encouraged to participate. However, your house will survive without improvements for several years. But a product or a service that needs to sell—that has a market—cannot. Consumers get bored. They want better. They are hungry for change. You need to feed them new characteristics and features to keep them happy. That is exactly what the phone manufacturers and software publishers do on a periodic basis. In some cases you might find the upgraded phone features seem superficial, or worse, inferior to the previous version. Remember that all this, the ideas and the improvement opportunities that are getting presented, is coming from the power of the ranks.

To be at the top, you cannot rely on magic. You need practical tools that you can use in various situations, something that aids in the outcome of the continual improvement process. In this section, we look at several tools that help in the process of identifying and delivering improvements.

Continual Improvement Register

Improvement ideas are generated during discussions, while working over a task individually or with a team or even during service reviews. Of paramount importance when ideas are generated is to record them in a reliable repository. We do not have to go so far as to say that it needs to be a single source of truth, but there must be a commonly accessible repository where idea generators can log it seamlessly.

This is perhaps the most critical tool; in ITIL it is referred to as the continual improvement register (CIR). The objective of this register is flexible; it needs to be a repository where ideas are logged, reviewed, prioritized, and delivered/rejected based on the quality of the idea and the circumstances.

An organization can have any number of CIRs: say, for example, a CIR for infrastructure related improvements, a CIR for the SAP team, and so on. As long as the CIR exists, and the staff and other stakeholders know about it (and have access too), it serves the purpose. Care should be taken though to compare the logged ideas to ensure that improvement ideas do not get delivered in isolation, which leads to reinventing the wheel.

In a typical organization, a CIR plays a similar role to that of a product backlog. The user stories in a product backlog are reviewed and prioritized regularly. Only the highest ranking priority items are identified for development and taken into the development cycle. Likewise, improvements go through the cycle of prioritization and reprioritization. An improvement idea remains actively in the CIR until the improvement is delivered.

Improvement Reviews

Once the improvements are logged, they need to be regularly reviewed to ensure that the ones that deliver most value are prioritized and realized at the earliest possible cycle.

An organization can choose any number of ways to review an improvement; it could be as simple as reviewing the business justification and making a decision based on gut feeling. Or it could be detailed and granular by attempting a strength, weakness, opportunity, and threat (SWOT) analysis. A balanced scorecard view also delivers a granular assessment on the improvement affecting various areas of the business. It is not uncommon to hand over the improvements to third parties for an unbiased assessment as well.

Development Methodology

The flavor of the decade is Agile, but that does not necessarily mean that all improvements get delivered in an Agile fashion. Horses for courses is the norm! Depending on the improvement that is being put through the grinder, an apt development methodology needs to be identified. Take, for example, delivering an infrastructure based on a new architecture. Doing this in Agile may take more effort and does not generate value, as the architecture is highly unlikely to change during development. In such cases, it is better to opt for a waterfall methodology.

The importance of this tool is to choose the right methodology for the improvement that is laid on the table. This essentially translates to the development team jumping back and forth between methodologies and adjusting their mindsets accordingly.

Deployment Approach

The final tool in the continual improvement armory is to decide on how the improvements are handed out to the users and other consumers of the service/product.

Experience tells us, similar to the development methodology, that deployments can be done either in a big bang approach or in a phase-wise manner. Not only this, there are several deployment approaches that can be employed, such as a canary release, blue/green, or A/B testing.

What is necessary is, to find the right approach for the right scenario. If you are dealing with a simple improvement, deploying it in a big bang approach makes sense because the impact if things going south is perhaps negligible. But if you are onboarding new online banking software, a cautious canary release would serve well.

Engagement with Service Value Chain

Table 10-1. *Continual Improvement in SVC*

SVC Activity	Involvement	Details
Plan	High	Planning activity leverages on continual improvement in plan formations and provides feedback to the practice on the improvement's relevance to the organization's direction.
Design and Transition	High	The ideas identified and ratified by the continual improvement practice are inputs to the Design and Transition activity for developing and transitioning the ideas into delivery.
Obtain/Build	High	The improvement ideas are designed, and in the Obtain/Build activity, they're developed and fed back to Design and Transition for transitioning into the product/service.
Engage	Medium	Continual improvement practice's scope involves third parties including suppliers and other involved stakeholders.
Deliver and Support	High	The improvements that are transitioned are delivered to end users and the product/service is supported through its life cycle.
Improve	High	The Improve activity in the SVC provides governance to improvement ideas in prioritizing and allocating resources to the identified improvements.

Knowledge Check

The answers are provided in Appendix.

10-1. Which of the following steps are not present in the seven-step model?

A. Take action

B. Where are we now?

C. What should be done?

D. Where do we want to be?

10-2. What is the importance of finding out where the organization is currently before embarking on identifying improvements?

A. A baseline serves as a starting point and as a comparison value for the progress made through improvements.

B. Understanding where we are currently helps us understand the mistakes that were made earlier.

C. It provides a balance in terms of the improvements that are taken before and after an improvement is delivered.

D. The ground realities provide an excellent value to assess the relevance of improvement ideas.

10-3. How does culture play a role in identifying improvements?

A. The culture of an organization enables collaboration and coordination that is decisive in coming up with improvement ideas.

B. Identifying improvements must come from all quarters. This is not possible if the organization does not give its staff the freedom to express and experiment.

C. A culture needs to be inculcated in an organization through the formation of a continual improvement team that is responsible for delivery of improvement ideas.

D. Culture provides the basis for services and products to improve and create value for customers.

10-4. Which is the ideal methodology for developing improvements?

A. Agile methodology provides the flexibility and the expressive freedom for improvements to be delivered as and when new improvement requirements are identified and ratified.

B. The waterfall methodology is employed for improvement, as the nature of improvements does not change the inherent requirements.

C. A hybrid model involving both Agile and waterfall methodology is to be employed, to ensure that the changing requirements are considered and the delivery timelines are adhered to.

D. A methodology for the delivery of improvement must be identified based on the improvement that needs to be developed.

10-5. What is the basis for maintaining a continual improvement register (CIR)?

A. It provides a comparison point for measuring the quality of improvements identified by the staff in an organization.

B. CIR is the repository for managing the artifacts pertaining to improvement ideas, related codes, and other documentation.

C. It is a repository that manages improvement ideas throughout its life cycle.

D. CIR is the product backlog for improvements. The only difference is that the identified improvements are stored in the CIR and the ideas are moved into the product backlog after reviews.

DAY 5

Approximate Study Time: 1 hour and 12 minutes

Chapter 11 – 1 hour and 12 minutes

Day 5 is an important day, as we delve into support practices: incident, problem, and monitoring and event management. These practices are commonly employed in the industry today.

CHAPTER 11

Practices to Manage Operations

The heart of ITIL lies in operations. This is the phase of service management where value is essentially created or lost, customers are awed or move away, and organizations thrive or barely survive. There may be a phase when enhancements or new developments could pause (maybe due to economic slump) but operations continue as long as the product's end of support exists or until the service that is offered to customers is active.

They say that you need to put your money where your mouth is. For a service provider, most of the action takes place during operations. Customers always tend to remember service operations over all other practices and activities, as their interactions mostly happen in this area. The service provider also bills the maximum amount of the total contract in the operations phase. Yet, this is not the best place to put your money, although the mouth is wide open. You will find out the reasons soon enough!

Operational activities deal with maintaining products and services that have been designed, built, and transitioned in the earlier activities of the service value chain. In this phase, no functional or nonfunctional modifications are performed to the service (any modifications performed will be done as an enhancement). A status quo is maintained, ensuring that the service runs as it was designed to. The operational practices run the longest in terms of timeline, are the biggest in terms of staff strength,

© Abhinav Krishna Kaiser 2021
A. K. Kaiser, *Become ITIL® 4 Foundation Certified in 7 Days*,
https://doi.org/10.1007/978-1-4842-6361-7_11

and, most importantly, the customer generally forms a perception of the service provider through the operational phase achievements.

If the strategy is innovative, the design is sound, and the transition is perfect, then you can expect service operations to be less noisy and probably peaceful. In reality though, this never happens. Strategies are bound to change over time, designs have flaws, either manmade or limitations owing to technology, and transitions are rarely event free. Technological innovations and advancements bring in changes to products and services. These changes are designed, built, and transitioned through the change control practice; after the transition, the modified specs of the product or service are maintained by the operational practices. With the advent of DevOps, product and service maintenance is far easier. Otherwise, there usually exists a period of transition and training of the support staff. In that case, since the support staff is new to the changes, you can expect support glitches and compounding problems for the customer. DevOps methodology has ensured that operations is a no-brainer and it is business as usual in the life of a DevOps team that builds and manages products and services.

I have worked in service operations for a good portion of my career, and it is not something that I would like to focus my memory cells on. The usual run-of-the-mill day included taking calls on the fly, sleeping when the customer is sleeping, and juggling vacation plans in sync with peers. Now the good part: service operations hire the most people in the service management industry. ITIL practitioners have job security as long as they are able to adjust to the flexibility needs of organizations. Remember that not all service provider organizations work in a DevOps mode, so there's plenty of work to be done in the next decade or so.

With DevOps, a service operations professional is expected to manage more than just service operations—like managing some of the CI-CD tools or getting your hands dirty with coding. But one thing is clear: you cannot expect to survive the IT industry as a one-trick pony. You need to be able to do multiple forms of activities. That is the way the future is shaping up, and it's an immediate trend that I am seeing in the industry today.

This chapter covers three practices:

- Monitoring and event management

- Incident management

- Problem management

The monitoring and event management's expectations from an examination perspective are a basic understanding requirement, while the incident and problem management practices have to be well understood. This is an important chapter from two angles: (1) as I mentioned earlier, operations are at the heart of ITIL and the chapter therefore demands maximum focus; and (2) a number of other practices interlink to these practices, so it is imperative that you get to the bottom of operational practices.

Exam Tip   Practices for managing operations is an important topic from the ITIL Foundation exam perspective. If you need to answer questions correctly, you need more than a cursory understanding of the topics. You can expect six to seven questions to appear from this chapter.

Monitoring and Event Management

There are various configuration items that contribute to a service. These individual CIs are responsible for the successful delivery of a service. So it is critical that if any of the CIs does not work as it should, then the relevant action should be taken to restore it at the earliest. The concept of keeping a watch on CIs is an example of monitoring in ITIL, and the action undertaken on the back of such changes (usually negative) in states is the essence of event management.

ITIL Definition of Monitoring and Event Management Practice

The purpose of the monitoring and event management practice is to systematically observe services and service components, and record and report selected changes of state identified as events.

The job of monitoring and event management practice is to ensure that a finger is placed on the pulse at all times. The objective is to notice abnormal behaviors at the earliest possible time in order to bring help. Think about it! The earlier you detect a problem, the sooner you can fix it, which translates to service outages staying at a minimum.

Some of the typical CIs that are monitored include infrastructure, applications, IT security, services, and business processes. A typical service could have thousands of CIs behind it. So, it doesn't make sense to monitor every single one of them. Typically, the critical CIs that will contribute directly to the workings of a service are monitored. If a server has an auto failover established (high availability architecture) through another server, the frequency of monitoring may be limited. Not-so-critical applications may not be monitored at the same breakneck speed as an Internet banking application. The idea behind this is to prioritize the services and CIs that need to be monitored and the subsequent actions that have to be taken in case of a failure. In the same example, if the Internet banking application is down, alarm bells could start ringing for the major incident management staff to pool technical resources to fix the problem at a rapid pace. Technical staff may be woken up from their sleep to jump into the issue. Now suppose internal time management software goes down; the downtime is probably identified when a staff reports it, and it may be fixed at its own pace. Clearly and considerably, the Internet banking application is prioritized over the time management software. It all depends on the impact and urgency to get the application up and running.

Types of Events

Before we go into the type of events, let us understand the meaning of an event.

ITIL Definition of an Event

Any change of state that has significance for the management of a service or other configuration item (CI).

An event is a change of state. My daughter going from hungry to full after a meal is also a change of state. So is the server not being accessible anymore. An event by itself is not a game changer but the significance behind an event is critical. What are the types of events that we possibly want to keep an eye out for? A user logging into an application successfully is an event that can be ignored, but an application used by security agencies registering a login from North Korea is worth taking note of and confirming.

Note   The definition of an event is one of the frequently asked questions on the ITIL foundation exam. The question will center on identifying the right definition from a list of choices. So, it is prudent for you to understand and memorize the definition verbatim.

All events are not the same. Most are informational and some indicate failures or about to fail conditions. Based on the application, events are broadly categorized as follows.

Exception Events

Exception events signify errors. They indicate a condition where the monitored subject is not performing as it should—in other words, there is possibly something wrong with a component or a service. They require the most attention. Therefore, they are classified in the topmost tier and normally require urgent action.

Examples of an exception event are:

- Server is unreachable

- Hard disk space has exceeded the threshold limits

- Administrator has tried to log in with an incorrect password

- PC scan reveals malware

Note   The definition of which events are exceptions and which are not is a decision of the organization in agreement with the customer. There is no universal categorization based on illustration of events.

Warning Events

You might have heard of the end of days apocalyptic events, wherein prophecies are foretold about the end of the world as we know it. The world has not ended yet but there is a warning ahead of time. The warning is meant to accelerate caution and take a corrective course before something bad sets in.

Similar warning events are defined in the monitoring and event management practice, and these events exist to warn about an impending exception. They throw out a warning stating that things will soon take a wrong turn if not dealt with quickly. They are important because they help an IT organization to be proactive and prevent exceptions/downtimes. The end of times may be a fantasy but warning events aren't. They have a high probability of materializing. Therefore, it is imperative that a service provides the same kind of urgency as for exception events.

Examples include:

- Memory usage is hovering close to the acceptable threshold.

- An application is running slower than normal.

- Turnaround time for a certain transaction is not within the optimized limits.

- Temperature in the datacenter is not at the ideal level.

Informational Events

If you are big on online shopping, you get those emails and messages when the package has been dispatched or when it is out for delivery. They don't mean much in terms of our response. I don't get ready to receive a package as soon as I receive an email in the morning informing that it is out for delivery. But I would definitely feel jittery if I didn't get this message.

In short, informational events convey information, particularly the information about a change of state—not necessarily an abnormal change or status or anomaly. These events do not call for urgent action from IT staff and are generally recorded and retained for compliance and audit purposes.

Examples include:

- User has logged in to a server

- New folder created on a SharePoint drive

- Application has processed a batch job

- Hardware technician has entered the datacenter

Note   A service provider organization must spend considerable time and effort in designing the events and the event conditions. They wouldn't like to get an event rather late in the day and they definitely don't want to spend additional time processing an informational event.

Key Activities

In the erstwhile ITIL framework, event management was a minor process. Although monitoring was a part of the event management, it wasn't explicitly called out. Although critical, it was considered minor because the scope and management of it was limited to few activities and most of it was driven through toolsets. ITIL 4 doesn't make such a distinction, and the practice has been called out to perform several activities in the service management group.

Monitoring Strategy

Monitoring is an activity carried out by the tools. Yet, it does not give organizations the freedom to monitor every CI and every node, for the simple reasons that it costs money to procure licenses and management of them will be nothing short of a nightmare.

There is a need for a strategy to be put in place to set the record straight and to provide direction and leadership to the management of events. The strategy puts down conditions on what CIs and services will be monitored, which will in turn be based on service criticality and the business impact.

Monitoring Design

We discussed the event types in the earlier section. During the monitoring design activity, a definite shape to each of these types of events is carved out. It essentially identifies the type of events that will go into each of the buckets.

Further, the thresholds for firing warning and exception events have to be defined. For example, if you are going to produce a warning event of hard disk capacity at 95 percent, it may not give the operations team sufficient time to work on the capacity issue at hand. Rather, giving a warning at 70 percent will provide ample time and enable prudent decisions by the operations team. Such thresholds are identified for different types of CIs: a warning event for a server will have separate conditions compared with a warning event for an application.

Solution architects employ empirical methods and trend analyses to determine thresholds and other design parameters. The monitoring tools as well are determined by them.

Policy Management

Now that the events have been designed, the next item on the list is the management of them. What are the policies that drive the management of these events? That is the essence of this activity.

Every type of event that is designed is supplemented with a policy and a process for its management. If there is a warning of a hard disk capacity of a server, what should be done? Should an alert be raised to the server team, or should an incident with low priority be created and assigned automatically? What should be the priority for exception events? Do all exception events have the same incident priority tagged to them? The answers to these questions are an outcome of this activity.

Implementation of Monitoring Tools

With the monitoring designs in place, the monitoring tools are implemented. Tools such as AppDynamics and Splunk rule the monitoring tool space, and this activity ensures that they are set up against the CIs, nodes, and services as per the design.

There are two types of monitoring that we normally employ: passive monitoring and active monitoring.

Passive monitoring is the native monitoring capability built into a CI; for example, a firewall has its own monitoring capability. When something doesn't work as it should, then its monitoring picks up the signal and takes appropriate action.

Active monitoring is a nonnative entity that performs monitoring. Nagios, AppDynamics, and Splunk provide active monitoring. These are featureful compared with passive monitoring, as they proactively monitor various parameters of a CI and a service. Say, for example, Splunk pings a server every minute and if there is no response back after certain number of pings, it raises an exception event. Let's say, in this case, the network is down. A server's passive monitoring tool does not come into play, as the loss of network does not give it a fair chance to create events.

Implementation of Processes

Processes are defined to manage events and the subsequent activities. Not only this, processes provide a framework for the maintenance of monitoring tools and the process efficiencies around them.

The event management processes are defined through the policy activity and get implemented through this activity. Event management even provides guidance to the implementation of automation, the threshold conditions, and the automation actions.

The activity is also responsible for identifying the process roles and their responsibilities. Their accesses must be sorted out. To perform their roles, they are tightly aligned with the defined policies and processes.

Automation Enablement

Most practices in ITIL are role and people focused. Automation is used in repetitive jobs and to generate efficiency. Monitoring and event management practice is the lone practice that bucks the trend. Its processes employ automation for its normal operations; without tools and automation, the practice fails to deliver. In other words, tools and automation form the backbone of the monitoring and event management practice.

Automation can be a part of the CIs through the passive monitoring feature that is built in to them. It can perform limited sets of activities and can come in handy in identifying configurational level changes. On the other hand, active monitoring tools employ automation to poll the CIs and to take necessary actions based on the response. Also, the changes identified in passive monitoring can be fed into the active monitoring tools for further processing such as raising alerts and incidents.

Engagement with Service Value Chain

Table 11-1. *Monitoring and Event Management in SVC*

SVC Activity	Involvement	Details
Plan	None	There is no engagement of the practice in the plan activity due to its transactional and operational nature.
Design and Transition	Medium	The data coming from monitoring CIs and services can influence designs.
Obtain/Build	Low	During environment development, its respective environments could come under the purview of the monitoring and event management practice.
Engage	Low	Based on the monitoring outputs, third parties could be engaged.
Deliver and Support	High	The crux of the monitoring and event practice performs in the Deliver and Support activity – which is the operational activity of the service value chain. Identifying anomalies and raising incidents are examples of its engagement.
Improve	Medium	The monitoring and event management practice keeps its ears close to the ground and is in an excellent position to provide data points for improvements.

Incident Management Practice

Incident management is one of the most popular ITIL practices, from the perspective of the number of jobs the process creates. Quite naturally, most ITIL professionals are aware of the principles that the practice lives by.

In addition, the practice runs the longest, and with maximum touch points with various stakeholders across the service value chain. The incident management practice is primarily responsible for customer satisfaction and the agility with which service interruptions are handled.

I have worked a number of years in the incident management practice area, some as an incident manager and mostly as the incident management practice owner. The incident management process is lively, and you always end up learning something new every time a new situation comes up. You cannot get bored with the process, as every situation is different; even in two similar situations, the potential responses could vary. It is also the process that has kept me up all night on certain days and has kept the senior management of the customer organization at the edge of their seats throughout.

If you need to be exact about the incident management practice, you can state that it is a reactive process with no proactive side to it. And I would agree. It reacts to situations, and its efficiency depends on how quickly and efficiently the service outage is managed. The customer does not get upset if there are service outages, but the customer would definitely become disgruntled when the restoration goes beyond the expectations set.

Note   It is a general habit or a practice to begin either the design or implementation of ITIL practices in an organization from the incident management practice. Whether this is the best practice to start with or not, I will reserve my comment for now. However, its popularity owing from break fixes that are the norms in the service or product industry has made the practice an essential part of every industry, including non-IT ones.

Before I get into the practice, let us understand the term *incident*.

ITIL Definition of Incident

An unplanned interruption to a service or reduction in the quality of a service.

Customers enjoy services, which provide value. If there is a disruption to the service, then the value that comes through the service is no longer there. Think about a salon in your area. You go there to get a haircut, which is a service. The value is good looks coming from well-groomed hair. If the salon closes down due to a water leakage, then the service gets interrupted. As a customer, you can no longer enjoy the service until the water leak is taken care of.

The disruption to the service is an incident. If the water leak is planned (I cannot imagine it can be, but for argument sake let's say it is), then it is no longer an incident.

The second criterion for an incident is subpar quality of service. If the barber in the salon gives you a haircut that's uneven and asymmetrical, then although you are getting the service, you are no longer deriving the benefits from it. You will be far from having good looks from a bad haircut. Such cases are considered as incidents as well.

Some IT examples could be buffering Netflix videos, unable to send emails, and hard drive failure on a laptop. In all these cases, the service is either completely unavailable or is of bad quality. Such disruptions are referred to as incidents.

Note   If you are a betting person, you should place your bets on the definition of an incident appearing on the ITIL foundation exam. The question will center on identifying the right definition from a list of choices. So, it is prudent for you to understand and memorize the definition verbatim.

Now we are ready to get into the incident management practice.

ITIL Definition of Incident Management Practice

The purpose of the incident management practice is to minimize the negative impact of incidents by restoring normal service operation as quickly as possible.

We know what an incident is: a disruption to a service. Incidents, although common, are bad. In our respective projects and organizations, we too don't want to have incidents on our plates. The management of incidents is all about keeping the incident rate at the lowest and ensuring that the lifespan of an incident is as short as possible. This minimizes the loss of a service and increases customer satisfaction.

Looking specifically at the definition, the incident management practice exists to reduce the impact of an incident, which is possible by quick resolution of incidents.

Considering the examples that I stated earlier, as a customer you would be happier if Netflix stops buffering and starts playing the movie—at the soonest possible timescale. We don't appreciate loss of a service even for a minute but when we compare, we would be happier to see services restored in 10 minutes rather than in 20 minutes. The essence is time. The faster the resolution, the more effective the incident management practice.

Leaders may say proactiveness is the way forward and the future. However, when it comes to the incident management practice, it is highly (or completely) reactive and the most looked after process in the service management industry.

Good Practices of Incident Management

Incidents happen. They cannot be avoided. They are a part and parcel of the life of a product or service. Some products and services often give rise to more incidents, while the rest could be relatively smaller numbers. It's like people falling sick with flu, cold, and cough. Everybody falls sick, some more than others. Sickness is like an incident. Two things can be done to manage them:

1. Find a fix (cure) so that the downtime (sickness) does not last long.

2. Find a preventive fix (immunity) so for the majority of causes, you remain protected from incidents (sicknesses).

Yet, you may get the occasional incident (common cold) where an application freeze (flu) can only be resolved through a server restart (paracetamol).

The trick is to manage incidents in a way that the downtime is minimal. It is difficult to define minimal downtime, as every user and every service has its own limits of withstanding downtimes. Most importantly, improvements that are put in the Improve activity of the SVC find opportunities that could potentially prevent incidents, like scheduling an auto-reindexing job of the database to prevent data search slowness.

Next up, incidents come in all shapes, colors and sizes. So the management of incidents must be able to pinpoint the area of concern and get the right team involved. For example, the team that manages servers is separate from the team that manages databases. And the team that manages applications is separate from the team that manages integrations. For all we know, these teams could be sitting in different business units and be a part of different organizations.

Here are some of the good practices in managing incidents:

1. Log all the incidents, including those identified by the internal IT staff.

2. Self-help is a great aid for organizations in hands-free operations. Activities like password reset should be carried out without human intervention.

3. Have an able service desk as a first point of contact for users and other stakeholders. Let them not be just a mouthpiece but rather be the first line of defense for the incident management practice.

4. Identify a functional escalation matrix where, starting from the service desk, an incident gets escalated through various teams for its resolution.

5. Keep a matrix of teams that are responsible for different categories of incidents. This is handy for quick handover followed by faster resolution of incidents.

6. Remember that all the stakeholders who support the service value chain can potentially resolve incidents— including suppliers who provide necessary enablers to a service.

7. Remember the commandos who are specially trained units helicoptered in for special missions. Build a team such as the commandos who can be relied upon when the impact and urgency is of utmost importance.

8. Use techniques such as swarming, where all stakeholders get together during the initial stages of resolution. Once they are able to identify which stakeholder needs to take it forward, others disperse and the stakeholder in charge continues to the end.

9. Some incidents could give rise to service continuity management practice (which is not covered as a part of this book), where the disaster recovery plans are invoked for a speedy resolution (or workaround) to be put in place.

10. Remember that all stakeholders are bound by a single principle: to keep all the updates recorded on an incident register. Without this discipline in place, it is impossible to realize the benefits of the other good practices that I have mentioned here.

The good practices I have stated here are just the tip of the iceberg and definitely not comprehensive, but I believe they should get you started in recording the good practices that work for you and your organization.

Note   Service continuity management comes into play when there is a disaster. Examples could be the COVID situation, floods, earthquakes, and riots. The practice ensures that the service endures in the wake of disasters. Some techniques employed could be replication of data in real time to a server in a different part of the world, and flying out people to different parts of the geography to work as normally as possible. While this is reactive in nature, proactively the practice will work on building resilience into services by ensuring that second and third lines of defense will come into the arena if the services were to come under the effects of a disaster.

Incident Management Life Cycle

There are several kinds of incidents. A unique incident can come up any day, even after providing the same service for a number of years. No matter what kind of incidents show up and what they specifically are, the process that delivers its management can be standardized. The incident management life cycle can be explained through the illustration shown in Figure 11-1. Remember that the life cycle steps varies between implementations. There are no specific steps or a sequence that needs to be followed. The example shown in Figure 11-1 follows logic in identifying and sequencing the incident management steps.

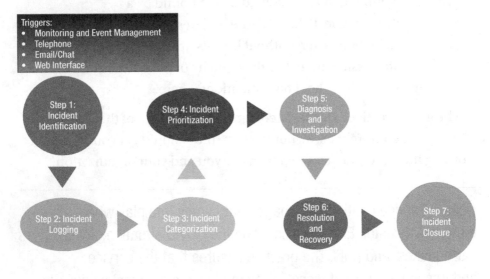

Figure 11-1. *Incident management life cycle*

Note   The steps showcased in this section may or may not appear on the ITIL Foundation exam. If you want to jump ahead, feel free to skip this section. However, if you are keen to understand how the process is laid out and what activities are performed and in which order, read on!

Step 1: Incident Identification

There needs to be a mechanism to identify incidents, they don't show up at the doorstep by themselves. Incident identification or triggering of incidents can happen in a number of ways. Remember that a process gets kick started when it is fueled by the identified triggers. It is important that all the triggers are identified during the process definition stage. The more the merrier, but controlling all the known triggers requires plenty of effort and could lead to misidentification of incidents if they are not curtailed. The most commonly used incident management triggers are:

- *Monitoring and event management*: Through the monitoring and event management practice, incidents are identified; and through integration between the monitoring tools and incident logging tool, incidents can be automatically logged.

- For example, a server that goes down raises an exception with an event management tool. The tool is designed to poll the server every minute; when it does not receive a response three consecutive times, an exception event is raised, which in turn logs an incident ticket.

- *Telephone*: One of the oldest forms of raising complaints is to pick up the phone and complain about a disrupted service. To raise an incident, users have the option of calling the service desk. The trigger in this case is the phone call by the users. It is also possible that IT staff could find a fault in one of the systems and call the service desk.

- *Email/chat*: Instead of calling in, users can opt for a passive form of communication through email or real-time chat. They would still be interacting with the service desk and getting them to raise an incident on their behalf. This form is quite popular at the time of writing of this book, and it lets service providers cater to multiple users through a single service desk agent.

- *Web interface*: In today's world of cutbacks, the service desk is often replaced by self-help mechanisms. ITSM (IT Service Management) ticketing tools provide the front end for users to raise their own tickets without the aid of the service desk. In a way, it is good that precious resources can be used elsewhere. But it could also lead to a good number of misidentified incidents that could add to the flab that you don't like to see.

Most organizations also allow users to create their own incidents through a web interface by building a wrapper around the ITSM ticketing tool. For the user, the form they fill out would be simple without the complications of an ITSM tool.

Step 2: Incident Logging

All incidents that are identified should be logged, with a timestamp that is unalterable. Incidents are generally logged directly into the tool by the user if there is a web interface.

And the event management tools can also create incidents, based on the threshold levels and the designed algorithms. The service desk raises incidents on behalf of end users when they call, email, or chat about their issues.

There are several ITSM ticketing tools that are employed to log incidents. Popular ones include ServiceNow, BMC Remedy, and CA IT

Service Management. ServiceNow is far ahead of its competitors. Its seamless integrations with other tools and flexibility to implement and run on optimized infrastructure make it an easy choice for organizations. Essentially, ITSM tools log different types of tickets, be it incidents, changes, or problems, among others. They also host CIs and CMDBs and knowledge databases. When an incident is raised, it can be mapped to the CI and, based on the incident summary, the knowledge base often pulls knowledge articles that could help with the resolution.

An incident ticket has a number of fields associated with it, primarily to support the resolution of the incident and to control the various parameters and pull reports as necessary. Some common fields that are found on incident tickets are:

- Incident number (unique)

- End user name

- End user team name

- Incident logger name

- Time of logging the incident

- Incident medium (phone/chat/web/email)

- Impact

- Urgency

- Priority

- Category

- Related CI

- Incident summary

- Incident description

- Assigned resolver group

- Assigned engineer

- Status

- Resolution code

- Time of resolution/closure

Step 3: Incident Categorization

Not all incidents fall into the same bucket. Some incidents are server based, some network, and some application/software. It is very important to identify which bucket the incident falls into, as the incident categories determine which resolver group gets assigned to resolve it.

For example, if there is an incident logged for the loss of Internet, you need the network team in charge of handling network issues to work on it. If this incident gets categorized incorrectly, say applications, the incident will be assigned to a resolver group that specializes in software troubleshooting and code fixes. They will not be able to resolve the incident. They are required to recategorize and assign it to the right group. But the effect of wrong categorization is that the resolution takes longer, and this defeats the purpose of the incident management process. So, it is absolutely imperative that the team that is logging the incident is specialized in identifying the incident types and categorizing them correctly.

In cases of autologged incidents, event management tools are designed to select a predetermined category that does not falter. User-raised incidents are automatically categorized based on the keywords mentioned in the incident summary and description. It is quite possible that the incident could be categorized incorrectly in this scenario, but in the interests of automation, this is the price we have to pay.

Step 4: Incident Prioritization

Consider a real-life scenario of a company that employs 100,000 employees and there is a support team of about 100 technicians. At any given time, around 1 percent of the employees raise incidents for issues faced by them—1,000 tickets. So you have 100 IT staff to handle 1,000 incidents. They cannot handle them all at the same time. They need to pick and choose which ones to work on first and follow up with the rest. How do they pick and choose? The answer is in prioritization of incidents.

Not all incidents carry the same weight in terms of their impact and urgency. Some are more urgent, some cause more impact than others, some may not be urgent, and some are neither grossly affecting nor urgent.

To state some examples:

- A finance application at the end of the month will cause a major impact and it needs to be fixed urgently.

- A finance application in the middle of a month will cause major impact but it may not be urgent.

- The PDF viewer not displaying in the right format for a single user is low impact and not urgent.

- Network connectivity for an entire floor of business users causes a great impact and is urgent.

- The email application not working for a VIP user is low impact but is very high on the urgency list.

Incident priority therefore can be determined based on impact and urgency:

Incident Priority = Impact × Urgency

Impact refers to the business impact, which is definitely a factor that drives the incident priority. Business impact normally refers to the following:

- Financial losses

- Productivity losses

- Loss of reputation

- Regulatory or legislative breaches

Urgency is a measure of how quickly or how swiftly the incident needs to be resolved. It may demand a majority of the staff be dedicated to a particular incident immediately or indicate resolution when IT resources become available.

To determine the priority of an incident, let's imagine a 3×3 matrix for deriving the incident priority based on impact and urgency, as shown in Figure 11-2.

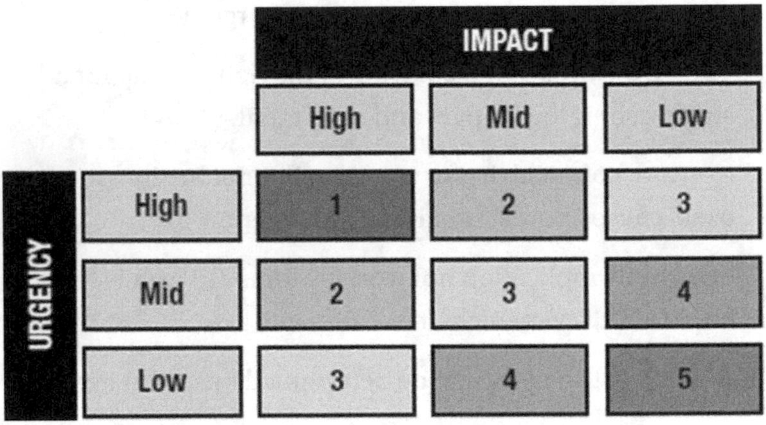

		IMPACT	
	High	**Mid**	**Low**
High	1	2	3
Mid	2	3	4
Low	3	4	5

(URGENCY shown along the vertical axis: High, Mid, Low)

Figure 11-2. *Incident priority matrix*

As per the matrix, a high impact and a high urgency incident would be classified as priority 1. A medium impact and urgency incident is prioritized as 2, and so on. The matrix shown here is too simple to be used in the real world. There are far too many permutations and combinations to consider in rating the priority of an incident, but the principle is the same.

Response SLA is the target set for technicians to respond to incidents, say by acknowledging and accepting the incident in their respective queues. For example, an incident was logged at 10 a.m. and the defined response SLA is 30 minutes. In this case, the technician is expected to accept the incident before 10:30 a.m.

Resolution SLA is the target set for technicians to resolve incidents. For example, an incident was logged at 10 a.m. and the defined resolution SLA is one hour. In this case, the technician is expected to resolve the incident before 11 a.m.

Now that we have the priorities considered and determined, each of the priorities comes with its own set of response and resolution SLAs. These SLAs are drawn during the service design phase under the service-level management process. A sample response and resolution SLA for various priorities is shown in Figure 11-3.

Response and Resolution SLAs for Incidents		
Incident Priority	Response SLA	Resolution SLA
P1	15 minutes	2 hours
P2	45 minutes	6 hours
P3	2 hours	1 day
P4	1 day	3 days

Figure 11-3. *Incident management SLAs*

In the example, the highest priority, P1, has a response SLA of 15 minutes and resolution SLA of 2 hours. This requires the technical team to acknowledge the incident within 15 minutes (start working on the resolution), and the P1 incident is required to be resolved before 2 hours. Say, for example, a very sensitive banking application that allows foreign exchanges to transact is down. This outage will cost the bank a significant amount of financial loss and the bank will lose customer perception. Also, it could face the government's wrath as well owing to regulatory norms. To ensure that such a scenario is contained, a P1 priority with stringent timelines will allow the maximum resources to be allocated at the earliest possible time to resolve the incident.

Incident priorities and parameters for setting the priority are different for every customer. The service provider is expected to adhere to the requirements put forth by the customer and charge them accordingly, based on the number of resources and assets utilized in fulfilling the service obligations.

The service desk measures the urgency and impact and sets the incident priority. Event management tools have the ability to set the right priority based on an algorithm. User-created incidents are normally assigned a default priority, and the resolver group changes the priority once it begins resolving the incident.

Incident priorities are not set in stone. They can be changed throughout the life cycle of an incident. It is possible that the end user has hyped the impact of the incident and could have gotten a higher priority incident raised. During the resolution process, the resolver group validates the impact and urgency and alters the priority as needed. Some critical incidents are monitored after resolution. The observation period could see the priority pushed down until closure.

Step 5: Diagnosis and Investigation

The service desk performs the initial diagnosis of an incident by understanding the symptoms of the incident. The service desk tries to understand exactly what is not working and then tries to take the user through some basic troubleshooting steps to resolve the incident. This is a key substep, as it provides the necessary data points for further investigation on the incident. It is analogous to a doctor asking you about the symptoms you have: Do you have throat pain? Do you have a cough? Do you have a cold?

Do you have a headache? You get the drift. Likewise, the service desk is expected to ask a series of questions to provide the necessary information to resolve the incident quickly, which is the objective of the incident management process.

Not all incidents can be resolved by the service desk. They get functionally escalated to the next level of support, generally referred to as level 2, or L2. The L2 group is normally a part of an expert group, such as the server group, network group, storage group, or software group.

The resolver group diagnoses the incident with the available information, and if needed, calls the user to obtain more information. It is possible that the service desk's line of questioning could be on the wrong path, and perhaps the resolver group must start all over again by asking the right set of questions.

Investigation of the incident digs deeper into the incident by understanding one or more of the following thought processes:

- What is the user expecting to obtain through the incident?

- What has gone wrong?

- What is the sequence of steps that led to the incident?

- Who is impacted? Is it localized or global?

- Were there changes performed in the environment that might have upset the system?

- Are there any similar incidents logged previously? Are there any KEDB articles available to assist?

Step 6: Resolution and Recovery

Based on the investigation, resolutions can be applied. For example, if the resolver group determines that a particular incident is not localized, there is no reason for it to resolve the incidents on the user's PC, but rather it starts troubleshooting in the server or network. Or perhaps it brings in the experts who deal with global issues.

The success of resolution rides on the right path of investigation. If the doctor you are seeing prescribes the wrong medicines because the line of investigation was way off, the chances of recovery are close to nil, aren't they?

For incidents that are widespread in nature (affecting multiple users), once the resolution is applied, various tests have to be conducted by the resolver group to be absolutely sure that the incident has been resolved. There is generally a recovery period to observe the incident and be on the lookout if anything were to go wrong again.

In some of the accounts that I have handled in major incident management, it was a regular practice to keep major incidents open for at least a week. This was done to observe, and to hold daily/hourly meetings with stakeholders to check the pulse and keep tabs on things that could go wayward.

Step 7: Incident Closure

When an incident is resolved, it is normal practice to confirm with the user before closing the incident ticket. The confirmation is generally made by the service desk, not the resolver group. So the process for postresolution of an incident is that the incident gets assigned to the service desk for confirmation and closure of the incident.

Some organizations feel that this step adds too much overhead to the service desk and prefer to forgo this confirmation. They keep the incident in resolved status for maybe three days. An email is shot out to the user informing him that the incident has been resolved, and if they feel otherwise, they are expected to inform back or to reopen the incident. If there is no response within 3 days, the incident would be autoclosed. I like doing this and have been a proponent of the autoclosure system, as confirmation can be overbearing; and, from a user's standpoint, it is irritating to the customer to receive calls just to ask for confirmation.

After an incident has been closed, a user satisfaction survey goes out asking for feedback on the timeliness of the resolution, the ease of logging incidents, and whether the user was kept informed of the incident status throughout the life cycle.

Major Incident Management

Major incidents, as the name suggests, are severely impacting incidents that have the potential to cause irreparable damage to the business. So the ITIL service management suggests that major incidents be dealt with through a different lens. This can be done by having a separate process, a more stringent one of course, with stricter timelines and multiple lines of communication. Many organizations institute a separate team to look into major incidents and hire those with specialized skill sets to be exposed to the pressure that this job inherits.

The people who work solely on major incidents are called major incident managers. They have all the privileged powers to mobilize teams and summon management representatives at any time of the day (or night). They run the show when there is a major incident and become completely accountable for the resolution of the incident. The pressure on them is immense, and it calls for nerves of steel to withstand the pressure from the customer, service provider senior management, and all other interested parties.

I once worked as a major incident manager and was heading a major incident management team not too long ago. The job entailed keeping the boat floating at all times, and any delays from my end could potentially jeopardize the lives of miners across the globe. During a major incident, there could have been two or three phones buzzing with action, emails flying daggers into my inbox, and chat boxes flashing and roaring. It was a good experience when I think about it in hindsight, and a time I will cherish.

In a typical organization, you will have the service desk working on low-priority incident resolution. I will discuss the service desk later in this chapter. To track, manage, and chase incident-related activities, there are incident managers who keep tabs on all occurrences. When a major incident hits the queue, none of these groups take responsibility, but they call in the experts (major incident managers) to manage the situation. In some cases, the service desk and incident managers might validate the incident priority before calling the major incident line.

It is a good practice to let the whole service provider team and the customer organization know that a major incident is in progress, to make sure that everybody knows that certain services are down and to avoid users calling the service desk to report on the same incident. A few good practices in this regard include sending out emails at the start and end of major incidents, flashing messages on office portals and on ticket logging pages, and playing an interactive voice response (IVR) message when users call the service desk.

Engagement with Service Value Chain

Table 11-2. *Incident Management Practice in SVC*

SVC Activity	Involvement	Details
Plan	None	The planning activity and the incident management practice do not necessarily have to work with each other.
Design and Transition	Medium	During transition (system tests and user acceptance tests), incidents do occur (depending on the definition set forth). Resolving them quickly will help in releasing the end product as per the planned scheduled.
Obtain/Build	Medium	Just as in having incidents in the test environment, they could happen in the development environment as well. Resolving them quickly will help in releasing the end product as per the planned scheduled.
Engage	High	Much of incident management is communication to stakeholders. They can be customers, users, or suppliers. It is a good practice to keep the statuses transparent, to build trust with the stakeholder community by setting the right expectations and obtaining confirmations upon resolution.
Deliver and Support	High	Incident management operates in the operate space, and the union between the practice and the service value chain is significant.
Improve	Medium	Improvement ideas are often generated on the back of incidents. Depending on the number of incidents and their impact, improvements are prioritized and delivered as well.

Problem Management Practice

Incident management is the first line of defense in providing immediate relief against the disruption of services and eventual downtimes. However, by no means does the incident management process get into the nitty-gritty of putting an end to the cause behind the incidents. Its purpose is to bring the services back up, even if the solution is a nonpermanent one.

The second ring of process governance ensuring permanence to solutions is the problem management practice. This is a process that deep dives into the cause of incidents and follows the problem to its root, ensuring that incidents related to the particular cause do not repeat.

To summarize, the incident management practice deals with correction, while the problem management practice focuses on prevention.

The problem management practice in the service management practices is critical for the product and the service to thrive. Incident management is good, but at the end of the day, the more incidents, the more downtime, and the more efforts required to bring the services back up. The customer gains zilch from the process, as it's trying to keep the support above water at all times but not really taking it to new places. There is a dire need to bring value to services, and value can be brought about only if stability is assured. One of the pillars for ensuring service stability is the problem management practice.

The problem management practice is academic in nature. It does not believe in happenstance and does not (in effect) try to resolve world hunger in one swooping move. There is a definite method to the madness around laying tombstones on top of the problems. I represent the problem management practice as the investigation unit of the IT service provider organization.

You might have seen the popular TV series CSI, where crimes are solved by following the leads and taking down the culprits. The problem management process is the CSI of IT service management, and you can compare incident management to the police squad.

Let's consider an example involving an application that crashes frequently when certain actions are performed simultaneously. An incident is raised. The incident is diagnosed, and the resolution is identified to be a complex one. But incident management focuses on helping users move on with their day-to-day activities involving services. Therefore, an incident analyst recommends a workaround whereby the user can perform actions on the application in a sequential manner rather than in parallel. The user's immediate issue is solved, but the impending problem exists. A problem is raised, and an investigation into the problem begins. The problem is recreated, the codebase is examined, and all the relevant logs are studied to debug the underlying cause. The investigation pays off, and the cause is identified and subsequently fixed. All the investigative activities are done under the auspices of problem management to identify the problem and find a permanent solution.

Before I move any further, I want to focus on the word *problem* that I have used in this section. It's a common English word but the meaning it derives is deep.

ITIL Definition of Problem
A cause, or potential cause, of one or more incidents.

There are unresolved incidents where the fix is yet to be determined. The resolution of these incidents is not possible until the root cause of the incident is known. Yes, one can shoot in the dark trying to do a hundred things, hoping that something sticks, like restarting the server as soon as the server goes down. But it's not always that simple. The resolution of incidents must be surgical. A problem comes into the play only when there are incidents where the root cause is unknown.

This is similar to a doctor prescribing medicines. If the doctor does not know the cause of certain symptoms, then the doctor will not be able to prescribe medicines. Well, he/she might guess, assume, and hope certain medicines work. When they don't, the doctor might prescribe another set. Through problem management, we want to avoid this behavior; as I mentioned earlier, it has to be surgical. In the medical analogy, the cause of the disease must be found and the right medicines prescribed. If it requires MRI scans, blood tests, and swabs, so be it. The thing that matters is to find out what is wrong and to find an apt solution.

In IT organizations too, to resolve incidents, the technical resolver groups must know the root cause of the problems. If they do not know the root cause, they start to guess by asking users to restart machines, uninstall and reinstall software, and other "fiddles" that may amount to a waste of time and resources. But, if the principles of problem management are applied and the root cause identified, the solution to follow will be a matter of routine.

A problem gets raised when the root cause of an incident is unknown. Or a bunch of incidents with a common thread is unable to be resolved, as the underlying root cause is yet to be identified.

Note   The definition of a problem is a must learn, not just from the perspective of the ITIL Foundation exam but also to get a better footing in the ITIL framework. On the exam though, you should expect to see a question asking you to identify the right definition from a list of choices. So, it is prudent for you to understand and memorize the definition verbatim.

Incidents vs. Problems

It is my experience that many IT professionals in the IT service management industry use the terms incident and problem interchangeably. This does more harm than good, especially if you are working in an organization that takes shape after ITIL and especially if you are preparing for the ITIL foundation exam. In this section, I will differentiate the two terms with examples, so as we move forward toward the process and other key terminologies, there shouldn't be any speck of doubt between incidents and problems.

Incidents are raised due to loss or degradation of services. They are raised by users, IT staff, or event management tools. When incident resolution is not possible, because the underlying root cause is unknown, the IT team will raise a problem. Remember that users and event management tools don't raise problems; generally speaking, they can come only through the incident. However, in a mature IT environment, we can configure event management tools to look for specific patterns of events and subsequently raise problems. But, let's keep this discussion out of the scope and restrict problems to be derived only on the back of incidents.

Let's consider the example of a software application that crashes when it is initiated. The user raises an incident to fix this issue. The software resolution team tries to start the application in safe mode, uninstalls and reinstalls the application, and finally makes changes to the OS registry, to no avail. When all hopes fail, they provide a heads-up to the problem management to find the root cause and provide a permanent solution.

The problem management practice, aided by experts in the software architecture group, debug the application loading and run a series of tests to find the triggers and sparks for the crash. They find out that the root cause of the crash is because of a conflict with a hardware device driver. They recommend a solution to uninstall the hardware device driver and update it with the latest driver. The recommendation works like a charm, and the software application that used to crash loads nicely without any fuss.

This is the problem management practice in action, working on difficult problems that can cause irreparable damages to the customer organization if not dealt with on a timely basis.

Other Key Terminologies in Problem Management

Problem management digs deep, and the process brings a certain amount of complexity to the table. The complexity begins with a few terms that are used quite often during various stages of the process activities. It is important that you understand all the terminology that I put forth here. It helps you use better terms at work and most definitely bags a few more right answers on the ITIL Foundation exam.

Root Cause

The root cause is the fundamental reason for the occurrence of an incident. Let's say that you are in a bank and the ATM does not disburse the money that you requested. The underlying cause or the root cause for the denial of service in this instance is attributed to a network failure in the bank. For every incident, there will be a root cause.

Only when you identify the root cause will you be able to resolve the incident. In the ATM instance, unless you know of the network failure, you cannot bring the ATM service back up.

Root-Cause Analysis

Identifying the root cause of an incident is no menial task. At times the root cause may reveal itself, but many times it will become challenging to identify the root causes of complex incidents. You are required to analyze the root cause by using techniques that commonly fall under the activity called root-cause analysis (RCA).

Remember that the outcome of RCA may not always result in identifying the root cause of an incident. In such cases, RCA must be performed using complex techniques and with experts pertaining to related fields of technology and management.

Known Error

Even when the outcome of the RCA procedure yields results and the root cause is known, it may not be always possible to implement a permanent solution. Instead, temporary fixes called workarounds are identified. Such cases where root causes are known, along with the workarounds, are called known errors.

ITIL Definition of Known Error

A problem that has been analyzed but has not been resolved.

There could be various reasons why solutions cannot be implemented. Commonly, permanent solutions come with an expensive price tag. Most organizations are price conscious these days and may not approve the excess expenditure. Other reasons could include a lack of experts or people resources to implement the permanent solution, or governance or legislation controls that could prevent implementation.

Note   The definition of a known error is important from the ITIL Foundation exam point of view. On the exam though, you should expect to see a question asking you to identify the right definition from a list of choices. So, it is prudent for you to understand and memorize the definition verbatim.

Known Error Database

Known errors are documented and are stored in a repository called a known error database (KEDB). The KEDB consists of various known errors, their identified root causes, and the workarounds that can be applied. The known error records are not permanent members of a KEDB. Known errors will cease to exist in this repository when the permanent solution is implemented.

Workaround

As I mentioned, workarounds are fixes to solve incidents temporarily. Each incident could have one or multiple workarounds, but none of them will alleviate the problem permanently, and it may be necessary to revisit the workaround applied on a regular basis.

> ### *ITIL Definition of Workaround*
>
> *A solution that reduces or eliminates the impact of an incident or problem for which a full resolution is not yet available. Some workarounds reduce the likelihood of incidents.*

For example, say a printer on your floor is not working and you cannot wait until the technician can get to it. A classic workaround, in this case, is to print from a printer on a different floor. The workaround will solve your problem temporarily by providing a way out, but it may not be a permanent solution because you may find it inconvenient to run down to the next floor every time. Another workaround could be that you don't print the document but instead send the soft copy to the intended recipient.

A workaround exists to provide immediate or intermediate relief from the service disruption. In some cases, if a permanent solution is not found (due to technical or financial reasons, et al), then the workaround could possibly be considered as a final solution.

Permanent Solution

When the root cause of a problem is known, the follow-up activity in problem management process is to identify a permanent solution. This solution permanently resolves the problem, contributes toward a reduction in the incident count, and avoids future outages.

As I mentioned earlier, permanent solutions come at a cost, and organizations may not always be willing to shell out the required capital. In such cases, permanent solutions are known but not implemented.

Problem Management Phases

The problem management process is made up of three phases that drive its objectives. They are indicated in Figure 11-4:

- Problem Identification
- Problem Control
- Error Control

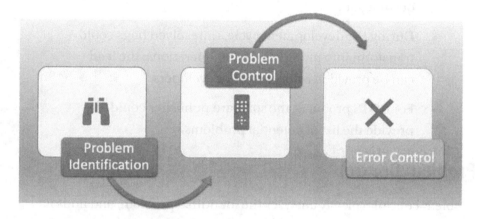

Figure 11-4. *Problem management phases*

Problem Identification

The first logical step in the problem management phases is to identify the problem. Identifying it is not simple or straightforward. Remember that there will be typically hundreds and thousands of incidents coming through for a decent sized organization. Sieving through it for a problem is going to be challenging unless, the rules of engagement are well defined. Here are a few, and the list is not comprehensive:

- Incident records should be analyzed on a regular basis to identify common elements such as similar incidents like occasional Chrome browser crashing, or it could be a particular CI that is breaking down multiple times.

- Through trend analysis of incidents, repetitive incidents can be identified, and the intel can be provided by users and IT staff as well.

- Suppliers and other third parties could also potentially provide intel around problems.

- All major incidents could be succeeded by the problem management process to ensure such incidents do not occur again.

- During the development cycle, unresolved bugs could transform into problems during operations; the lead can be provided by testers and developers.

- For COTS products, the software publisher could provide the list of potential problems.

Problem Control

Problem control typically analyzes the identified problem, and finds its root cause and a permanent solution if possible. If there are a handful of problems, then perhaps all problems can be analyzed. If there are several, an activity of prioritization is done to pit problems against each other in the order of impact and its probability, which is nothing but the risk it poses.

The riskiest problems are analyzed to identify the root cause. We employ a few techniques to get to the root of the problem. Some techniques are:

Brainstorming

The technique that has been used, misused, and underused at times is the power of using our brains to focus on areas of investigation. The brainstorming technique involves focused thinking without any inhibitions.

In the brainstorming technique, there are no bad thoughts. Every single thought must be weighed, and then a decision must be made. In other words, ideas are not tagged absurd or made fun of; everything is accepted, examined, and then acted upon based on the results of the examination. Let me explain brainstorming in the form of an example. If thinking is a car, then in this car I take out the brakes because I don't want the thinking to stop or be impeded. There must be no action taken to stop the flow of thoughts. I use only the steering wheel to steer my thoughts toward the goal I want to achieve. The more thinking, with the right steering, the closer I will get to my destination.

Brainstorming can be done on your own or in a group. The more the merrier, right? Not always. It is possible through group brainstorming sessions that the clear thoughts in your mind could get defocused, so group brainstorming must be done with caution and with a process to keep it in a framework. Osborn says in his book that group brainstorming sessions are more effective than individual ones, as he firmly believes that quantity breeds quality. The assumption is that a greater number of ideas generated provide a better probability of striking gold.

Five-Why Technique

One of the most used and misused techniques in the problem management process is the five-why technique. It is used during the investigation of a problem, specifically during the root-cause determination stage. The technique is so commonly taught and retaught to problem management personnel that it has become a de facto standard in the activity of root-cause analysis.

The five-why technique involves asking the question "why?" to the problem on hand five times to arrive at the root cause. It was conceived by Japanese industrialist Sakichi Toyoda, the founder of Toyota Industries in 1930. But it wasn't until the Toyota Production System became popular that the technique became more widespread in the 1970s. The technique's principle relies on being on the ground to find out the reasons rather than in the comfort of an air conditioned office (a "go and see" philosophy).

The part that makes the technique popular is that it is extremely simple to use and takes a short amount of time to process and execute. Figure 11-5 is an illustration of using the five-why technique for identifying the root cause of the problem.

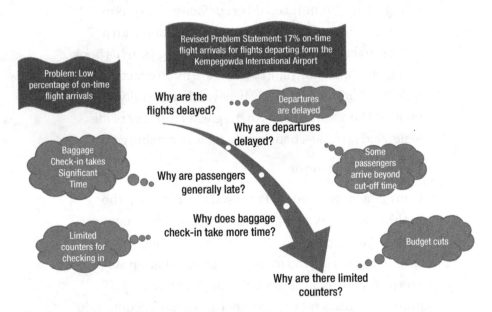

Figure 11-5. *Illustration of the five-why technique*

Ishikawa

An Ishikawa diagram is known by multiple names such as fishbone diagram, fishikawa diagram, and herringbone diagram, among others. The diagram consists of a central spine that represents the problem. Several branches jut out of the spine to indicate possible causes. The arrangement of the spine and branches looks like a fishbone.

The causes are not arbitrary, as discussed in the five-why technique. There is a method to the madness in the Ishikawa process of the root cause of determination. Each branch is designated to a category of cause, and the thinking behind it is to follow the category lead to determine the root cause. One of the popular fishbone models used in the manufacturing industry is called the 6M model. The six categories of causes are modeled are as follows:

- *Material*: causes related to the material used in the manufacturing process

- *Method*: the process

- *Machine*: the actual machinery, technology, and so on

- *Mother Nature*: the environment

- *Measurement*: the measurement techniques employed in deriving metrics

- *Man*: the people involved

There are other models as well, depending on the type of industry. Figure 11-6 is an illustration of the Ishikawa technique.

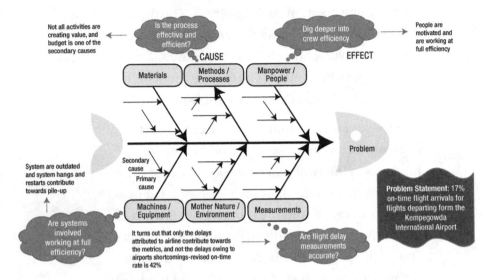

Figure 11-6. *Illustration of the Ishikawa technique*

The outcome of any of the techniques could result in the following options:

- No root cause

- Root cause and permanent solution known

- Root cause known but no permanent solution

If the root cause is not determined, then the technique needs to be altered and reprocessed to identify the root cause. When the root cause and the permanent solution are known, then a determination needs to be done whether the permanent solution needs to be implemented or not. A number of factors could influence it: commercial, collateral risk, etc. If the root cause is known but not the permanent solution, the next best thing to do is identify a workaround that will hold the fort until the cavalry arrives (permanent solution).

Error Control

An error or a known error comes up if a permanent solution to a problem is not implemented. As I mentioned earlier, there could be several reasons why a permanent solution is not implemented: it may not be technically determined yet, it may be commercially unfeasible, or the collateral risks could outweigh the benefits.

Managing errors is done though a KEDB. The exercise involves regular assessments of the known error to identify potential permanent solutions and to ensure that the known errors are well socialized with the user and IT staff community. The assessment is done on the basis of impact to customers, the cost of implementing a permanent solution, effectiveness of the permanent solution, and the effectiveness of the workarounds identified.

Engagement with Service Value Chain

Table 11-3. *Problem Management Practice in SVC*

SVC Activity	Involvement	Details
Plan	None	The planning activity and the problem management practice do not necessarily have to work with each other.
Design and Transition	Low	Problem management inputs may be used during testing, and knowledge transfer activities during transitions.
Obtain/Build	Low	The output of problem management might lead to detection of product defects, which is fed back to the Obtain/Build activity for providing the fixes.
Engage	Medium	Problems are fewer but may not be limited to the IT community alone. Long-standing problems could be made visible to customers and end users who may like to be a part of the problem resolution process. The supplier likewise may be involved if the problem could be caused due to them or if they have a role to play in its resolution.
Deliver and Support	High	Problem management has the highest play in the Deliver and Support activity—through the activities involving incident reduction and problem resolution.
Improve	High	Problem management is the other side of the improvement activity. Both the Improve activity and problem management practice are set out to make the product/service more stable and incident free (read incident reduction).

Knowledge Check

The answers are provided in Appendix.

11-1. Which of the following is the correct *event* definition?

    A. Any change of state that is significant for a service or product or related CI

    B. Any change of state that triggers changes to the other operational processes

    C. Any change of state for CIs that correlates risks and issues to the service and service management processes

    D. Any change of state that has significance for the management of a service or other CI

11-2. Which of the following is the correct *incident* definition?

    A. A problem that has been analyzed but has not been resolved

    B. Interruptions to a service are referred to as an incident

    C. An unplanned interruption to a service or reduction in the quality of a service

    D. A method for overcoming a problem or limitation in a program or system

11-3. What kind of a tool should be used to log incidents?

    A. A tool that is specialized for registering incidents, and carries attributes such as incident summary, incident description, priority, category, etc. Also, there must be room provided for customizing the fields.

B. A tool that provides access to all IT staff, users, and the service desk and that is available on demand

C. A tool that provides links to CIs, problems and known errors

D. A tool that can be used for self-healing of incidents and that can provide quick resolution

11-4. Which is the difference between a problem and a known error?

A. Problems are created to identify root cause of incidents; known errors are created when root cause of an incident is known but a permanent solution is yet to be implemented.

B. Problems are created to identify root cause of incidents; known errors are created to identify the product bugs that are released from the development cycle.

C. Problems are created to identify a permanent solution to an incident; known errors are created when the permanent solution to an incident is yet to be implemented.

D. Problems are created to identify a permanent solution to an incident; known errors are created to track and identify product bugs that come from the development cycle.

11-5. Which of these is not a valid problem identification technique?

A. Performing trend analysis of incidents

B. On the back of a major incident

C. Five-why analysis

D. Analyzing recurring issues

11-6. Which of the activities is a valid *error control*
activity?

A. Applying workarounds to incidents

B. Identification of permanent solution

C. Analysis of root cause of known errors

D. Analyzing recurring issues

DAY 6

Approximate Study Time: 1 hour and 34 minutes

Chapter 12 - 42 minutes
Chapter 13 - 52 minutes

On day 6 we study the practices that manage changes to services: service request management and change management. We also delve into the release and deployment practices that follow the change management practices.

CHAPTER 12

Practices to Manage Changes

While operations keeps the services afloat and maintains status quo, for a service or a product to stay alive, barely surviving is far from enough. It needs to change, it needs to evolve, and it needs to transform. Without changes, a service or a product is as good as dead. Think of a service or a product that have stayed the same for a number of years. Hard, right? Impossible to name a couple? Yes, that's true. Even a simple product like the day to day confectionaries changes because customers get bored and crave something new. Think about the avatars of Haribo or any of your favorite chocolates. Very few have stayed the same, and they keep the change constant. One other anomaly in this regard is "classic" coke. Although the old made way for the new, popular demand meant that the company had to bring the old formula back to revive the fortunes of the company.

Coming back to the products and services in IT, anomalies are rare to extinct. Every product or a service can survive by introducing improvements and making it better with every release. But bringing in the new and discarding the old cannot be done like we junk our old television sets. There needs to principles, processes, practices, and procedures to make it happen. After all, there will be several users who are accustomed to using products and services in a certain way, and change for them is going to be painful. Not only from the user perspective, changing

© Abhinav Krishna Kaiser 2021
A. K. Kaiser, *Become ITIL® 4 Foundation Certified in 7 Days*,
https://doi.org/10.1007/978-1-4842-6361-7_12

a service must ensure that disruption from change is nil to minimal. Although the desire to change is high on the requirement index, the appetite for taking risks with service uptimes and availabilities is quite low. So, we need ITIL to provide a safe passage for changes to be done in the least disruptive manner, and here you go: this chapter deals with practices that manage change.

This chapter covers two practices:

- Service request management

- Change control

In both practices, we shall delve deep to understand their nuances, and the expectation is that you get a good grip on both practices. From your career perspective, these practices are invaluable—especially change control. It is considered an equal next to the incident practice, and interviewers testing your knowledge of ITIL may start at incident management but will pass through or end at the change control practice.

Exam Tip Practices for managing changes is an important topic from the ITIL Foundation exam perspective. If you need to answer questions correctly, you need more than a cursory understanding of the topics. You can expect anywhere from seven to eight questions to appear from this chapter.

Service Request Management

Service request management is a minor practice in the ITIL framework and is often confused with the incident management process. Before I get into the muddle of this confusion, let us consider the definition of the service request management practice.

ITIL Definition of Service Request Management Practice

The purpose of the service request management practice is to support the agreed quality of a service by handling all pre-defined, user-initiated service requests in an effective and user-friendly manner.

The service request management practice exists to ensure that service requests are fulfilled based on the agreed service levels, and the service requests themselves are well defined. The term service request is used in a number of industries; it usually means carrying out an activity that is predefined. It is pertinent to understand what is meant by a service request.

ITIL Definition of a Service Request

A request from a user or a user's authorized representative that initiates a service action that has been agreed as a normal part of service delivery.

Service requests are predefined deliveries that are agreed with customers. They can be requested by users or their delegates. A service request is not a complaint that you register when a service does not function. Although it is concerned about a part of a service, it is not related to a part or complete service going down. Examples will provide a fairly good understanding about what I am talking about:

- A customer can call a bank or use an online banking system to request a checkbook. The exhaustion of the previous checkbook is not considered as a service failure. Requesting a new one is a delivery that is agreed, and it gets done as per the predefined set of activities and predefined timelines.

- You could call your company's service desk and request open source software to be installed on your laptop. Installing software is a service, and as a user you are entitled to request it. Likewise, requesting a laptop, mobile phone, or a monitor are examples of service requests.

- Suppose you need access to a portal; you raise a request to get the requisite access. This is an example of a service request as well. You are seeking something that you do not have, and you are asking for something that is already defined and you're entitled to.

- If you did not know how to get to the train station, you could call the people concerned and ask for information (directions in this case). The request for information is another example of a service request. The information could be anything that falls under the ambit of the services offered.

- Finally, compliments, complaints, and feedback provided for the offered services or the people involved in offering it also fall under the service request definition.

Note   The service request management practice was referred to as request fulfilment management in ITIL V3. In fact, it was called service request management back in ITIL V2. In my opinion, calling it request fulfilment didn't go too well with companies, users, and practitioners, as the norm is that management of incidents is done through incidents and management of changes is done through change control. So why not service request management for managing service requests?

Service Catalog and the Confusion with Incidents

Service requests have to be predefined. A user cannot request something that has not been defined. They cannot call the service desk and say: "I want you to book a cab." If booking a cab is not defined, then the team responsible for fulfilling service requests will not fulfill the request.

How does a user know what he can or cannot request? All the agreed and defined service requests are part of a service catalog. Generally speaking, the service catalog must be socialized with the user community so they know about services they can avail themselves of.

There was a time when incidents and service requests were put into the same bucket and treated similarly. I say this as though this practice does not happen anymore, which isn't true. It still does, but the two sets of tickets are now better understood to define separate processes and manage them separately through their respective processes.

By clubbing incidents and service requests together, the service provider organization is doing gross injustice to those who have raised incidents, because incidents pertain to loss of service. And as we have established, service requests are not loss of service but rather getting something additional to what users already have.

The trouble with treating incidents and service requests the same is that the time taken to resolve incidents will go up. That leads to additional downtime, and generally a loss of service leads to productivity loss and hence financial losses. The implications from a service request are not on the same scale. Therefore, clubbing the two and not differentiating between them leads to higher service downtime and unhappy users, and it introduces inefficiencies in the system that are best avoided.

Note   There is a practice called service catalog management, which delves into the processes and nuances of defining and managing the service catalog. However, the practice is outside the scope of ITIL Foundation.

Fulfilment of Service Requests

All service requests are predefined. In an ideal scenario, all the service requests are listed for the users to see. They can simply go in, select what they need, and submit it. For every service request, the steps required to fulfill it are well known, defined, documented, and proven to work. As they are predefined, it makes it much easier and straightforward to formalize them with standard operating procedures for initiating service requests, obtaining approvals, and to fulfill them.

Consider the illustration that I have put forth in Figure 12-1. In this example, the service catalog consists of three service requests:

1.   Request for a laptop

2.   Request for open source software to be installed

3.   Request for an experience letter from the HR dept.

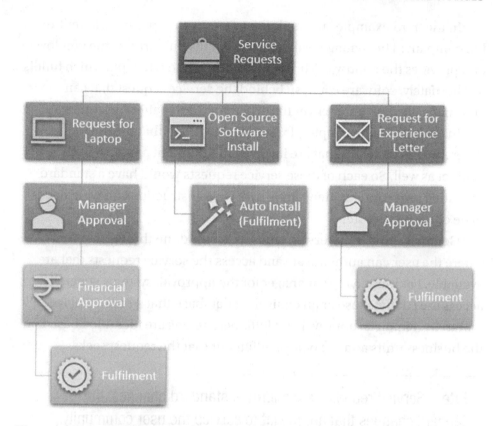

Figure 12-1. *Fulfilment of service requests*

Each of the service requests in this example follows a separate path. The laptop request has the most steps, as every request raised goes for a manager approval, and the next approval sought is a financial approval. Once the finance head clears the financial part of the request, the request goes to the team that allocates a laptop to the user.

In the next service request, open source software that is approved by a company for general installation by its users requires no approvals; in fact, it does not require any humans to fulfill it. As soon as the user requests it, it gets autoinstalled through preconfigured scripts and software that pushes the software to PCs.

In the third example, an employee requests an experience letter from the company. The manager validates the details put forth by the employee and provides the approval. The request flows to the HR dept., which fulfills it. Alternately, software could sit behind the service request that can automatically draft and deliver the experience letter after the approval.

In each of these examples, I wanted to highlight that the flow is different and the teams that are involved in fulfilment are most likely distinct as well. So each of these service requests would have a standard operating procedure written, along with clear instructions on what needs to be done at every step.

Generally, initiating service requests is best done through a portal where the user can authenticate and access the service requests that are available. For identifying a manager for the approval, systems generally access the HR database or an equivalent database that stores employee hierarchy. Financial approval and fulfilment teams are identified based on the business units and the type of fulfilment that the request seeks.

Note   Service requests are a form of standard changes: the standard changes that are meant to service the user community. For example, a standard change for installing a security patch on a server is generally categorized as a standard change, and a software installation on a laptop as a service request. In principle, both follow the same set of guidelines: predefined, well known, and almost zero impact.

Guidelines for Implementation

Service request management is meant to be a process that is straightforward. Unknowns are close to nil, and a mature practice ensures that the processes involved are streamlined and socialized with the user and fulfilment community. There are a few guidelines that are defined to ensure that the service request management practice is seamless, efficient, and effective:

1. A clear boundary must be drawn through applicable policies that define the length and breadth of service requests. In other words, there must be no confusion about what qualifies as a service request, what is an incident, and what is a change.

2. Every service request must be defined, and no shortcuts must be undertaken during the definitions phase.

3. The service catalog must be made available to all users, preferably on a portal for users to choose from. For each of the service requests, the service levels associated with it must be defined, as well as the number of hops (approvals, etc.) that are involved.

4. Service request flows must be standardized as much as possible unless certain service requests require special flows. For example, most of the service requests should be routed to the immediate manager for approval and not pick and choose managers, based on the service request type.

5. There must be a conscious and sincere attempt made toward automating all the service requests that do not require human intervention. The example that I shared earlier of an experience letter is an excellent candidate for automation.

6. The service request practice should come under the
    ambit of the Improve activity, where improvements
    can be introduced for increasing the effectiveness
    and efficiency of the practice.

Engagement with Service Value Chain

Table 12-1. *Service Request Management in SVC*

SVC Activity	Involvement	Details
Plan	None	There is no engagement of the practice in the plan activity, due to its transactional and operational nature.
Design and Transition	Medium	During transition, certain service assets could be moved into production on the back of a service request.
Obtain/Build	Medium	Service assets and components for the lower environments could be obtained through the service request management practice.
Engage	High	There is plenty of interaction between the practice and the user community in setting expectations and ensuring transparency of the hops and approvals.
Deliver and Support	High	A good chunk of service delivery comes from the service request management practice. The fulfilment of service requests is an inherent part of this activity.
Improve	Low	While service request management itself can go through the Improve churner, the practice is a medium for users to reach out to share complements, complaints, and improvement ideas. Many of these could be inputs to the Improve activity.

Change Control Practice

They say that change is the only constant. They also say that anything that does not grow withers away. This is so true in the IT industry. No matter how old the product or the service is, changes to it happen all the time. No matter how legacy the service is, it still needs to be maintained and made current to the organizational needs.

Changes are inevitable in any industry; therefore, the onus is on management. The question is not whether we make changes or not but rather how do we do it without impacting the product or service negatively.

It is also true that a majority of incidents are caused by mismanagement of changes. So, that is all the more reason that we need to tighten up the change management process to increase the overall uptime and reduce the number of outages.

The word *change* means quite a few things in several contexts; it could be changing seasons, changing clothes, or making changes to the furniture upholstery. From an ITIL perspective, a change revolves around services and pertains to changes to all things that make up a service.

ITIL Definition of Change

The addition, modification, or removal of anything that could have a direct or indirect effect on services.

A service is made up of various individual components; it could be servers, switches, software, middleware, mobile app, and networks. Changes done to any of these individual components or to the overall service itself constitute a change.

Note   Change control is a popular topic on the foundation exam. You should likely see a question pertaining to the definition of a change appearing on the ITIL foundation exam. The question will center on identifying the right definition from a list of choices. So, it is prudent for you to understand and memorize the definition in verbatim.

Here are some examples of changes:

- Implementation of fiber optic Internet service to the customer organization

- Transition of email services from Exchange to Gmail

- Decommissioning of mainframe computers

- Adding extra memory to servers

- Changing ownership of a core switch

- Adding an IP to a blacklist on firewall

- Modification of a batch job

- New version release of an iPhone app

- Upgrade of an enterprise application

Then there are other layers that make up a service, be it processes, governance, capability, or IT staff, among others. Changing any of these aspects indirectly affects a service, so in principle they can be considered changes; but the majority of organizations do not consider them as changes, or they manage these changes separately.

ITIL Definition of Change Control Practice

The purpose of the change control practice is to maximize the number of successful service and product changes by ensuring that risks have been properly assessed, authorizing changes to proceed, and managing the change schedule.

The change control practice exists solely to govern the changes to products and services. The objective of the governance is to ensure that the changes that go through are thoroughly vetted to ensure that all risks are known and mitigated, and to increase the probability of changes succeeding.

In IT as in life, nothing in guaranteed. So, any change proposed comes with associated risks. If an organization fears the effect of the risks and stops the changes in their tracks, then that organization will not improve their products and services and is doomed to fail. So, changes are necessary evils, and the art of change control is to control the changes to ensure that the beneficial aspects are amplified while minimizing risks through adequate mitigation actions.

For example, a bank's online banking application has been upgraded using newer technologies and features. With over ten million customers, when the new application takes the incumbent's place, any risk would have a profound effect. So how does the change control practice ensure that the risks are minimized? There are several options; one common option is to use a technique called canary testing. We release the application in parallel with the old application but for certain users only; say about 100 users agree to use the new version instead of the old. The new application gets used by its limited users and the chinks in the armor are detected and dealt with, before releasing the application to its entire user community.

The change control practice does not perform any of the technical activities, nor does it manage the technical activities. They are the gatekeepers of changes going into products and services. They ensure that adequate controls are in place, and when they are satisfied with the tests, approvals, and mitigations, they authorize changes to be implemented.

Scope of Change Control

ITIL per se does not specify the boundaries under which the change control practice is triggered for governing changes in the system. The actual scope definition depends on the service provider, the customer, and the suppliers.

An IT service can have multiple elements, including making use of the supplier's network and data, among other dependencies. It is managed by IT professionals, and the service documentation also is critical. Does changing any of these peripheral components call in a change? Yes, but it depends on the agreement between the service provider and customer organization. Managing more items requires more time and resources, which adds to expenses. If the customer wants to have absolute control over the IT services, then yes, every single element that makes up a service must come into the purview of change control. In the real world, this is often not the case, owing to the financials. Many of the indirect components are ignored in the interests of reducing expenses, and some companies find innovative ways of controlling the peripheral objects using standard changes and service requests.

From my experience, there is much more to change control than addition, removal, and modification of IT services. Take the example of running an ad hoc report. You are not adding, removing, or modifying anything, just reading data from the database. Yet, you possess the power in your hands to break systems with the wrong set of queries that goes searching in each and every table, that utilizes the infrastructure's resources, and could potentially cause performance issues to the IT service. In this case, if you bring this through to change management, they can possibly identify the resource-consuming queries and shelve them or schedule them to be run during off-peak hours.

To define scope, ITIL takes a holistic approach to define what can be categorized as a change. It scopes changes based on the following aspects of design:

1. New or modified services, where functional requirements are changing, translating to resources and capabilities

2. Management information systems (reporting and communication) and tools

3. Technology and management architecture

4. Policies, processes, and components derived from processes, such as templates, guidelines, etc.

5. Measurement systems, metrics, key performance indicators (KPIs), and associated methodologies

---

Note   The biggest success for a service provider comes from its scope definition of change control. And the best way is to synchronize the business goals and objectives with the services, and that to the scope of change control. What drives a customer and what is most critical to a customer need to be governed with utmost scrutiny. If the change control practice can do it, then the major battles would have been won.

Types of Changes

One size does not fit all the changes that happen in services. They come in all shapes and sizes. Therefore, you cannot use the same yardstick for all changes. You need a different set of protocols, policies, and processes to handle various types of changes. Say, for example, you trip over a water pipe and hurt your shoulder. You go to the hospital, and a doctor tends to you and does what is necessary with minimum fuss. Instead, if you were in a car wreck that required stitching you up and putting some dislodged organs back in their place, this process will require an operation, surgeons, an anesthesiologist, and nurses among others to be present, to ensure you survive and the operation is a success. Between the two instances, the processes carried out are expectedly different. One instance requires a host of professionals, utmost care, and some amount of planning, while the other can be done as and when needed with a basic medical skill set.

For the trip-over patient, you do not need to assemble surgeons and others. Likewise, in change management, some changes need to be done with proper attention, planning, and care, while others can be carried out with minimum scrutiny.

In ITIL, there are three major types:

- Normal changes
- Emergency changes
- Standard changes

Note   For your organization, you can define as many types of changes as you need. ITIL is not prescriptive, so the types of changes serve at best as a guideline. I once worked for an organization that had a fourth type called an urgent change that was placed between a normal change and an emergency change

---

Normal Changes

Let's say that a patient is ailing from a heart problem and needs to have open-heart surgery. The doctors and surgeons involved carefully and meticulously make all the plans, reserve the facilities, and then carry out the procedure. These are planned surgeries, and in the change control world, such changes that are planned in advance are called normal changes.

Most changes in any organization are normal changes, as no organization wants to make changes without proper plans in place. Such changes are often lengthy because of the planning sessions, stakeholder visibility, and approvals, and to ensure that all the dependencies are managed. In other words, they follow the entire process, which includes authorization, reviews, and scheduling.

Normal changes are generally associated with all the bells and whistles of the change control practice and are often well analyzed, tested, mitigated, and verified. The maturity of an organization's change control practice is often measured through the normal change process, and the metrics and KPIs associated with it.

Normal changes will be associated with a priority to help focus on changes with maximum risk over others. For example, refreshing an Internet banking application will be a major change that would require the highest levels of reviews and assessments. Authorization will change authority and other dependent teams along with the customer organization review and approvals. Conversely, changing a configuration on an application to change a field from nonmandatory to mandatory will be done briskly with minimal stakeholder approvals.

Examples of normal changes include an application refresh to a newer version, a server migration from in-house to a cloud service provider, and the decommissioning of mainframe applications and servers.

All normal changes have to be registered; this is called a change request. They are logged on an ITSM tool such as ServiceNow. Then they go through the steps of prioritization, and based on the prioritization, the amount of scrutiny is decided. In the case of application of continuous deployment in a DevOps project, a single change request will be raised giving high level overview of the kind of changes that will be performed over a period. So in essence, for every change performed, there will be no new change raised. This will differ when the change is major.

Every type of a normal change can be further broken down based on the technology involved, personnel, customer requirements, and change management policies. For example, the steps involved in introducing a software upgrade and replacement of a hard disk are different. A single standardized process to incorporate all types of changes, irrespective of the technology involved, will not present the best that the change control practice can offer. So it is necessary, in the interests of the service provider to improve delivery, to create change models for different types of changes. Let's consider an example of a change model for a software upgrade and for a hard disk replacement, as indicated in Figure 12-2.

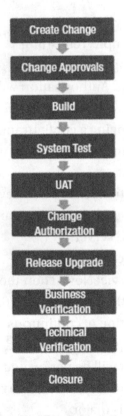

Change Model for Software Upgrade

Change Model for Hard Disk Replacement

Figure 12-2. *Change model*

A change model is a repeatable way of dealing with a particular category of change. A change model defines specific agreed-upon steps that will be followed for a change of this category.

Not all organizations opt for change models. They run with change control processes that are standard for all technologies, teams, and customers. This has its limitations, although the concept of standardizing sounds good on paper. Tailoring the process through change models helps improve delivery and provides better control and governance of changes. Every change model must contain the following:

- Individual steps for processing changes, including mitigation and risks

- Identifying dependencies and chronology of change activities

- Identifying responsibilities and accountabilities (basically RACI [responsible, accountable, consulted, and informed]) for individual activities

- Relating SLAs and KPIs for every activity

- Escalation matrix associated with the process

Emergency Changes

During his REM sleep, a man clutches his chest in pain and starts to sweat. An ambulance is called, and he is transported swiftly to a nearby hospital. The doctors diagnose a series of heart attacks that were caused by a blockage in his heart. They don't have the time to plan a surgery but rather need to do it right away if the patient is to survive. So, with minimum planning, they carry out the surgery. Such changes that are done during such firefighting exercises are called emergency changes in the change control practice.

Emergency changes are necessary to urgently fix an ongoing issue or a crisis. These changes are mostly carried out as a resolution to a major incident. The nature of such changes requires swift action, whether it is getting the necessary approvals or the testing that is involved. Generally, emergency changes are not thoroughly pretested, as the time availability is minimal. In some cases they may go through without any testing, although this is not recommended even for an emergency change. As much as possible, it is recommended that emergency changes go through the same level of scrutiny as normal changes but on an expedited schedule. However, the documentation portion of the change can be done retrospectively, and some shortcuts in testing are undertaken to restore services at the earliest.

The success of emergency changes reflects the agility of an organization and the change control practice to act on disruptions in a time-constrained environment. and to come out unscathed in the eyes of the customer and your competition.

Emergency change control practice supports the incident management practice in the resolution of incidents, especially major ones. Emergency changes are generally frowned upon and are not preferred. The number of such changes in an organization reflects poorly on the organization's stability of the services it offers.

Examples of emergency changes are the replacement of hardware infrastructure and restoring customer data from backup volumes.

To manage emergency changes, it is possible that a separate governing authority is put in place that works closely with the operations team, and this governing authority is available round the clock.

Standard Changes

A patient with failed kidneys gets dialysis done multiple times a week. The process for carrying out a dialysis procedure is well known and rarely can it go south. Most patients set up dialysis treatments at home and do them fairly regularly. The risks involved are low, and if something goes wrong, the impact too is on the lower end of the spectrum because there are multiple workarounds available. Such changes for IT services that pose no danger to services and are low key are referred to as standard changes.

Standard changes are normal changes that are of low risk and low impact in nature. The categorization of changes as standard is at the discretion of the service provider and customer organizations. These types of changes are well understood, thoroughly assessed, and documented in detail. They are preapproved changes: not every single change but the type of changes. For example, if we consider blacklisting an IP address as a standard change, the action of blacklisting IPs is authorized. Then every time a new IP address is identified for blacklisting, the team involved simply raises a standard change and blacklists the IP without having to seek approvals.

Under service request management practice, I talked about service requests as being a type of standard changes. Service providers often take the route of service requests when dealing with individuals, and standard changes while dealing with service level changes.

Standard changes have distinct advantages and create value for customers. They follow a process that is less stringent and is free from the multiple approvals and lead times that are often associated with normal changes. This provides the service provider with the arsenal needed to implement changes on the fly, which increases productivity and also helps deliver better value to the customer.

Examples of standard changes include minor patch upgrades, database reindexing, and blacklisting IPs on firewalls.

It is believed that the maturity of the service management process of organizations offering services can be determined based on the number of standard changes in the system. That's true, as standard changes present a system to segregate difficult changes from the usual ones. The commonly performed changes are like a well-oiled machine. It operates smoothly and can be relied upon in most circumstances. Around 60 percent to 70 percent of the changes in any organization are common, repeatable, and straightforward. If all these changes are standardized, imagine the number of approvals that don't have to be sought and the number of meetings, telephone calls, and waiting around that can be skipped.

The advantage with standard changes is such that in most situations it can be done on the back of any defined trigger. When a team wants to perform a standard change, they don't have to go to the change management team or to the change authority for authorization to present their change. They simply log a standard change in the system (yes, records are an absolute necessity), and then they can carry it out. Once it is successfully implemented (which is expected), the change is closed. Voila! There's no need to do any post-change reviews.

Examples of standard changes can be anything and everything under the IT sun that is repetitive in nature and does not pose major risks. That sounds like every single deployment we do under DevOps, doesn't it? Do you now see the connection between standard changes and DevOps? Typical examples include installing security patches on operating systems, running batch jobs, and performing nonintrusive backups.

Championing Standard Changes

I started my career as a service management consultant, and over the years, I earned the reputation of creating value for my clients through my designs and improvements. Implementing standard changes was one of my secret weapons. These are the first things I look at during an assessment:

Does a robust change control practice exist?

Are there provisions for standard changes?

How many changes are implemented as standard changes?

Are standard changes monitored and audited regularly?

Standard changes are the low-hanging value creation fruit for clients. Most service management experts and consultants have yet to come to grips with it, and that hurts their clients' chances of making a difference through service management.

When I worked as an enterprise change manager for a retail organization in Sydney, Australia, I noticed that the organization did not have an active standard change process. A team of change managers reviewed and processed anywhere between 150 and 200 changes each day. They knew the changes so well that by reading the change summary, they would just scroll down to where the approval task became visible and hit Approve.

What struck me first was why this human effort was even required, as it amounted to a process to be followed rather than any visible value through the additional pair of eyes. I got down to work by pulling data for the past couple of years and identifying such changes that could potentially be categorized as standard changes. I did some arithmetic and some guesswork to crunch some numbers, and according to my analysis, the organization could save anywhere between 25 hours and 40 hours every single day. I considered modest numbers for my calculations, and this was the minimum savings that the organization could do, based on 200 hours of weekly savings and the average wages for a week typically in Australia being about $2,500 ($12,500 for the 200 hours saved). This saving translates to a monthly savings of around $50,000 ($12,500 × 4 weeks). Out of nowhere, the company could save over half a million every year, and they jumped on it, not without a number of warnings from the company old-timers.

I managed to convert about 60 percent of the overall changes into standard changes within 4 months, and the benefits showcased the power of Agile and DevOps. A number of business people in this organization were relieved not to have to worry about getting approvals for all their changes. The best part was that they did not have to bundle their changes into releases, so the changes went quickly to production and provided maximum benefits to the business.

Change Advisory

The change control practice alone may not have the necessary skills to judge changes on their merit. So, a body called change authority is set up to advise the change control practice on the risks posed by the change. They have the power to authorize changes for implementation or reject them, and the change control practice usually considers their judgment.

The change authority can be described as an extension of the change management role, and it exists to ensure that the proposed changes are nondisruptive, scheduled to minimize conflicts, prioritized based on risk and impact, and analyzed for every possible outcome to the hilt.

Earlier, an organization consisted of the change authority, which was dynamic in nature, but since the change control was central, the change authority too operated centrally. Today, in the swift decision-making world, having a single change authority is a bottleneck to speedy turnaround. Therefore, it is quite common to decentralize the process of change approvals through local change authorities. For example, an application portfolio may have its own change authority, and cloud infrastructure could have its own decentralized change approval system in place. This helps in moving ahead quickly and also to have decision makers who know the system, such as product and service owners. The primary change control or the policy making body could still be central, which can impose change freezes and other enterprise-wide policies and processes such as processes to define standard changes.

In a typical change authority meeting, a change representative (usually the technical lead) presents the change. Based on the presentation, the committee might choose to seek clarifications; ask questions; and approve, defer, or reject the change—purely based on the merit.

Note   In ITIL V3, the change authority was referred to as the change advisory board (CAB). Both the change authority and the CAB are the same in principle and spirit; they only differ by name.

Change Schedule

The definition of the change control practice talks about a change schedule, which is an important terminology in the change control practice. A change schedule refers to a change calendar that consists of the changes that are in the pipeline, approved upcoming changes, and the changes that are implemented. Look at it through the eyes of a calendar. We use our calendars to plan the day, propose new slots for conflicting meetings, and delegate people to certain important meetings that we cannot make. Likewise, a change schedule is used for planning of the changes, especially where dependencies exist between one change and another; assigning resources to oversee and implement changes; and communicating to appropriate stakeholders on the change lifecycle. Conflicts in changes are quite common, and a calendar (change schedule) helps in identifying and mitigating them.

Other practices also leverage the change schedule. For example, the incident management practice uses the information to identify the changes that have been implemented, to identify the source of a cluster of incidents. That helps in identifying the cause of an incident and resolving it swiftly. Problem management too could use this information to identify the root cause of problems. The change schedule could be seen from the upcoming changes perspective as well, to identify the product bugs that are getting fixed. The applications of a change schedule are endless. It is important that an organization maintain a centralized change schedule to help identify conflicts and dependencies effectively.

Note   In ITIL V3, change schedule was referred to as forward schedule of changes (FSC). Both the change schedule and the FSC are the same in principle and spirit, and only differ by name.

Engagement with Service Value Chain

Table 12-2. *Change Control Practice in SVC*

SVC Activity	Involvement	Details
Plan	Low	Making changes to plans—and its derivatives such as policies, processes, and frameworks—is governed by the change control practice.
Design and Transition	High	When there are design changes to products and services, or when new products and services are introduced, changes are created to bring them into production. The majority of the change transition activity is run on the back of a change ticket.
Obtain/Build	High	Products and services that are developed go through the change control practice to become operational.
Engage	Low	Some changes may call for an engagement of customers, suppliers, or users in providing oversight for changes or taking a place in the change authority.

(continued)

Table 12-2. (*continued*)

SVC Activity	Involvement	Details
Deliver and Support	High	It is no secret that changes are one of the primary sources of incidents, leading to increased deliver and support activity. And resolution of incidents and problems piggybacks on change control for implementation.
Improve	High	Improvements that are recommended go through the change control practice for vetting against risks and to weigh the benefits against the depth of changes being introduced.

Knowledge Check

The answers are provided in Appendix.

12-1. Which of the following is the correct *change* definition?

A. Any change of state that is significant for a service or product or related configuration item

B. The addition, modification, or removal of anything that could have a direct or indirect effect on services

C. Any change of state for configuration items that correlates risks and issues to the service and service management processes

D. Any change that has significance for the management of a service or other additions, removals, and modifications

12-2. Why should incidents and service requests be treated separately?

    A. Incidents are raised by monitoring tools and service requests by users, so the levels of service are different and therefore need to be treated differently.

    B. Incidents are service disruptions, and service requests are additional requests. So, in order to avoid further service disruption, incidents should be prioritized over service requests.

    C. Loss of service requests result in incidents being raised. So service requests need to be given priority.

    D. Incidents and service requests should not be treated differently. Both provide inconvenience to the end users, so it is paramount that both of them be resolved at a quick pace.

12-3. The service request management practice exists for this reason:

    A. To support the provisioning of services through the change control practice

    B. To ensure that the services are restored to the end user to support in increasing the end user's productivity and effectiveness

    C. To support the agreed quality of a service by handling all predefined, user-initiated service requests

    D. To provide an overarching framework for managing service requests and standard changes that are predefined and established

12-4. Which of the following is not a valid type of a change as per ITIL?

A. Urgent change

B. Normal change

C. Standard change

D. Emergency change

12-5. What is the primary role of change authority?

A. Advise the change control practice on the risks posed by the change

B. Approve or reject changes based on the change schedule

C. Authorize standard changes that are due for implementation

D. Provide recommendations to the change control practice for creating change requests

12-6. What does a change schedule consist of?

A. Approved changes

B. Approved and pipeline changes

C. Approved and rejected changes

D. Standard and emergency changes

CHAPTER 13

Practices to Manage Releases

The cycle generally starts with the design, followed by build, test, and transition. Transition activities involve the management of moving a built object into production. Before this can happen, there needs to be a streamlined process to manage the movement of packages from the lower to higher environments. There should be precise policies, principles, and processes that guide the releases to ensure that the activity does not become an ambiguous chaotic method. While these represent half the story, there is the technical aspect of moving the packages: the methods we use to deploy to minimize risks and maximize predictability.

In the waterfall world, releases and deployments happened very few times, and the periods were defined in blood and followed to the hilt. So the onus of a process to drive it, procedures to deploy, and the means of deployment were not as significant as the process of development and testing.

© Abhinav Krishna Kaiser 2021
A. K. Kaiser, *Become ITIL® 4 Foundation Certified in 7 Days*,
https://doi.org/10.1007/978-1-4842-6361-7_13

Today in the DevOps industry, things are not what they used to be. The final production units of releases and deploys have become one of the pillars of development and operations. They happen all the time, and without human supervision as was the case earlier. So, it is imperative to tighten the processes and rein in the activities through automation to allow the two sets of activities to be seamless and not act as blockers, because in DevOps, speed is everything. And blockers/impediments are meant to be bulldozed one way or the other. This is an important topic from DevOps, Agile, and ITIL perspectives.

This chapter covers two practices:

- Release management

- Deployment management

Note   In ITIL V3, release and deployment management practices were combined into a single process. In ITIL 4 the context has changed, and the world has become more digital, with a lot more releases and deployments. So, it makes full sense that there are dedicated practices to give both the topics the due respect they command.

Although ITIL does not specify that in-depth knowledge is necessary from an examination standpoint, I shall dig deep because they are critical pieces from whichever industry you consider and look at them from. I will ensure that you get a good grip on both practices.

Exam Tip   You can expect about one or two questions on the ITIL Foundation exam from the release and deployment practices. You will be tested on your cursory understanding of the topics.

Release Management

Release management is a practice that is common to both the development and operations activities of a program. In other words, you do releases for items that are enhancements and you do releases for break-fixes as well, especially those that aren't urgent.

Before I get into what the release management practice does, let us take a closer examination of the term *release*.

ITIL Definition of a Release

A version of a service or other configuration item, or a collection of configuration items, that is made available for use.

The definition might sound cryptic but it will not after I explain it.

The enhancements or a new product or service that is being introduced get developed in a lower environment such as a development environment. The access to it would sit with the developers alone. After completing the development and unit testing it, developers promote it to a higher environment, say, a test environment. A test environment is accessed by the testing teams that perform testing against the functional requirements (and technical design). Testing could be done by humans (manual) or by machines (automation). If tests are satisfactory, then the developed software is moved to the next higher environment, say, the acceptance testing environment where users perform testing similar to what the testers did in the testing environment. If all is well, the software is packaged as a release; on a preset and agreed date, it is moved to the highest environment, which is production. This movement to production is referred to as a release. In the release, you might have just this software, or a few software pieces clubbed together, and often packaged along with nonurgent incident fixes as well. When the release goes into production, the released software is available for general use, which is generally access controlled. I considered an example here of a software, but it is quite likely that along with the software there could be hardware changes going in as well; maybe enhanced processor capacity or a set of servers being load balanced. So it is important to imagine a release as a package that could contain software enhancements, new service introductions, break-fixes, and hardware changes. It's a package where a number of changes go into the system during the same window, referred to as a change window.

Why are we pushing a number of such changes at once in a package, you might ask? Isn't it likely to fail or act as a massive point of failure? In most industries, the business prefers that the production be untouched with changes for the most part. This gives the business a sense of stability and in some cases, given the sensitivity of the business, they are right in setting such expectations. Therefore, to reduce the number of touchpoints or the number of times changes are introduced into production, releases are designed to be done maybe once a month, which is most popular, or at least once a quarter.

ITIL Definition of Release Management Practice

The purpose of the release management practice is to make new and changed services and features available for use.

Change Control vs. Release Management

I have conducted several trainings in a classroom setting and online as well. The most asked question when I start talking of release management is this: what is the difference between change control and release management? It seems that what the change control practice does is the same as the release management; that is what I get asked about. This section is dedicated to those questioners. In this section, I will not differentiate between release and deployment management practices as the story drawing a thin line between change and release is straightforward if release and deployments are considered together.

In the illustration in Figure 13-1, I have considered a simple process starting from requirement gathering until production deployment. All the process activities have been segregated as either change control or release management. Although some activities like requirement gathering are considered as a part of business analysis, in software development they come under a common umbrella of release management—to ensure seamless flow between requirements to production deployment.

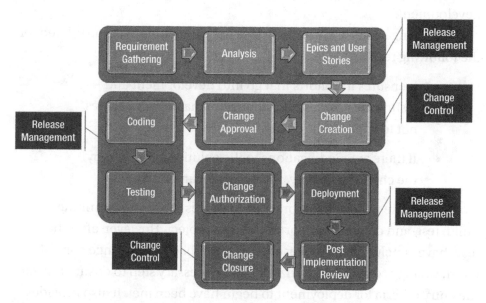

Figure 13-1. *Change control vs. release management*

Change control is a process that is responsible for obtaining all approvals and authorizations from relevant stakeholders and controlling what changes go in. The release management practice, on the other hand, deals with the management of technicalities of the changes. For example, let's say that a change has been raised to deploy a new version of the software. The change control process exists to put the change in front of the jury (change authority) and to help obtain approvals and authorizations so that the change can be deployed seamlessly. The release management practice manages the requirement gathering, coding, testing, and deployment activities of this change.

The change control and release management practices work closely together, exchanging information from related activities during various activities, as showcased in Figure 13-1. Setting the scope, creating a plan, and gathering the requirements all come under the auspices of release management. Once there is a plan in place, including the known dependencies and impacts, the change control people do their bit of formal vetting and approval before giving the go-ahead to begin development.

The change control approval before the development is considered for the following reasons:

- It ensures the efforts that go into development and testing are not wasted if change management decides not to approve the changes.

- If there are modifications to the solution proposed by the change authority, then rework can be avoided.

The release management practice manages the overall planning, build, test, and deployment portions of the project. However, after the tests have concluded, the release status is put back into change control's court. Change control's authorization is a necessary step to ensure that all the entry criteria for deployment to begin have been met. It also provides oversight before changes to production are set to begin.

The deployment and postimplementation review activities are owned by the release management process, and the results are duly reported to change management for change closures with the appropriate status.

In this sample process, the release has been ping-ponged between release and change control practices at least six times. It can go higher; the higher the number of exchanges, the better it is for ensuring the quality of governance and sharing accountabilities.

Release Fundamentals

I have broken down release fundamentals into chunks for ease of understanding.

Release Components

As discussed earlier, releases include both hardware and software components that go into production. Well, that is not all. As a part of the release, there are other components that need to be refreshed as well. Training, for example, is a critical aspect. If certain functionalities of the software are changing, then the end users need to be trained before the release, the documentation needs to be updated inline with the enhancements and new services, and accesses may need to be sorted. This list is different for every application that is going through the release cycle.

Not all release components come from the service provider alone. Third parties at times provide packages or components that can go into the release. An example could be a package that is needed for an existing integration to work in the upcoming versions of the third-party software that integrates with the service provider managed application. Not only third party but COTS and open source products making it to the release is possible as well.

The scope of release management therefore is spread as far and wide as the service stretches; they need to look at risks coming from third-party systems, the infrastructure that hosts the software, and all components of the service.

Types of Releases

Releases come in various sizes and cycles. You may be making a small change to a functionality that is almost harmless, or you could be refreshing software including its architecture. Or you may be moving your software components from an on-premises infrastructure to cloud, which is quite impactful if things were to go south. Or you could be making changes to a middleware, which could potentially impact 20 applications that are feeding off of it.

Examples of release types are minor releases, major releases, and emergency releases.

Major Releases

Major upgrades to software generally come under major releases. The business impact of major releases can be anywhere between high and critical. This type of a release is the mother of all releases and takes priority if there is going to be a minor release happening at about the same time. A number of resources are usually dedicated to the building and executing of a release, and from a compliance angle, all the hawks should watch it with extra attention.

In my experience, major releases are few and far between. In most cases, they are done on an ad hoc basis, with some organizations deploying at least four major releases in a year. For example, you might notice the updates being applied to the Windows operating system. Some changes are quick and may not even demand a restart. However, additions, modifications, or the removal of integral features happen on the back of major releases that could require several minutes of installation followed by multiple restarts.

Minor Releases

As the word minor suggests, minor releases include release units that are small and do not usually bring down the business if the release goes south.

Minor releases are usually carried out as often as a weekly basis or as late as monthly. It all depends on the number of changes that are getting pumped in and the number of resources available to work on them.

Emergency Releases

Emergency releases are the planning and execution counterparts of the emergency changes. They come into play on the back of an emergency change and are deployed (usually) to fix an incident and to avert negative business impact.

The number of emergency releases reflects negatively on the organization and the project. Therefore, this is a type of release that's not preferred or planned but rather gets imposed by the turn of events. It is also not uncommon that the release policy allows emergency changes to be helicoptered in only between releases, say, between two minor releases.

Release Schedule

Releases normally have a period associated with them. If they're not, or if they are carried as and when needed, these releases are referred to as ad hoc releases. At times, to put in a break-fix that has a major impact, unscheduled releases are made. These are done on the back of emergency changes and are referred to as emergency releases. Then there are scheduled ones, which could be daily, weekly, monthly, quarterly, half-yearly, yearly, and so on. Daily, half-yearly, and yearly are quite rare. Even the other periodic releases may have a theme associated with them, like weekly releases for security patches, monthly for configuration changes, and quarterly for major changes.

All these periodic releases are soon to go out the window with DevOps taking over. In DevOps, releases will be done in a modular fashion and as and when the testing of the piece of functionality is completed. Nobody is going to wait to assemble the pieces for a fine sunny morning. It gets pushed to production as it gets fully tested.

We looked at the change schedule in the last chapter, which consisted of all the changes that are in the pipeline and in approved status. A release schedule also exists that is similar in nature but contains all the releases that are in place. It's a schedule that has a visibility between a customer and a service provider. The common practice is for the customer and the service provider to discuss and come to an agreement on what a release schedule will look like, and to chart out the dates along with the themes. A release schedule for the entire calendar year can be published in the final quarter of the previous year. This gives a semblance of predictability for the business on when the releases are expected, and when the enhancements and other changes are due to go in.

Release Reviews

Releases and changes are similar. Like a postimplementation review for a change, a similar exercise called a release implementation review is conducted after every major release. The objectives are to understand how things played out and to identify missteps, and subsequently the lessons learned from the release. This will help better the upcoming releases, and takes the service provider a notch above in the maturity scale.

Waterfall vs. Agile/DevOps

Let me explain how releases work in a waterfall project, compared with a project that is run in Agile/DevOps mode.

Consider there are three features that are to be developed. In a waterfall approach, all the three features are developed first, then tested, and then deployed/released into production.

If the same project was to be executed in an Agile/DevOps fashion, the development, testing, and deployment of the three features are done iteratively. If the release plan demands that the three features be deployed to production in a single release, then each of the features are independently deployed into lower environments, packaged, and released all at once to production.

The waterfall vs. Agile/DevOps approaches are illustrated in Figure 13-2.

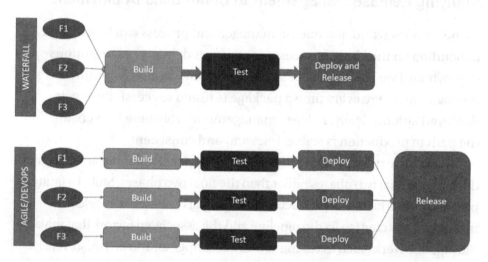

Figure 13-2. *Waterfall vs. Agile/DevOps releases*

Release Management in Agile/DevOps

In Agile/DevOps projects, release management has not been completely transformed. It has become stronger through iterations. The activities in release management are now viewed by a different lens that's ready to accept the facts based on the things at hand, rather than foretelling the future.

Using Agile Release Trains

The range of planning that we have started to do under releases is not limited to a sprint alone, which is the Agile/Scrum way of working. However, using the SAFe framework and applying release management to Agile release trains (ARTs) gives us a steady plan for the upcoming 10 to 12 weeks. The entire ART represents a release with software packages pouring in every couple of weeks at the end of each sprint. When we put the sprints together along with their outcomes, the end product is the release package.

Applying Release Management to Continuous Deployment

In the DevOps world, the release management process can be adapted depending on the kind of process (continuous delivery or continuous deployment) we leverage. Let's say that we plan to employ continuous deployment where every time a package is tested successfully, it gets deployed automatically. Release management's role here is to ensure that the path to production is stable, relevant, and consistent.

The release management process will have a lot of planning and execution during the initial two phases rather than the final two phases. Still, if a faulty package makes its way to production, the ball falls back into the release management's court to fix the pipeline and the associated factors that make the pipeline work (such as testing scenarios, scripts, and so on). Also, release management has to identify multiple release windows for the deployments to take place because the possibility of deployments happening multiple times a day is routine in a continuous deployment process.

Applying Release Management to Continuous Delivery

In continuous delivery, however, sanity can be maintained to a certain extent. The release management process becomes bimodal, with release planning and builds/tests using the iteration model, and deployments and reviews taking the traditional sequential approach.

The plan for continuous delivery works well with ART, with the planning exercise being done once every 12 weeks and refined as the sprints go along. The sprints are executed in iterations with the software packages, getting them to a state of readiness but not getting deployed. When all the pieces of the release are developed and integrated, the deployment happens (sequential) followed by a review of the release.

Most organizations will tend to go with this approach, mainly because it gives people in charge a sense of control. Since continuous delivery still commands a manual trigger before deployment, the decision makers feel comfortable in opting for a process that not only accelerates production but also awaits a formal order before hitting production.

Maturity is leading the way toward continuous deployment. The decision makers, after a few releases, will realize that their decisions have always been backed by the figures, that the releases put forth in front of them have always been good for production, and that their decisions have become just a formality. So, the end game will always be with continuous deployment.

Release Management Techniques

Although in DevOps we intend to be brave and encourage experimentation, the core principle of reducing risks for existing services is not sacrificed. While we make rapid changes to the service, the software, the hardware, and other pieces of the services that users enjoy, the transition to the upgraded service should be as seamless as possible. To achieve this, we leverage a few techniques that help us mitigate the risks that come with making changes to stable environments.

Proof of Concept and Pilot

While making major changes to a product or a service, we first test the waters by carrying out a proof of concept (POC). The purpose of a POC is to prove that the path you are embarking on does work and to avoid progressing too far ahead with development and testing, only to find out that the end result you are trying to achieve is not possible. POCs are generally carried out if you are making architectural changes, technology changes, and introducing new concepts.

For example, a bank moving from mainframe technology to a SAP-based technology for running their banking engines would like to see some critical transactions demonstrated on a SAP platform before they can give their go-ahead for full blown development. If you are introducing test automation on a product, you probably would like to see if it works through a POC before start making a full-fledged journey. Likewise, changes that are transformational in nature could take the POC route to give the sponsors confidence that the solution does indeed work.

Well, POC is just half the battle in convincing the sponsors and other stakeholders that a particular solution does work. After the success of a POC, stakeholders often initiate the next phase of development, called the pilot phase, and not full blown development.

A pilot is the next step in the development process after POC, where the idea is to take a piece of the functionality, develop and test it, and run it against real data. A successful outcome further proves that the path taken indeed does work. The pilot release testers will be limited; call them a private group who test the developed functionality and give their feedback.

Note   Do not get confused between pilot and beta releases. Both are different. In a pilot release, you only develop a small piece of functionality to prove that the overall solution will follow suit. A beta release is generally buggy, meaning the testing and fixing is still in flight. A beta release will consist of either the entire solution or a solution that is reaching completion.

Blue–Green Release

Seeking downtime for releases is a thing of the past. In DevOps projects, carrying out deployments without downtime is the norm, and release management must do this at a minimum. There are a number of ways the process could achieve this. One such example is the blue-green deployment approach, where two environments are run in parallel (each of the environments is designated with the color blue or green). Figure 13-3 illustrates the blue-green release approach.

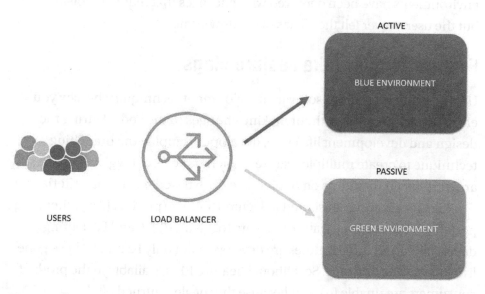

Figure 13-3.   Blue-green release approach

We have two parallel environments, designated as blue and green. Both the environments are identical; however, one of them is active and the other passive. In this example, let's say that the blue environment is active and the green is passive. This refers to the load balancer routing all the user requests only to the blue environment and not to the green environment.

Let's say that we have a release on hand that requires mandatory downtime to install and configure packages, followed by elongated sanity reviews. In this scenario, the passive node (green) gets deployed first. As there are no user requests getting routed, there is no question of seeking downtime. The users continue to operate normally in the blue environment. When the deployment is successful and the environment is production ready, the load balancer routes all the user requests to the green environment. While users are busy operating in the green environment, the blue environment goes down, gets deployed, and becomes production ready. The load balancer can either be set back to blue or be shared between green and blue; this is a decision of the architects. Voila! Both the environments have been deployed with packages that required downtime, but the users never felt the effects of the downtime.

Feature Toggles (aka Feature Flags)

Using feature toggles is a software development technique whereby you effect feature changes without making changes to the code. During the design and development life cycle, developers employ the branching technique to create multiple feature branches. Feature toggles (switches) are introduced that turns on or off the feature based on certain criteria.

Take the example illustrated in Figure 13-4. The product (say a shopping portal) consists of three features that are toggled: F1, F2, and F3. During development, all three features are developed but only F2 and F3 have gone live for users to consume. So, although feature F1 is available in the product, consumers are unable to use it because the toggle is turned off.

Come December when Christmas shopping sets in, feature F1, which is designed to introduce certain promotions to attract buyers, is activated (i.e., toggle turned on). Users will be able to see feature F1 in action. All these feature changes were introduced without making code changes; all that was done was changes to the toggle switches through a configuration file.

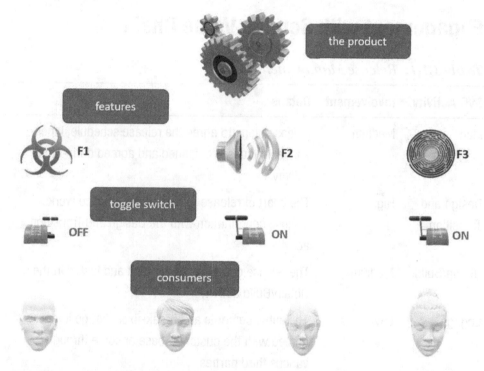

Figure 13-4. *Feature toggles illustration*

Use of feature toggles is an effective technique to minimize the risks that are introduced due to changes being introduced in the system. Imagine that during the Christmas shopping time, you make a code change and a bug in the system brings down the entire portal for 20 minutes. The downtime results in losses to revenue and portal reputation. To avoid such misadventures, feature toggles are introduced well ahead of time and, as and when they're needed, are turned on and off.

This is not the only application of feature toggles. You can segregate your user community based on various criteria, be it the level of service that is subscribed, geography, etc. Using feature toggles, users in the UK get features F1 and F2, users in the United States get F2 and F3, and users in India can enjoy all the features (F1, F2, and F3), for example.

Engagement with Service Value Chain

Table 13-1. *Release Management in SVC*

SVC Activity	Involvement	Details
Plan	Medium	Release plans to agree the release schedule, types, and techniques are defined and agreed during this activity.
Design and Transition	High	The heart of release management practice works in close coordination with the Design and Transition activity.
Obtain/Build	Medium	The release components are built and tested in the Obtain/Build activity.
Engage	Low	The enhancements and break-fixes that go in are agreed with the customer base or come through various third parties.
Deliver and Support	Medium	Releases change the existing service, and this requires updated documentation, training, and new methods of providing support. Release management practice provides the required artifacts and knowledge needed for support.
Improve	Low	Improvement items also go through the cycle of design, build, and release.

Deployment Management

Deployment management is one of the three technical management practices. It is a new practice from the ITIL perspective, or an accurate expression would be that deployment management was clubbed with the release management in ITIL V3.

ITIL Definition of Deployment Management Practice

The purpose of the deployment management practice is to move new or changed hardware, software, documentation, processes, or any other component to live environments. It may also be involved in deploying components to other environments for testing or staging.

The practice exists to provide guidance around deployments. A general misunderstanding is that deployments refer to moving packages to the production environment alone. However, it is not true. Moving software packages to any of the lower environments as well are deployments. Deployment essentially means movement from point A to point B. The point A is most likely an artifact repository and point B could be any of the environments that are under the scope of the deployment management practice.

Also, deployments are generally referred to as software package movement to environments. From the ITIL 4 point of view, deployment of infrastructure also comes under the practice's purview. Deployment of infrastructure is an infrastructure-based activity, so how does it relate to moving from one place to another, you might ask. Today, most of the infrastructure in vogue is in the cloud, and provisioning infrastructure is generally a coding exercise. Using a code (referred to as Infrastructure as Code), infrastructure can be built in the cloud. So you are basically moving the resources from a generic pool to a specific pool and provisioning dedicated infrastructure for a dedicated use. This is essentially deployment of infrastructure, hence its inclusion in the ITIL 4's scope under the deployment management practice.

To reiterate, the scope of the deployment management practice covers:

1. Deployment of software packages to lower and production environments

2. Deployment of infrastructure for lower and production environments

Deployment Approaches

As discussed earlier, deployments are moving packages from point A to point B. The concept is simple enough, but think about the volume, complexity, and constraints that might exist. Compare it with a courier company such as DHL that needs to ship packages across the globe. How do they move their couriers around? Do they ship out every customer's package separately or do they bundle their customers going to a particular location together? What if there are dangerous goods? Will those be sent on a plane along with the other packages, or will they go via a ship or other means. While you start thinking along these lines, you can understand how deployments are quite complex and why they warrant a separate practice, rightfully so.

Based on various mitigating circumstances, there are multiple approaches to deployments. Some of the popular ones are:

1. Big bang deployment

2. Phased deployment

3. Continuous delivery

4. Pull deployment

Big Bang Deployment

The big bang option is derived from the big bang theory, which states how the universe came into being from a single super force. Likewise, when software is deployed, it gets deployed to everything that's under the scope at the same moment. In other words, all users will get to experience the software (or the trauma of deployment) at the same time.

This type of deployment is referred to as big bang deployment. It is also called parallel deployment. Generally, a pilot deployment to a sample set of users is followed up by a bigger deployment—in this case, a big bang one. In the illustration in Figure 13-5, the release package gets deployed to regions 1, 2, 3, and 4 at the same time.

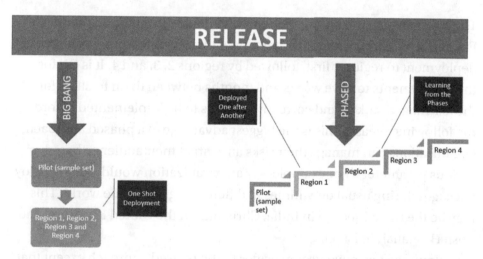

Figure 13-5. *Big bang and phased deployment approaches*

The upside is that all users will be in a position to enjoy the upgraded services at the same time, and the service provider can claim to be consistent with its services. This is generally preceded by a pilot (or multiple pilots) to ensure that the software does work.

When the pilot is deemed successful, a time is set and the users are made aware, and then the entire scope of the targeted system will receive the release package.

The big bang option is almost never considered in these modern times. You might have noticed that releases happen to certain smaller regions first (pilot) followed by, say, the United States. iOS updates are known to follow this pattern. The downside of deploying to everyone at once is pretty significant. Any screw-up will result in a disaster, and the negative business impact that follows is unbearable. Therefore, no organization likes to take chances by pushing everything out worldwide in one go.

Phased Deployment

The alternative to the big bang option is to deploy in a phased manner. In Figure 13-5, an initial pilot to a sample set of users is followed by a phased deployment to region 1 first, followed by regions 2, 3, and 4. It is OK for the deployments to have weeks and months between them to allow for the learning to sink in and corrective actions to be implemented before the following release. This is the biggest advantage of a phased approach. Organizations can manage their risks and target their audience based on various parameters. For example, say an organization would like to deploy packages during usual downtimes in different regions of the world. This may be the Diwali season in India, Christmas in the United Kingdom, and Rosh Hashanah in Israel.

I don't see any obvious downsides to the phased approach except that it requires a lot of continued planning and differences in release version between users, so this may end up being a support challenge. But there are a number of ways to mitigate this.

There are multiple variations of phased approaches that can be conceived, apart from the geographical deployments described earlier:

> Different features are deployed separately, so users can enjoy certain features first and then get the rest later.

> All users face downtime at the same time, although the deployment happens in phases. This usually refers to a deployment taking place right on the tail of a previous one.

> A combination of geographical deployments, feature-wise deployments, and downtime for all

Continuous Delivery/Deployment

We discussed continuous delivery and continuous deployment in Chapter 2. The piece of software that gets built and tested is ready to be deployed (or is deployed) into production. So the deployment does not wait for any of the parameters, or for other packages to be clubbed together, before deploying into production. It gets developed and upon successful testing, gets deployed into production—straightforward. This is illustrated in Figure 13-6.

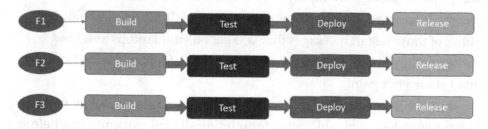

Figure 13-6. *Continuous delivery/deployment*

The simplicity exists because there are no constraints that hold the developed piece of functionality going into production. This is an ideal scenario that eases the way packages are delivered to customers with no frills or thrills. As you already know, in continuous delivery a manual trigger is needed to deploy into production; in continuous deployment, deployment into production is automated, meaning no manual triggers to move packages into production.

It is simple and straightforward. But it is not without its rank of risks. There is the burden of getting things right the first time, and the risk of exposing flaws to end users demands careful determination and perhaps quality checks; the role of humans in this process would be minimal. There is also an (over) dependence on automation to keep the pipelines flowing from the development's continuous integration cycle until it is deployed into production. But getting continuous delivery to work is an outcome based on deep thinking and maturity of the organization in running DevOps and automation.

Pull Deployment

The previous three approaches we looked at were push approaches, where the packages were pushed from a tool to either production or to an end user machine. The end user did not have much of a choice other than to accept these packages. What if the end user was in the middle of a client presentation when a software package is pushed that is overt in nature. Think of those restart messages that you get on your laptops and how annoying they can be when you are in the midst of some activity. I can say that I share your pain!

Imagine if you had the power to install the packages when you needed rather than when they —like after completing all your work and just before you are about to log out for the day. That would be wonderful, in my opinion.

The pull deployment option does exist, although it's not as popular as the other three approaches. In this approach, software packages are made available to users and users are notified of it. So users will basically follow a set of instructions (like clicking a specific link) to pull the packages at their own time. The software packages usually reside in a software repository called a definitive media library (DML), and the users will be provided access to download a package and permission to install it on their laptops.

One of the common processes to achieve this is through the service requests management practice. Say that a user wants some software and he is required to log a service request with appropriate details. After the service request gets approved, an email gets shot out with a link or a notification message from a pull deployment software pop-up. The user can choose to trigger the software package installation/movement at their convenience. This method is effective in ensuring that the user's productivity does not get affected and to ensure maximum customer satisfaction feedback.

This might not be an all-weather option. If there are urgent security updates that need to go in sooner than later, then pushing in a big bang way is possibly the best option. In conclusion, an organization needs to have all the options up its sleeve and should use the approaches in appropriate circumstances.

Note   The term deployment could also refer to retiring certain features, which necessarily means cleaning up of code and updating the older packages with newer ones.

Deployment Process

Deployment management is a practice from the technical management group in ITIL. It should not be mistaken for a practice that deals with tools and techniques only. There are process aspects that are critical to making the practice's objective a success.

I can break down the deployment process into three major activities:

1. Deployment planning

2. Deployments

3. Review and close

Deployment Planning

A good plan wins you half the battle. When it comes to deployments, it is no different. You need to plan the deployment in terms of the timing, the approach, and the people involved in carrying out the deployment. Next, the mode of deployment is also important. Is it manually done or through automation or a mix of both?

Sort Out Ownership

First and foremost, the ownership needs to be sorted out. Who is going to perform the deployments? Common sense says that the team responsible for the operational aspects of the environment must carry out the release activities. This is an ideal way to keep the accountability with a single team and not keep the environments vulnerable to changes by multiple groups.

Complex Environments

How do you deal with an environment where multiple suppliers are involved?

It is important to start drawing the boundaries and responsibilities for every supplier. Your outcome will likely say, for example, that supplier A is responsible for all changes pertaining to an SAP system. All packages that are to be deployed into SAP need to be vetted by the SAP team.

This can be achieved with a strong CMS in place. Unless you have a good CMS in the organization, you wouldn't know what systems exist and how they interact with each other. Without this information, you would be shooting in the dark at best.

Keep Processes Consistent but not Common for Environments

There are multiple environments in any organization where software packages move. The same level of scrutiny is not needed for all the environments. A different process for every environment is practical. However, keep these processes consistent for all the deployments that go in.

For example, for a test environment, you may seek a one-step approval from the development manager before a package is moved to the environment. The approval is a stamp that all the bugs that are identified in the development environment are fixed to satisfactory levels. For moving to the UAT environment, you may require two sets of approvals: one from the test manager and the next from a product owner. Moving the changes to production may follow the change control process. So, you will find that the process to move packages is different for every environment but it is consistent for all suppliers and teams that are involved.

Infrastructure Deployments

Infrastructure deployments work similar to software packages. The service provider generally holds the ownership to infrastructure. As and when new infrastructure components are needed, they are spun up; every new component deployment can be controlled.

What about deployments that the suppliers carry out? For example, Microsoft installs security patches and VMWare carries out urgent patches as well. If the supplier has a free run of installing patches as needed on host machines, then how does the service provider retain control of the infrastructure deployments?

It is imperative that either the suppliers provide the information (and seek approval) of patches that are being rolled out in advance, or provide the patches to the service provider to plan the deployments on their own. This way, the service providers will still remain in control, which is the right position to be in. You would want the owner to be fully in control of the changes that are proposed and that are going in.

Deployments

The actual deployment that is to be carried out is done during the change window for production deployments and during designated times for nonproduction environments; this is led by the processes for the particular environment.

The deployments are carried out based on the approach that has been agreed and the tooling that is identified. It is important that the people involved in deployments are the teams that have the ownership of deploying to the environment, and they will work closely with the other teams whose packages are getting moved. For example, if a supplier wants to install a COTS product plug-in into a production server, the supplier technician will also be present during the deployment activity, along with the operational team that has the ownership of the environments.

It is also a good idea to keep track of all activities performed during deployments. Keep a log that is timestamped, to help in future analysis as needed.

Deployment Reviews

Similar to conducting postimplementation reviews after carrying out a change, deployment-specific reviews must be employed as well. This provides an insight into the health of the deployment and a tool for learning and improving the maturity of the deployment process.

In DevOps, there is plenty of weight given to learning and experimentation. One of the best ways to learn is to record what was done and then review the logs to find inconsistencies.

Definitive Media Library

The DML is a repository for storing all licensed copies of procured software and software that has been developed in-house. The repository can be an online one or a physical one, but it needs to be access controlled.

The software that gets accepted into the DML is controlled by the change control practice, and only those copies that are authorized by change control into the DML are allowed to be used during the release and deployment management processes. The software that gets into the DML is expected to be analyzed, quality tested, and checked for vulnerabilities before getting accepted.

In the case of a physical DML where CDs, DVDs, and other storage media are used, it is expected that the storage facility is fireproof, can withstand the normal rigors of nature, and is secure against media thefts.

The DML is ideally designed during the service design life cycle phase, and the following are considered during the planning stages:

- Medium to be used and the location for the master copies to be stored

- Security arrangements for both online and offline storage

- Access rights, including who has access and how it is controlled

- The naming convention for the stored media to help in easy retrieval and tracking

- What types of software go into the DML, for example, source codes or packages

- Retention period

- Audit plan, checklist, and process

- Service continuity of DML if disaster strikes

Deployment Tooling

Deployments are carried out generally using tools. The days of manual deployments are soon approaching extinction.

The tools either are automated using an integrator tool such as Jenkins or Bamboo, or triggered manually by deployment personnel. Today, the preference is to build a pipeline wherein deployments are a part of the pipeline, to ensure consistency and avoid human intervention and hence errors.

Deployment tools are often integrated into the development suite such as Azure DevOps, where the Microsoft tool includes aspects of code management, user story management, and manages deployments as well, along with a host of other functionalities.

No matter how the tool is built or set up, there are a few qualities that all tools must possess:

1. Tools must have the functionality to store audit logs, which is critical for analysis and problem management activities

2. There must be easy integration with the change control practice: say, for example, every deployment must be able to confirm the change request number and the status before it can trigger deployments.

3. It goes without saying that deployment tools must be easy to use and stable to ensure consistency.

4. Deployment tools must be flexible enough to integrate with the various development tools that are on the market, and also expose APIs so that even the bespoke tools, if any, could leverage the deployment tools.

5. Integration with service request management tools will help in pull approach deployments, which has been discussed earlier.

6. Integration with configuration management tools will ensure that the deployments are governed by the foundational practice, which is ideally the single source of truth.

Engagement with Service Value Chain

Table 13-2. *Deployment Management Practice in SVC*

SVC Activity	Involvement	Details
Plan	None	Deployment management practice does not feature directly in the overall planning, as this is generally carried out through the release management planning.
Design and Transition	High	The deployment management practice plays a critical role in Design and Transition, as the practice is at the center of moving packages to environments.
Obtain/Build	High	In a DevOps project, the difference between Obtain/Build and deployments is nonexistent, as the incremental nature of development and deployments ensures close collaboration between the two.
Engage	None	Deployment management does not have a directly role to play with end users or other stakeholders.
Deliver and Support	None	Deployment management does not have a direct role to play with the delivery of services or its support.
Improve	Low	Improvements, like other enhancements and changes, go through the cycle of release and deployment.

Knowledge Check

The answers are provided in Appendix.

13-1. Which of the following is the correct *release* definition?

A. A version of a service or other configuration item, or a collection of configuration items, that is made available for use

B. A service that is deployed into an environment that is used by users

C. A deployment that consists of software and infrastructure packages that change the functionality of the service

D. Any change that has significance for the management of a service or other additions, removals, and modifications

13-2. Which of the following is not a type of release?

A. Major release

B. Standard release

C. Emergency release

D. Minor release

13-3. What is the difference between a POC and a pilot?

A. A POC is conducted to prove that the solution can be implemented. A pilot develops and implements a small piece of the functionality.

B. A POC is conducted to provide ample proof that the services are still valid. A pilot is used to ensure that the service is fit for purpose.

C. A POC is done to ensure sponsor engagement and to provide valid proof that the solution is valid. A pilot provides functional specifications that further provide proof that the solution is on the right path.

D. A POC is used to bring about transformation changes to a product or a service. A pilot is leveraged to identify a functionality that can be developed and tested successfully.

13-4. Which of the following is not a valid type of deployment approach?

A. Phased deployment

B. Continuous deployment

C. Continuous delivery

D. Emergency deployment

13-5. What is the role of a DML?

A. A repository where the software code is stored and is pushed to the pipeline for further building and testing

B. A repository that stores IT spares and software that can be accessed by valid personnel only

C. A repository for storing all the software used by the organization to provide services to end users

D. A repository for storing all licensed copies of procured software and software that has been developed in-house

DAY 7

Approximate Study Time: 1 hour and 7 minutes

Chapter 14 - 46 minutes
Chapter 15 - 21 minutes

On the final day, we look at the service desk practice, which is the final practice to be covered on the examination. Tips and tricks are provided to help you on the exam and also to answer some of the frequently asked questions from an ITIL career perspective.

CHAPTER 14

The Service Desk

The service desk is an integral component of the ITIL framework, and most ITIL implementations prioritize the design and implementation of the service desk and its associated practices over others. It is more of a people-led practice than a process-led one. So far, the practices that we have looked at are defined by their processes. The service desk practice is different from the rest.

The service desk acts as the face of the service provider organization to users, suppliers, other service providers, and even customers. The service desk is the single and first point of contact for the identified stakeholders. If you have a problem with your mobile phone bill, you call your cell phone service provider, and the person on the other end of the line is from the service desk.

As the service desk serves as the single and first point of contact, it often becomes the face of the service provider organization. Therefore, it becomes an activity of utmost gravity to ensure that the service desk is fit to represent the service provider organization with professional etiquette. Generally, an organization's image depends on the service desk. Just think about it. If the service desk of your cell phone service provider gives you a cold shoulder for a genuine problem that you are facing, do you measure the service provider's performance based on this interaction? Definitely you would, even if the service had been immaculate up until then, because a single interaction can break a solid foundation built over the years. I will get to the juicy bits of the service desk practice later in this chapter. This is the last of the practices that are included in the ITIL Foundation exam.

© Abhinav Krishna Kaiser 2021
A. K. Kaiser, *Become ITIL® 4 Foundation Certified in 7 Days*,
https://doi.org/10.1007/978-1-4842-6361-7_14

Exam Tip   Although we are going to discuss a single practice in this chapter, it is a key practice and you can expect about three or four questions on the ITIL Foundation exam about the service desk practice. You will be tested on your in-depth knowledge on the topics of the service desk practice.

Service Desk Practice

In the incumbent ITIL framework, the service desk was included as a function along with technical management, application management, and IT operations. A function is a team or group of people who have specific skill sets and were required to be process practitioners.

ITIL 4 has reimagined the service desk as a practice, on the same plank as the rest of the practices; there is no distinction between processes and functions, as the end goal is to be responsible for defined deliveries and set objectives. Before I go further, let us look at the definition of the service desk practice.

ITIL Definition of Service Desk Practice

The purpose of the service desk practice is to capture demand for incident resolution and service requests. It should also be the entry point and single point of contact for the service provider with all of its users.

The service desk serves as the first line of support for the service provider organization, apart from being the first point of contact. If the service desk is unable to support the resolution of an incident or fulfilment of a service request, it gets escalated to the second line of support and then the third if the second line is not in a position to resolve. In an organization that supports an application, generally the first and second lines of support offer configuration changes. If the resolution requires changes to the code, it gets pushed to the third line of support. The third line of support is a part of the product/DevOps team. This is represented in Figure 14-1.

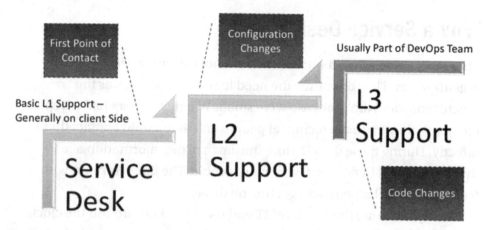

Figure 14-1. *Typical support lines in a DevOps organization*

According to the purpose of the service desk, there are two main bits:

1.   Act as a conduit for logging incidents and service requests

2.   Act as a single point of contact for users

All organizations have a place for a service desk in one form or another. There is a special place for them, even if they are manned by machines. The service desk presents itself as the face for customers; perhaps in most cases it's the only face, or in other words, the single point of contact for customers or users. When users reach out to them, they do it with a purpose: either they are facing an issue or two with the services/products or they are calling in to request something. The service desk, while acting as the single point of contact, is also one of the trusted channels to log incidents and service requests. It is not just the act of logging but rather the action of logging and providing a reference number for tracking, which gives the user/customer confidence that somebody is looking at the issue. The same trust is very much diminished or absent when an automated message pops up confirming the registration of the issue.

Why a Service Desk?

There was a time when a service desk did not exist in service providing organizations. They didn't see the need for one at the time, as the organization and the user base were small. Whenever users had to report incidents, they knew the technical people and they would contact them directly. During those days (before the dawn of the information age), the numbers of IT end users were manageable. The direct rapport with technical teams helped them get the job done.

Today, there are thousands of IT end users working around the clock, in multiple locations, and using various IT devices to carry out their work. If the times when no service desk was available were to be imagined, think of all the calls that technical team would start to receive. How would the technical team ensure that the load was spread across the team? How would the technical team know whether the user was calling the right technician? How would they decide on the priority: which issues to work on first and which ones to pick up later in the day or week? The answer is that it is impossible to think of IT service management functioning without a service desk. It channels triggers and routes them to the right groups of people. It prioritizes incidents and service requests to aid technical teams in acting on higher priorities first.

There was a time when IT service providers were required to provide a business case for installing service desks. Not anymore!

Here are the other benefits of having a service desk:

- Improves accessibility to IT staff for IT end users, customers, and suppliers

- Optimizes usage of IT resources

- Improves customer service and customer excitement

- Provides faster turnaround on service requests

- Optimizes the cost of providing IT support

Let me explain the last item here. The people who work at the service desk are not required to possess much experience, nor are they expected to be technically sound. It is a position that opens its doors to fresh college grads and those who wish to start their careers in IT. One of the main requirements for working at a service desk is good communication skills, both telephonic and writing.

I mentioned that the cost of providing IT services is optimized. The service desk hires entry-level job seekers who are paid less than an experienced technical professional.

So, by hiring less skilled resources, the operational costs are reduced, and this provides a win-win situation for the fresh graduates, IT service providers, and the customers (as the benefit of cost reduction is passed on to the customer).

Business and Technology

Not too long ago, when IT started to boom, the concept of a service desk was first seeded to help users call and register their issues. It wasn't called a service desk back then; the most commonly used term was a help desk. Even today, many organizations refer to their service desks as a help desk.

Nomenclatures aside, a help desk was meant to serve one function only: to function as a single point of contact for users to report issues. When ITIL was reimagined in its second being, a service desk was given a wider reach to not only be a single point of contact for users but also to suppliers and customers. It was meant to be a one-stop-shop for all things in IT; for any issue with IT, reach out to the service desk, no matter what your status is. This concept worked wonderfully well, with the service desk handling various functions including acknowledging the callers, classifying incidents, taking ownership of them, and also acting as the first line of support. A mature service desk was imagined to independently manage about fifty percent of the overall tickets that came through the system. It was a big success, especially because of the presence of less skilled resources, which meant that they could be set up in a country where labor was reasonable.

While the gulf between business and IT closed, and both joined at the hip, IT went from a service provider to being a partner sitting at the table that made decisions. While IT started to take some of business' space, it was time to return in kind. The interface between IT and business, the service desk, was reimagined yet again. How about the service desk not only existing for IT issues but also for other issues like janitorial, electrical, administrative, etc. The service desk's tentacles spread to every nook and corner of the business, and in its current state it is not restricted to logging and providing resolutions for technical issues alone but also for a host of other types of issues.

Most organizations have harped on this model, creating a single-service desk. For callers, IVRs route your calls to service desk personnel who have specialized skills they are reaching out for; the same service desk is being manned by people of different skill sets. Each person has a main skill set and a secondary one. If a caller is calling about travel, then the service desk agent who is trained and skilled on travel-related queries picks up the call.

Channels to Reach Service Desk

Business and IT processes have simplified over the years, which is unquestionably a goal that is being met and recalibrated to be achieved. Either organizations make more money or save through optimization. There are the sales and consulting units of the organization that get into making money and growth, and optimization is expected to happen from within, which is reasonable and logical. Everybody who uses the process or has a role to play in a process has valid inputs toward optimization measures.

Users reaching out to the service desk is one such activity that has simplified over the years and continues to do so. There was a time when users had to walk up to the service desk (and they still do in some extreme cases) to log incidents and service requests. Phones came into the picture, which put the users in a queue while the agents went through their first in, first served principle in connecting with the users. The time spent either visiting the service desk or calling them was time lost, which resulted in lost productivity, and the chain reaction of losses for the organization kicked in. So there came measures to save these efforts lost; one primary action was to enable users to help themselves through various knowledge bases and self-help tools. The classic example is the password reset process. There was a time when the service desk used to do it. Turning this into a self-help feature saved plenty of hours not only for the users but for the service desk staff. The principle that was applied was that anything that did not require human brain power could be automated. I will talk about the service desk and automation later in this chapter.

A few of the channels to reach a service desk are listed here, and at the time of writing, they are relevant. New means could be designed and implemented by the time you read this section. I would also like to add that the channels to reach the service desk that are mentioned here are not comprehensive but rather the ones that are widely used.

Walk-Ins

The service desk personnel used to sit in a group, and I remember the days when we visited them on an upper floor and we logged our incidents in a physical register. The service desk coordinator used to check the register every hour and assign incidents to agents accordingly. The setting up of this service desk was touted as a breakthrough improvement, as the practice earlier was to reach out to technical team members directly. I am not talking about a small IT shop but a major one.

To my knowledge, walk-in service desks do not exist anymore, although there are other forms of walk-in technical support that exist. Yet, the walk-in means of reaching the service desk deserves an honorary mention as we get into some modern ways as we sift through the list.

Telephones

When you do a Google image search for a service desk, you will find that majority of the images that you see are of a person talking over a telephone with a headset. Telephones and service desks have become synonymous with each other. This was the case 1 year back and it does not look like it is going to change in the next decade.

Reaching the service desk by phone is by far the most popular means. Although most IT organizations have tried to shun it, traditional businesses and governments swear by it even today.

The problem with telephones is twofold. The user who is calling in must go through the IVR options and then choose the right nested option. This could easily take a couple of minutes. I particularly hate calling banks' service desks over a telephone, but they do not give me much of a choice for raising certain service requests and grievances. While the IVR option is painful—the wait time before we talk to a person and the time spent identifying ourselves, explaining the problem, and the eventual resolution—imagine the time that gets drained. If I were going to implement the lean framework in an organization, this would be one of the axes for sure!

All that being said, talking to a human over a telephone is the next best thing to talking face to face. It gives the user a level of comfort that cannot be gotten through other modern means. While I might detest talking to the service desk, it remains the most popular means because the comfort users derive and the possible immediate resolution that could result during the same conversation is assuring.

Emails

Emails have transformed the way we communicate. Although they are passive, the trusted delivery of messages from point A to point B and the option to respond on one's own schedule have made it a de facto standard for communication. Reaching out to the service desk to register incidents is a form of communication, and popular meets popular with users reaching out to service desks via email.

There are pros and cons on both sides. From the user's perspective, sending an email is as easy as it can get. I send close to four dozen emails in a normal day, so one more to the service desk is a drop in the ocean. If the incident faced is not of immediacy, it's okay from a user's outlook. The user does not feel like his time has been wasted, when compared with the telephonic means. The resolution comes when it comes, which is bound by the SLA, and the user can look at the resolution when she/he has free time. No more holding up meetings while talking to the service desk!

The service desk on the other hand need not worry about the queues and call drops, which is one of the KPIs they are forced to face. They can get to the email and respond as they see fit. The advantage is that they get the additional time to think and respond, which may not always be possible on a telephone, where the answers must be thought of in runtime. The other advantage is that the service desk could maintain templates for certain common resolutions, and all they need to do is copy and paste— voila! How the telephonic service desks wish that their voices could be recorded and played back as soon as they identify the common problem that the user faces?

The service delivered through emails is relatively slower, but for nonurgent issues and service requests, it's the best channel.

Chatting

My favorite channel to reach the service desk is chatting. It is quite like a telephone, only we don't talk to them in real time but chat away. It's nonintrusive, as I could chat with the service desk as I sit in a meeting where my active participation is not called for. The service desk on the other hand does not get tied up, with an agent held up by a user. An agent can be chatting to five users at the same time. The productivity may not go up by five times, but it would definitely be much better than the telephonic option. The user on the other end does not feel like he is sending out a one-way communication, and could end up chatting with peers as well as with the service desk.

It's a win-win situation for everybody. As a user, my first preference is to reach for the chat option. Plus, I can save the transcript for future reference. That is a necessity these days, as service desk agents are known to be inconsistent with their solutions—especially the likes of Amazon. As an IT consultant, I recommend that my clients promote chat over the other options.

Portals

As self-help became a norm, service portals where users could raise their own incidents on a web form became a new normal. The principle is: why do you need a human to do your dirty work when you can articulate it better?

Many service management tools provide an interface or a wrapper for the user to log in incidents or service requests. It could be as simple as a form where the user populates relevant data, or it could be backed by an artificial intelligence engine that can understand the reported problem and route it directly to the correct team.

In fact, very few organizations route tickets coming through a portal to the service desk. Most try to skip the service desk all together, to reduce the hops and to reduce downtime. There are pros and cons with the approaches, like skipping the service desk does not bring uniformity in prioritizing incidents, and categorization could be a hit and miss game.

The advantage obviously is that the right team picks up the incidents right away, and they are best suited with specialized skill sets and can resolve issues rapidly.

Messaging

Twenty-first century technologies have made it possible to report incidents and service requests through a mobile phone. While the user is agile and dynamic, why make them constrain themselves to a laptop or be glued to a phone to raise tickets.

Users can now raise tickets using Whatsapp, and the chitty chatty service desk on the other end of the conversation uses the same platform to provide resolution.

The other messaging option is to use the short messaging service (SMS) to report incidents and service requests. This is more of a traditional approach that basically makes you interact with a computer program that receives inputs and gives you a ticket number in return. A service desk agent picks up the details and may choose to reach out to you by a phone, email, or if your day is not going well, can send your resolution through a text message.

Using text messages is still in vogue with a few businesses but with more and more users not opting for it, the service will soon be disbanded. Using Whatsapp on the other hand is picking up, and Whatsapp has provided a different product called Whatsapp Business that eases the communication channel and is no longer a phone to phone communication. On the other end, the service desk agents use laptops to interact just as they would over chat. Some organizations use bots as well to provide information that you may already know. What use is it, you may ask? I am still seeking answers to this question!

Social Media

Every possible communication channel has been taken over to reach the service provider organization. The last on the list are the social media channels, the most popular ones being Twitter and Facebook.

Users can interact with the service desk by raising issues through Twitter or Facebook, and the responses too are sent back on the same channel. It is good to use existing channels, but what fun is it if you must wash your dirty laundry in public. I do not like to tell the world that I am unable to fix my laptop and am reaching out to somebody else for resolution.

Since everything is in the public domain, users are often discouraged from utilizing social media channels, as the interactions they make are not on private messaging channels but rather on the public page. Yet, it is a feature that is available to reach the service desk.

Service Desk Structures

Compare your current organization's service desk structure with the structures from other organizations. There will definitely be distinct differences between the structures and the way they operate. Why do organizations choose to build their own structure and not follow a set structure based on certain standardized principles? The answer is strategy.

Strategy drives how organizations are structured. Some structures work better than others, while others might bring in synergy, generating more value with the same set of people. It is observed that traditional organizations typically opt for a highly hierarchical structure, while start-ups and new age organizations go for flat structure. There are advantages and disadvantages with both. If the advantages outweigh the disadvantages, organizations are convinced of their justification to opt for it.

As the service desk is manned by people, lots of them, it is imperative that the structuring needs some serious thinking. There are several ways a service desk can be structured. If the core objectives of the service desk are met, it can be structured as needed. In this book, I will discuss three common types of service desk structures. This is an important topic from the service management perspective and from an examination standpoint.

The three most widely used service desk structures are:

1. Local service desk

2. Centralized service desk

3. Virtual service desk

Local Service Desk

As the structure nomenclature indicates, a local service desk has a limited boundary and serves a subset of the overall function. It is a service desk that is for a specific office/location/region. This type is shown in Figure 14-2.

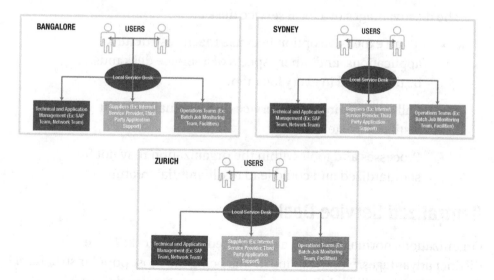

Figure 14-2. *Local service desk*

I have considered three distinct locations that an organization is set up in, which is quite common these days: Bangalore, Sydney, and Zurich. Each of these locations houses a service desk. The service desk in Bangalore caters to the Bangalore location only, and the Sydney and Zurich location service desks cater to their respective locations as well. Within the location, the end users, technical teams, suppliers, and operations teams reach out to their respective service desk.

The advantages of a local service desk are:

- The service desk, end users, and the teams involved generally speak the same language, which leads to better understanding of the problem and the feedback provided by both the parties.

- Sharing a similar culture helps develop rapport and reduce differences.

- VIP users can be better served through customized service.

- Increased customer satisfaction

The disadvantages of a local service desk are:

- It's an expensive option because the infrastructure, applications, and other aspects of a service desk must be duplicated in every location.

- Call volumes in a local service desk normally do not justify its existence.

- Processes and tools within the organization may not be standardized and could lead to differential treatment.

Centralized Service Desk

Organizations normally opt for a centralized service desk. There are distinct advantages, which has led to this being the most popular structure. An organization will mobilize and station a single service desk at a strategic location. This is shown in Figure 14-3.

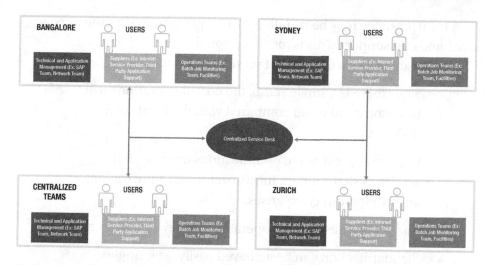

Figure 14-3. *Centralized service desk*

A centralized service desk is formed with a single service desk, instead of having a service desk at every location. In this example, the locations Bangalore, Sydney, and Zurich have no individual service desk, and a centralized service desk is formed that caters to all the locations. The centralized service desk could be formed in any one of the existing locations or in a new location altogether. It does not matter where the centralized service desk is set up; what matters is that the organization has only one service desk as a single point of contact for all end users and other stakeholders.

It is possible that the technical teams and suppliers are still localized. Yet, when they must reach out to the service desk, they need to call the centralized service desk. In most organization setups, there are centralized technical teams that handle respective technologies from a central location as well. These central teams, if they need to, reach out to a centralized service desk.

A local presence may be installed if the organization sees the need to have hands-on support. This is totally optional.

The advantages of a centralized service desk are:

- Since there is a single setup, the cost of operations will be economical when compared with the local service desk setup.

- Cost savings extend to optimizations made with the service desk resources, infrastructure, administration, and other indirect expenses.

- The service desk can be operated with fewer resources.

- Standardization can be achieved easily, as a single team following the same set of protocols is easier to achieve than multiple teams following a single set of processes, procedures, standards, and scripts.

- Management has a better overview on the performance and effectiveness of a service desk in the centralized setup.

The disadvantages of a centralized service desk are:

- The local flavor, language, and culture will be lost on the users.

- Some users may prefer proximity and personal touch for their support needs, and a centralized service desk may not provide this option for all the organizational locations.

Virtual Service Desk

A centralized service desk is a good idea. But how easy or difficult is it to find the people, a location, willingness to work through the night, friendly regulatory controls to support 24/7 operations, and other bells and whistles that make it a reality? Through technology, we can achieve a centralized service desk without the colocation factor for service desk employees. We could have a centralized service desk even when service desk agents sit in different parts of the globe and operate as one unit. Let us look at how this is achieved.

Figure 14-4 represents a virtual service desk, and it is almost like the centralized service desk. It looks the same, as the underlying principle between the two setups is the same. But in a virtual service desk, we achieve centralization through technology. And the virtual service desk enforces usage of a common service knowledge management system (SKMS) to ensure standardization and easy exchange of information.

Virtual Service Desk

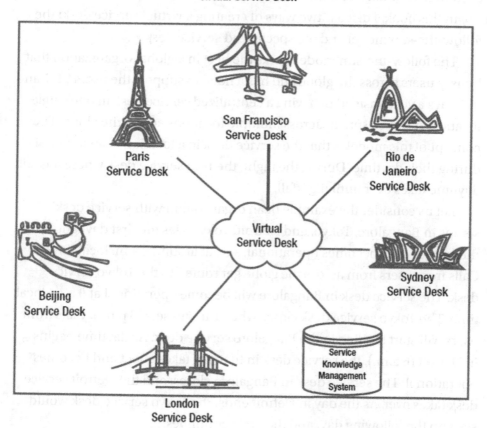

Figure 14-4. Virtual service desk

Today, we have the technology to bring service desk agents onto the service desk platform from the comfort of their homes. Several housewives are working at call centers from their homes. The phone calls are routed to their personal lines or come in through voice over Internet protocol on the agent's personal computer. The end user will notice no difference between a centralized service desk and a virtual service desk, as the technology seamlessly integrates disjointed bits into a single unit.

Likewise, organizations are off-shoring, near-shoring, and outsourcing several service desks to countries where talent is available in plenty and where the operational costs are marginal when compared with the customer's market location.

In this book, I discuss two ways of creating a virtual service desk: the follow-the-sun model and the specialized service desk.

The follow-the-sun model works the best in a global organization that houses users across the globe and has a need to support the users 24/7 and 365 days a year. Instead of having a centralized service desk in one single location, it can be spread across multiple locations across the globe. The concept of this model is that the service desk in a location is operational during their daytime. During the night, the next service desk where it is still daytime takes over until nightfall.

Let us consider the example of an organization with service desk setups in Bangalore, Tokyo, and Detroit. Tokyo sees the first daylight, and the service desk becomes operational, say, at around 9 a.m. local time. Calls from users from across the globe get routed to the Tokyo service desk. The service desk in Bangalore will become operational at 9 a.m. local time. The Tokyo service desk closes when the sun sets (6 p.m.). Calls from users will start landing in the Bangalore service desk. As daytime begins in Detroit (6 a.m.), the service desk in that city takes effect and becomes operational. The service desk in Bangalore closes, and the Detroit service desk takes over. As the day in Detroit ends, the Tokyo service desk would start up the following day, and the cycle continues.

This model is in vogue with some major organizations. When you call the customer care line, you will notice that the call sometimes gets picked up by those with foreign accents (multiple accents), and at times by those with local accents. This, you may have observed, happens during a particular period. Say, when you call at night, somebody in India will be your service desk agent. And when you call during the day, you might hear a service desk agent speaking American English. This is virtualization chugging its wheels in the background; you, as the user, will have called the same number each time, and all the technicalities of call routing are done in the back end. Isn't it cool?

The next type of virtual service desk is not based on time, zones, or daylight. It takes shape based on the expertise in an area. In this service desk, it is possible to house different types of experts in different locations. And, through the power of IVR and routing, it is possible to route the call to the respective expert sitting across the globe.

Let's consider an example of an organization with the specialized service desk setup. When a user calls in, the IVR prompts him to select the type of problem that he is facing: laptop, desktop, network, storage, or application. When the user selects laptop, the call gets routed to a laptop support group sitting in London. They will talk to him and take care of the resolution. If the user selects application, the call gets routed to Manila, and application experts who are seated in Manila are responsible for the resolution of the user's application issue. Likewise, it is possible that expert teams are spread across the globe, and depending on the issue on hand, the respective service desk takes over.

This type of a setup is common in IT services organizations, as they normally tend to hire specific skill sets for locations.

The advantages of a virtual service desk are:

- Organizations can become resilient with virtual service desks, whereby they can bank on one or the other service desks if one was to fail and eliminate the single point of failure.

- It can be a less expensive option compared with the centralized service desk, as deploying home-working professionals can reduce the resourcing costs.

- It can also be less expensive if the organization does not have to shell out infrastructure costs, because the service desk agents are working out of their homes.

- There are rules in some countries to pay an additional wage if professionals are made to work beyond a certain time, which can be eliminated with a virtual service desk.

The disadvantages of a virtual service desk are:

- Aligning all service desks on common processes, procedures, terminologies, and language is an onerous task and requires plenty of training, course corrections, and constant management.

- Coordination between virtual service desk teams and technical teams can be challenging.

- End users may feel a difference in service quality, as when they reach different service desks.

- Plenty of management efforts are needed, and there is a need for automation to transfer tickets from one service desk to another.

Qualities Expected from Service Desk Staff

The service desk is the first point of contact for users. It is also a point of contact for various teams. So, it is imperative that communication and soft skills are the most desired talents that are expected from the service desk staff. The success of a service provider organization depends on how well the service desk is mobilized and trained.

Communication to Begin With

Consider an example where the email application server is broken. Most organizations run on emails, so effectively this disruption is bound to perturb the users and many would call the service desk numbers. While the service desk receives numerous calls seeking answers to the broken email system, they must remain calm headed and assure the users that the issue has been identified and engineers are troubleshooting the issue. When getting repeated calls from multiple users, it is natural for anybody to feel irritated. But when they face users, they must put on a mask and talk to them as though it was the first phone call of the day. In the back end, the service desk staff must keep seeking updates from the engineers involved to provide the estimated time of resolution. So in essence, a lot of communication from multiple channels is to be expected, and the staff hired for this role must be able to pull this off.

Technically Oriented

That is not all. The service desk is seen as the first line of support, which necessarily means that the staff involved must be technically oriented as well. They must be aware of the troubleshooting steps, the technical elements involved, and be good enough to resolve at least 50 percent of the overall issues that flow in. Of course, most organizations today have built knowledge base systems that help the service desk staff in asking the right questions while dealing with issues. But, at the end of the day, finding the cause and troubleshooting issues requires intelligence and technical skills. This too is mandatory. The service desk staff must be able to understand the issue and prioritize it correctly, because you want an email incident that's affecting a thousand people resolved faster than an individual who is unable to log his time. Next up, the service desk must understand the nitty

gritty of the incident quite well to escalate it to the right functional group if
they are unable to resolve it. For example, if the service desk is not able to
resolve an Outlook issue, they should know whether the incident needs to
be sent to the exchange team (central) or to the field team that can address
the problem in person.

Probing Toward Success

Probing the users in my opinion is one of the foundational skill sets
required for the service desk. The person who asks the right questions
is most likely to get the answer fast and correct. I dug deeper into the
art of communication for IT folks in my first book, *Workshop in a Box:
Communication Skills for IT Professionals* (Impackt Publishing, 2015),
where I brought to light the various communication skill sets that an IT
practitioner needs to reach for the skies.

Empathizing with Users

Last but not the least important of the skill sets is to show empathy with
users who are suffering from IT outages and who are unable to deliver to
their targets. I am not exaggerating the issue. Business users who cannot
get their jobs complete due to a technical issue are bound to be angry,
upset, and unforgiving. To deal with such users, service desk staff can
truly serve them by understanding their problems, and that is just the
beginning. I was once angry with Amazon because a product I returned
hadn't been refunded. While I chatted with several agents, they told me
the status and gave an authorization to prove that it has been refunded,
and some agents asked me to check with the bank. The bank confirmed
that they had not received a refund to this effect. I called Amazon and was
served by a service desk staff who sounded aged: not one of the younger
voices. She apologized profusely for me having to contact Amazon so
many times and the eventual delay. She not only refunded the amount

using a gift voucher but also topped it off with £10 for the delays and the experience I had to go through. While I was happy to get the amount back in my account, the topping off assured me of the high quality of customer service that I can expect at Amazon. All the ill feelings disappeared in a moment—not because of the topping off but because of the gesture and the empathy she shared. Another skill that is strongly associated with empathy is social intelligence, and these skills can truly separate the finest service desk staff from the rest.

Service Desk Under Automation Cloud?

Automation has made its mark in every part of our lives; it sometimes feels that we cannot function effectively without automation. I cannot possibly remember to pay my credit card bills on time, but automation will help ensure I do not end up paying late fees. I don't want to find out one fine day that my ink cartridges have run out, so I want somebody to monitor it for me and send me a new one when I am about to run out (HP's instant ink subscription is an example).

We are in a competitive world. There are several organizations offering the same services, and consumers get the same level of service from multiple service providers. How do they choose which one to latch onto? The kicker is the price. The service that costs the least is most preferred, while maintaining similar levels of service. The onus is on the service provider to reduce costs. They cannot just reduce on a whim, as there are service-providing costs, overheads, and dependencies that must be factored in. It is true for most services that most of the service costs go toward people, but reducing staff or hiring people with cheaper salary does not guarantee good service levels. The best option is to employ automation that can mimic people and carry out repetitive activities that people usually did. Although there might be a capital investment, in the long run this is bound to provide major benefits to the service provider. Voila! The automation solution could take down multiple birds with one stone. This will help service providers reduce their service costs; they then can also pass on the benefits to consumers, which will attract more consumers and make the business more profitable.

Yes, there are several benefits from automation apart from the service cost angle. One of the areas where automation has been applied is in the service desk. It is becoming harder these days to talk to a real person. When you call the service desk number, you are asked to go through a maze of IVR loops and in the end, every one of them ends up with the system as opposed to a human. The point is not to debate about human vs. machine, but rather look at it from the outcome perspective. While talking to the machines, does the user get the answers they are looking for? If the answer is yes, then automation is a great substitute. If the answer is no, then the company posing the machines as their first point of contact is sure to take a hit on its customer satisfaction ratings.

In my professional opinion, automation is great for a service desk; not entirely, but in certain processes. When you call a bank, the process of verifying your identity when done through automation is great, but you need a human on the other end of the line if you have a question about a particular transaction. Machines can never replace humans when it comes to communicating at a personal level and showing empathy where it matters—at least not until now. Personally, I would never chat with chat bots, because the information they provide can generally be obtained through other areas such as from the tracking monitors and account areas. Why go through the human-like experience when you know that you are talking to a computer program?

My opinion aside, technology has come a long way. This is the age of artificial intelligence, robotic process automation (RPA), and machine learning. We are getting to a place where the Terminator movies have taken us to already. The machines are learning fast and trying to be human-like in all things we do. There are artificial intelligence systems today that can learn and code from a human. So next time, we do not need a developer to write programs. A computer program can be trained to reproduce into developing new applications.

IBM's artificial intelligence engine Watson tied up with Japanese telecom giant SoftBank in 2015 to teach Watson to learn and speak Japanese—a language considered most difficult for machines to learn. The outcome of this is to replace the customer service channels of the company through robots that are powered by this AI.

Engagement with Service Value Chain

Table 14-1. *Service Desk in SVC*

SVC Activity	Involvement	Details
Plan	None	The service desk is not involved during the planning activities.
Design and Transition	Medium	The service desk is often leveraged to communicate to users the changes and new services introduced to users. They are also a part of the early life support and other release-related activities.
Obtain/Build	Low	During the Obtain/Build activity, the service desk could be leveraged for logging incidents and service desk pertaining to lower environments.
Engage	High	The service desk engages with users and with other stakeholders, and acts as a single and first point of contact, playing a central role in most processes.

(continued)

Table 14-1. (*continued*)

SVC Activity	Involvement	Details
Deliver and Support	High	The service desk plays a central role in coordinating with users during the resolution of incidents and communicating to various involved parties.
Improve	Medium	The service desk is an able channel to receive feedback from users that could translate into improvements. The service desk also comes under the ambit of continuous improvement, where its processes and activities are improved through the Improve activity in the SVC.

Knowledge Check

The answers are provided in Appendix.

14-1. Which is the purpose of the service desk?

A. Act as a first point of contact for customers

B. Provide first line of support to users

C. Capture demand for incident resolution and service requests

D. Act as a channel for communication between third parties and IT staff

14-2. Which of the following is not a typical service desk structure?

A. Virtual service desk

B. IT service desk

C. Centralized service desk

D. Local service desk

14-3. Which of these skill sets are most necessary with service desk staff?

  A. Empathy

  B. Communication

  C. Technical

  D. All of the above

14-4. Which of the following channels help users get the current status of tickets?

  i. Portal

  ii. Social media

  iii.IT staff

  iv. Chat bots

  A. i, ii, and iv

  B. i, iii, and iv

  C. i and iii

  D. i, ii, iii, and iv

14-5. Under which of the SVC activities does the service desk play a major role?

  A. Obtain/Build

  B. Design and Transition

  C. Improve

  D. Engage

CHAPTER 15

Tips and Tricks for Taking the ITIL Exam

The ITIL Foundation examination is one of the most sought-after examinations in the IT industry. It is one of the certifications that are considered mandatory during the time of employment.

I attended ITIL v2 training when I got started with IT service management. This was 15 years back. I did not pass the practice exam. I was flabbergasted. Then I sat down for the next 2 days trying to decipher the question pattern, the clues, and the giveaways. In the next practice exam, I scored 80 percent; and on the paper-based ITIL exam, I got just one question wrong. Still, I hadn't recovered from my failure in the first practice exam. I felt that it was the trainer's responsibility to help in the preparations for the certification exam. The trainer should have been there and done that, as he/she would be in the best position to provide an overview of the lay of the land. This is exactly what I plan to do in this chapter.

My experience as a trainer has helped deepen my knowledge of the ITIL 4 Foundation examination. I sometimes feel that I can read the question setter's mind. Not really! The tips that I share in this chapter are the ones that I generally would share in a training session with my students, and more than 90 percent of my students have passed the examination on their first attempt. Moreover, a good number of my students have opted for my training in advanced ITIL certification courses as well.

© Abhinav Krishna Kaiser 2021
A. K. Kaiser, *Become ITIL® 4 Foundation Certified in 7 Days*,
https://doi.org/10.1007/978-1-4842-6361-7_15

While ITIL certification examination is one half of the story, what happens next is a question that most people ask me on my LinkedIn network and on my blog. In this chapter, I will answer the most frequently asked questions pertaining to ITIL careers.

ITIL 4 Foundation Exam: Tips and Tricks

I first became ITIL Foundation certified in its second version: ITIL v2. At the time of taking the exam, I was fresh to ITIL. Next up was ITIL V3, which I took after 4 years of working experience. The world was much different in those 4 years: the way I perceived and read the exam.

I had a lot more distractions with ITIL V3 because I had the experience. I started to relate the topics to my work activities, and the processes at work weren't exactly as defined in ITIL. In short, with experience behind my back, it was a lot tougher than without experience.

ITIL 4 is a new exam on the block. It behaves similar to ITIL V3 in the exam pattern, style, and the way questions appear. So if you have ITIL V3 behind your back, you've been there and done that! If you are new, read along the next section to get some of the tips and tricks that I feel will help you out. This, by no means, is comprehensive and these tips are formulated based on my and my trainers' experiences. Remember that with an exam for which you prepare hard, the joy is in the result. It is heartwarming when the PASS result is displayed on the screen—that is, if you take a computer-based test instead of paper.

Preparation

This book is all that you need in the form of reading material. Rest assured, you don't need to refer to anything outside of it. Read the book in its entirety. The information provided in this study guide is based on the ITIL Foundation examination syllabus. There is a lot more to ITIL than what I have touched upon. The practices that are outside the ITIL Foundation exam, you can be found on my blog: http://abhinavpmp.com.

For the sake of the exam, stick to the contents of the book and you will be in good shape. When you are ITIL certified, then start reading the ITIL material from other sources; that way you do not get distracted between necessities and embellishments.

Being an engineer by academics, I have developed several bad habits (duh), but the one that matters is when I read. I used to study (and at times open the book for the first time) the previous evening for my internals and exams. I did something similar when I wrote my ITIL V3 Foundation certification; in fact, I came back home a little earlier than usual and studied for about 5 hours. This is not the best way to study for an exam, so I cataloged parts of this book to be read across seven days. Some days require more work than others. But the intent is to encourage you not to study like an engineering student.

Here are some other tips and tricks that you can use for preparing for the exam:

1. The only way you stick to a schedule is if there is a target ahead of you. You can set yourself a target in the future, and go ahead and book your exam before you start reading the book. This helps you stay on track and be focused on your target. Schedule the ITIL Foundation exam from one of the examination institutes (EIs). At the time of writing, PeopleCert was the designed EI; they have online options where the proctored exams are available.

2. The book is planned to be read after work, since most of us work from mornings until evenings. I felt that 7 days were sufficient, and based on the feedback I received from the first version, it was ideal for working professionals. So I stuck to the same plan in this version.

3. The ITIL that companies follow may not be word for word as in the framework; remember that ITIL is nonprescriptive. So, the biggest pitfall is that the trainees answer questions based on their experience rather than the framework. It is absolutely a necessity that you decouple work processes from the framework's. Unlearn what you have learned from your work experience. From the examination perspective, it is only the contents of this book that matter and not anything else. I tell my students who have sufficient experience that fresh graduates from college find it easy to pass the exam because they start from zero, while experienced folks start from a negative position.

4. Take plenty of notes. Although all the information you need is in printed form, it is not nearly equivalent to writing down your own notes, in your own hand and in your own words. Make notes at every juncture, including the tips and tricks that I am offering you in this chapter. Research has proven that taking notes helps you understand concepts better and helps you ask the right questions.

5. ITIL is old school when it comes to definitions and keywords. Success on the exam stems from identifying the right keywords in the questions and the answer choices. So, it is imperative that you learn the definitions for ITIL concepts, or at least be familiar with the keywords. Follow my exam tips in the chapters, where I have highlighted the frequently asked definitions. For example,

an incident is an unplanned interruption to a service. The keywords to remember are *unplanned interruption* in this case. Likewise, find the keywords, circle them, highlight them, underline them, do whatever is going to help you commit them to memory.

6. ITIL is best learned through examples. I have provided ample examples in this book. I encourage you to come up with your own examples (and not anything else) to help you understand the topics better.

Mock Exams

It is common with any certification that you attempt a few mock papers after you have studied all the topics. The same goes with ITIL Foundation exam. Here are some tips in relation to taking mock exams:

1. Axelos has provided a full-fledged sample paper that you can download from their web site: `www.axelos.com/certifications/sample-papers`. You are required to register before you can download it.

2. Do not attempt the ITIL sample question paper before you have completed reading this entire book. Sample papers must be used to gauge where you stand in terms of understandability, and it is best leveraged when this entire book has been read, understood, jotted down, and digested.

3. Answer the Axelos sample immediately after you have completed this entire book. This will give you a good handle on how well you have understood the ITIL Framework. The real exam will be in the same pattern as this one, so in all probability, you can expect to find a few questions directly picked from the sample paper as well.

4. There are a number of ITIL questions available on the Internet. Try to answer as many as possible. I cannot guarantee all the questions will be of the same quality as the exam questions. While you search for ITIL Foundation questions online, it is quite possible that you will bump into ITIL V3 questions as well, as the incumbent version was active for over 12 years. Stay away from it. There are plenty of differences between the two frameworks. Also attempt the exercises presented at the end of each chapter.

On the Exam Day

D-day brings in plenty of permutations: what ifs rule and the succeeding thoughts blur the machinations of ITIL that you have ingested over the past week or so. So, it is my rule of thumb to get plenty of sleep the night before, and then on the exam day, I don't review the material, and will probably watch a movie or a TV show to keep my mind off the clutter. Some of these tips are generic (you can use it for any exam) and some are specific. I am putting it all out here.

1. Try to schedule the exam in the first half of the day, when you are fresh and energetic.

2. It is important for you to know that the ITIL Foundation exam does not pose trick questions, wherein questions are twisted in a way to confuse candidates. The questions are straightforward, as they are trying to test your awareness of ITIL concepts.

3. The ITIL Foundation exam is a test of your awareness of the concepts. The trickiest questions that you will encounter are those with negative connotations: Which of these is NOT a . . . ?

4. Read the question fully, completely and accurately. Understand what is being asked. Check and double-check whether the question is in a negative connotation. After you understand the question, look at the answer choices.

5. Remember that ITIL is a guidance and not a rule book. So answer options with keywords like only, always, never, must, and others are likely incorrect.

6. Don't be in a hurry to finish the exam. Beating the clock isn't a criterion for passing the exam. Answer all that you can in the first skirmish, and then go through the ones that you aren't confident of. I learned this tip when I took my PMP exam and it helped immensely. I spent minimum time on the questions I could answer and the maximum amount of time on the questions that needed some thinking. Don't leave the exam hall early. Review the answers until the last possible minute.

7. It is also possible that you may be looking for an answer option after reading the question and it may not be there. Don't panic. Understand the question and each of the choices. Identify the closest answer and go with your gut. Also, one of my students who is in the habit of earning certifications (the last I spoke to him, he had 57 certifications) told me that verbose answers are generally the right answer in such situations. Maybe, this is something to keep in the back of your mind?

8. You have 60 minutes to complete 40 questions. That's 1.5 minutes for every question, which is plenty of time in my opinion. Around half the questions on the exam would be straightforward, which can help you move on within half a minute. And there are some (in minority) that will make you think. Take time where you need it.

9. There will be some questions that you may not be confident of and need some time to think over. In such a scenario, leave the question unanswered and move ahead. Take on the easy and simple ones first, and then go back to the tougher ones.

10. There are no negative markings; a wrong answer does not end up deducting marks from the overall score. So you should at least attempt to answer all the questions.

FAQs on ITIL-Based Careers

On my blog and on my YouTube channel, many IT professionals, with experience ranging from debuts to ten years, often ask me questions related to ITIL-based careers. Though hundreds of queries have come my way, the nature and direction of the queries are similar. In this section, I will provide a list of frequently asked questions (FAQs) regarding careers in ITIL and answer them.

How Different Is ITIL from Project Management?

ITIL is a framework for service management. The activities that are performed as part of service management are generally perpetual, meaning that you will not have a definite end date. Project management, on the other hand, is finite. It has definite start and end dates. The project ceases to exist after it has ended, and then you generally move on to another project. To summarize, ITIL and project management are in different hemispheres. However, both the project and service managements have been brought under the DevOps umbrella.

Do I Need an IT Background to Become ITIL Certified?

The short answer is no, you don't need an IT background to become ITIL Foundation Certified.

Here's the long one. You don't become ITIL certified for the heck of it, right? You try to find a role in line with ITIL and become employable through the certification. If you do not have an IT background, you can become ITIL Foundation certified, as long as you understand the concepts. However, for you to just start working in an ITIL organization, it would be a massive hill to climb. ITIL concepts are used in the workplace closely with the IT topologies and frameworks, and the disability sans IT knowledge will leave you wanting in every activity hurdle that you come across. My advice is that you enroll yourself in some IT training as well to become aware of the IT infrastructure, networks, and applications. To summarize, there is no ITIL without IT.

I Am in Software Development. I Want to Change My Career to ITIL-Based. What Can I Pick Up?

In the age of DevOps, all roles must be aware of the Agile processes as well as the service management practices and processes. Without the understanding of the entire DevOps framework, it is not possible for the one team to emerge. If you are in software development or in any other role in a DevOps project, irrespective of having to change your careers, learn ITIL. When you are ready to switch, it makes it all the more easier as you would be a pi-resource having multiple skill sets, which makes you more employable.

For software development roles in non-DevOps projects, my answer is the same. Learn DevOps to have a fruitful career; the option to switch will always be available, and your experience with software development will help in managing services (like in SaaS).

Diverging on this topic, I find ITIL as a shortcut for those keen on moving to the management table as opposed to a technical one, as ITIL is filled with a number of management roles that are up for grabs. For example, you can aim at managing incidents by working as an incident manager or managing changes by working as a change manager. In short, on the management side of things, the roles are pretty interchangeable if you have the right kind of mindset for it.

For example, if you are a methodical and organized person, I recommend a change to a manager's role. If you are a communicator who can bring parties together, and if you like action, incident manager is the role to move into. And if you are the investigative type of person, problem manager should be your pick.

What Are the Entry-Level Roles in ITIL?

Service desk is the most popular entry-level role in ITIL. Other roles that are offered to start are service reporting, operations control (monitoring batch runs), request fulfillment, and access management roles.

However, every organization might tag certain roles as entry level, depending on their maturity and the expectations of their customers. I have seen certain organizations hire IT professionals with barely a year of experience as incident and problem managers. I have my reservations against hiring inexperienced professionals for such roles. I believe that these roles are developed with experience, and a less-experienced person may not see all the aspects that an experienced campaigner would be able to address.

What Is the Normal Role Progression in Service Operations?

Service operations offers the greatest number of jobs in any service provider organization. When it comes to progression, service desk followed by service request and access management are considered junior-level roles. The next role hierarchy in service operations is an incident manager followed by a problem manager. In some organizations, incident management is placed above problem management, because incidents are viewed as critical over problems. Incident management roles are divided into incident managers and major incident managers. The major incident managers are often experienced professionals with over ten years of ITIL experience under their belts.

Although change management is a process under service transition, for most practical purposes the roles are considered as service operations. Change manager roles are considered in line with the problem manager roles.

What Are the Technical Roles in ITIL?

There are a number of technical roles in ITIL. The practices that come under technical management (deployment management, infrastructure and platform management, and software development and management) offer a host of roles that are technical in nature.

Examples include DevOps and cloud engineers who are responsible for configuration management and application integrations, and software developers who work in the application management area.

I Am Excellent at Customer Service. What Role Should I Aim for?

I recommend customer-facing roles for those who have a natural ability to connect and build rapport with people. These roles include the service-level manager, business relationship manager, and service delivery manager. Also, you will have sales roles in all organizations, where you are expected to meet customers and showcase the service management capabilities.

What Is the ITIL Role That You Have Enjoyed the Most?

This question was posed to me about eight years ago. My answer was different then; it was different when I wrote the first version of this book; and now it is completely different.

My answer in the first version was: I enjoy working as a consultant. My job involves finding a solution to a business or management problem, and providing all the plans necessary to implement it. The job involves plenty of customer interactions, makes full use of my ITIL expertise, and the short terms associated with consulting projects ensure that I don't get saturated over time.

My current answer is: I no longer work full time in the service management line. I only work as an architect or a consultant when a challenging project comes my way. Due to my know-how of ServiceNow and other tools and bridges, my architecture involves process integration specifications and all the necessary design decisions.

APPENDIX

Answers to Knowledge Checks

Chapter 3

3-1.

   C. This is the definition of an organization.

3-2.

   B. Utility is fit for purpose and warranty is fit for use.

3-3.

   B. A service consumer must be transparent about their needs if they intend to get a service catered for them.

3-4.

   C. Outcome refers to the results achieved by the stakeholder/ customer/consumer.

3-5.

   D. This is the definition of a cost. It is not a service offering. The remaining three are related to service offerings.

© Abhinav Krishna Kaiser 2021
A. K. Kaiser, *Become ITIL® 4 Foundation Certified in 7 Days*,
https://doi.org/10.1007/978-1-4842-6361-7

Chapter 4

4-1.

D. The primary focus is to create value by increasing efficiency, which is done through cutting down wastes.

4-2.

A. Organization and people focuses on organization structure even in the supplier organization. It's not the partners and suppliers dimension.

4-3.

A. Organization and people focuses on organization culture.

4-4.

C. Delivery model is a consideration for value streams and processes dimension

4-5.

A. There is a clear separation of roles for suppliers, as the relationship is transaction based. The focus is not on relationship.

Chapter 5

5-1.

B. Four dimensions is not inherently a part of the service value system.

5-2.

A. Represents options or possibilities to add value for stakeholders or otherwise improve the organization.

5-3.

A. The Engage activity deals with all things stakeholders—be it users, customers, or third parties.

5-4.

C. The Obtain/Build activity primarily exists to secure all resources needed to build services and develop the services.

5-5.

C. See Figure 5-9.

Chapter 6

6-1.

B. As you try to improve and remediate, the best option is to start with the current position.

6-2.

C. Complex processes and bureaucratic practices are quite common in organizations. This leads to more chaos and reduced productivity. By keeping things simple and as necessary, productivity can be increased and resource costs can be lowered. Optimize and automate is the next best option.

6-3.

D. When you have multiple work streams on a single product, it is critical that all teams point to true north. They must share a common knowledge management database and common artifact repositories. Most importantly, they must talk to each other if they are stuck. A collaboration tool that creates visibility of work will help identifying conflicts.

6-4.

A. While the customer makes up their mind on the final product makeup, the team can start building the base product. This is best achieved through Agile ways of working, and the guiding principle that relates to it is *progress iteratively with feedback*. As the features are finalized, it can be taken into development in iterations.

6-5.

D. A recommendation that guides an organization in all circumstances

Chapter 7

7-1.

A. Release and deployment management was a process in ITIL V3 and does not figure in ITIL 4.

7-2.

A. Service management practices started in IT service management organizations and were organized into best practices in the form of ITIL.

7-3.

B. Program management is not a general management practice.

Chapter 8

8-1.

D. Identification, Analysis, Monitoring, and Continual Improvement are the four stages of relationship management.

8-2.

B. A supplier provides support to deliver of services through a service provider. Generally, suppliers are a service provider's service provider.

8-3.

B. Relationship management engages customers at a strategic and tactical perspective.

8-4.

D. Service level management agrees on the various service levels with the customer, and they are tracked on a regular basis.

8-5.

C. While the feedback can come through any activity, the primary responsibility lies with Engage to liaise with customers and to understand the pulse.

8-6.

B. Service levels, metrics, and key performance indicators are inherent to an SLA document. However, service objectives are generally included in a formal agreement (in most cases, a contract) between a customer and a service provider.

Chapter 9

9-1.

A. To protect the information needed by the organization to conduct its business

9-2.

D. Any financially valuable component that can contribute to the delivery of an IT product or service

9-3.

D. A CMDB is a database of configuration items that have relationships built between them. In a CMS, there could be multiple CMDBs. So in this sense, CMS is a superset and CMDB is a subset.

9-4.

D. While all the options are correct to a certain level, this option is the primary objective of having a service map to start with. While it is desirable to have an architectural view that helps in planning and making decisions, on the ground, technicians would benefit the most when faced with incidents, and when the change managers have to make a decision while approving changes. For identifying orphan CIs, you don't necessarily need a service model; you could do it with the CMDB directly.

9-5.

B. Any financially valuable component that can contribute to the delivery of an IT product or service

Chapter 10

10-1.

C. *What Should Be Done* is not one of the defined steps in the seven-step model.

10-2.

A. It is the starting point or a baseline that gives the organization a reference point that serves two purposes: (1) as a measurement baseline, and (2) to design the improvement actions to take us from the current situation to the desired state.

10-3.

B. Improvements cannot be identified in a vacuum. It cannot all be done by a specific team. The organization must come together to identify improvements. For this to happen, a culture that orients people into thinking of improvements must be set; this essentially comes from fearlessness and expressiveness.

10-4.

D. There is no one universal methodology that is ideal when it comes to development of improvements. Every improvement is different, and the trick is to keep the methodology selection flexible in identifying one or the other depending on the nature of work.

10-5.

C. CIR is a repository for registering ideas. The ideas remain in the CIR throughout its life cycle.

Chapter 11

11-1.

D. Any change of state that has significance for the management of a service or other configuration item

11-2.

B. Interruptions to a service are referred to as an incident

11-3.

   C. The incident logging tool most importantly must provide the capability to link to problem tickets, change tickets, configuration items, and other types of service management records. Through these linkages, identifying improvements, defining changes, and carrying out problem management activities can be achieved.

11-4.

   A. Problems are created to identify root cause of incidents (which is the first step before implementing a permanent solution); when the root cause is known but a permanent solution is yet to be implemented, then a known error is created to keep track of known errors in the service/product

11-5.

   C. Five-why analysis is performed to identify the root cause of a problem that has been already identified.

11-6.

   B. Identifying permanent solutions to known errors in the KEDB is one of the major activities that are carried out in this phase. The objective of this phase is to ensure the reduction of known errors by either finding a permanent solution or by making the applied workaround permanent.

Chapter 12

12-1.

   B. The addition, modification, or removal of anything that could have a direct or indirect effect on services

12-2.

   B. Incidents pertain to loss of service. Service requests are not loss of service, but rather getting something additional to what users already have.

12-3.

C. To support the agreed quality of a service by handling all predefined, user-initiated service requests in an effective and user-friendly manner. Although the answer in the choices is not the complete definition, it is thus far the closest and most appropriate definition for service request management.

12-4.

A. Urgent changes don't exist in ITIL. I stated this as an example of a customized change type in an organization that I was associated with.

12-5.

A. Change advisory is a body that provides guidance to change control on changes, the risks they pose, and to identify potential changes that could be malicious.

12-6.

B. A change schedule consists of all approved changes and the changes that are in the pipeline seeking approvals; this includes changes that have been implemented as well.

Chapter 13

13-1.

A. A version of a service or other configuration item, or a collection of configuration items, that is made available for use

13-2.

B. Standard release is not a type of release. It is, however, a type of change.

13-3.

A. A POC provides substantive proof that the solution that is conceived is on the right path. A pilot takes the POC further in developing a small piece of functionality, thereby providing further proof.

13-4.

D. We have emergency releases but not emergency deployments. Deployment approach is about how we carry out the deployments and not about urgency or timing.

13-5.

D. A repository for storing all licensed copies of procured software and software that has been developed in-house

Chapter 14

14-1.

C. The purpose of the service desk practice is to capture demand for incident resolution and service requests. It also acts as a single point of contact for users. Answer A is incorrect because it refers to being the first point of contact with customers.

14-2.

B. While all the structures cater to IT, a structure called IT service desk has not been so named.

14-3.

D. A good service desk staff needs be good at communicating, empathetic to users, and must be technically sound.

14-4.

A. Generally, users can obtain updates to tickets either through a service portal, on social media channels that service providers have enabled, and through chat bots. Reaching out to IT staff may or may not get you the updates you are looking for, and it is not preferred that users contact IT staff directly.

14-5.

D. Engage: The service desk engages with users mainly and with other identified stakeholders, which is a central function within the Engage activity

Index

© Abhinav Krishna Kaiser 2021
A. K. Kaiser, *Become ITIL® 4 Foundation Certified in 7 Days*,
https://doi.org/10.1007/978-1-4842-6361-7

Printed in the United States
By Bookmasters